Clinical Data-Mining

POCKET GUIDES TO
SOCIAL WORK RESEARCH METHODS

Series Editor
Tony Tripodi, DSW
Professor Emeritus, Ohio State University

IRWIN EPSTEIN

Clinical Data-Mining

Integrating Practice and Research

OXFORD
UNIVERSITY PRESS
2010

OXFORD
UNIVERSITY PRESS

Oxford University Press, Inc., publishes works that further
Oxford University's objective of excellence
in research, scholarship, and education.

Oxford New York
Auckland Cape Town Dar es Salaam Hong Kong Karachi
Kuala Lumpur Madrid Melbourne Mexico City Nairobi
New Delhi Shanghai Taipei Toronto

With offices in
Argentina Austria Brazil Chile Czech Republic France Greece
Guatemala Hungary Italy Japan Poland Portugal Singapore
South Korea Switzerland Thailand Turkey Ukraine Vietnam

Published by Oxford University Press, Inc.
198 Madison Avenue, New York, New York 10016
www.oup.com

Oxford is a registered trademark of Oxford University Press.

Library of Congress Cataloging-in-Publication Data
Epstein, Irwin.
Clinical data-mining : integrating practice and research / by Irwin Epstein.
p. cm. — (Pocket guides to social work research methods)
Includes bibliographical references and index.
ISBN 978-0-19-533552-1
1. Medical social work—Evaluation. 2. Evaluation research
(Social action programs) I. Title.
HV687.E67 2010
361.30285'6312—dc22
2009011024

Printed in the United States of America
on acid-free paper

To the practitioners and students with whom I was fortunate enough to work.
To my wife Fran—the practitioner I was fortunate enough to marry.
To my mother Rachel—the source of social work within me.

Acknowledgments

This book is about social work practitioners using available agency data for practice-research purposes. In 2001, I first called this process "Clinical Data-Mining" (CDM). Looking back, my initial experience doing CDM preceded by decades my writing about it as a research method. In fact, it was the basis of my first professional publication. Co-authored with Richard Cloward, "Private Social Welfare's Disengagement from the Poor" (1965) was, in retrospect, a CDM study and arguably the best paper I ever wrote. Employed as Cloward's research assistant, I did the drudge work of gathering, sorting, and analyzing available client and service data "mined" from agency archives throughout New York City. The central thesis was his, but the empirical evidence I dug up expanded and challenged his thesis in ways neither of us anticipated. Our paper was widely cited and often vilified. My career as a social work researcher and critic was launched.

Ironically, the first publication about using available "material" for social work research was authored by Ann B. Shyne in 1960. What makes it ironic is that Shyne was one of the prominent social work researchers who were outraged by Cloward's and my empirically-based assertion of social work's abandonment of the poor. Equally ironic, I had read Shyne's paper as a graduate student, copiously underlined it, internalized its lessons, and until Rick Grinnell recently reminded me of it, conveniently ignored Shyne's impact on my CDM efforts. Thanks for that Rick. Spare me the psychoanalytic interpretations.

Three decades after my use of it with Cloward, I resurrected Shyne's method. However, instead of employing it to *critique* practice, I applied it *with* practitioners to *inform* their knowledge of their *own* practice. In so doing, I was helping social workers incorporate research methods and findings into their practice. Whether our findings were welcome, troubling, or simply surprising, we were *collaboratively* using available data along with traditional research logic and analytic techniques to describe, evaluate, and reflect on their practice. In using CDM as a practice-research consulting strategy, I took a more balanced and appreciative perspective toward practice—cognizant of the seriousness of practitioners' commitments to their clients, the organizational and ethical constraints within which they worked, as well as the strengths and limitations of every research paradigm. Maybe I had mellowed. Maybe not. Either way, by writing this book, I acknowledge the enormous debt I owe to both Cloward and Shyne.

But I have more current debts to acknowledge. This book was written while on sabbatical from Hunter College School of Social Work where I teach mainly in the Doctoral Program and where I occupy the Helen Rehr Chair in Applied Social Work Research (Health & Mental Health). I thank Jacqueline Mondros, Hunter's Dean who graciously provided the sabbatical and Helen Rehr who generously endowed the Chair. The mission associated with the Chair is the promotion of practitioner research. In seeking that objective, Helen was and is a true pioneer. I simply follow her path.

Much of the work described in this book took place over many years as a practice-research consultant at Boysville of Michigan and at Mount Sinai Medical Center in New York. For the work at Boysville, I gratefully acknowledge Br. Francis Boylan, Tony Grasso, Paul Neitman, and Edward Overstreet. For the work at Mount Sinai, my gratitude goes to Susan Bernstein, Susan Blumenfield, and Ken Peake, who supported my consultations and staff seminars, and to Gary Rosenberg, who brought me to Mount Sinai in the first place. In both organizations, the many research-oriented practitioners with whom I collaborated provided research exemplars and learning experiences that I draw upon routinely in my teaching and throughout this book. Thanks go as well to the doctoral programs in which I have taught and/or given CDM dissertation workshops—the City University of New York, the University of Hong Kong, and the University of Melbourne. Here, I wish to acknowledge Michael Fabricant, Cecilia Chen, and Elizabeth Ozanne, respectively, for their continuing support. I am especially indebted to the doctoral students at these far-flung universities for their willingness to follow my methodological lead in conducting their innovative and paradigm-stretching, CDM dissertations.

Admittedly, this book is intended as an instrument of modest paradigmatic change as well as a promoter of a particular practice-research method. Whether or not my research orientation has changed since my graduate student days, research certainly has. Advances in information technology have made research more accessible to practitioners as well as to academics. Historically emerging practice-research integration "movements" culminating in the presently ascendant Evidence-based Practice (EBP) reinforce the belief that practitioners are professionally and ethically obliged to integrate research into their practice—if not as *producers* of knowledge at least as *consumers* of research and *implementers* of research-based interventions. This book is about practitioners using CDM to perform all three of these functions and about researchers helping them to do so.

Though not always successful, my professional mission has always been about finding routes to the integration of social work practice and research. CDM is one. Sadly, some who have accompanied me most enjoyably on my utopian journey are no longer with me for the rest of the ride. Rebecca Donovan, Tony Grasso, Larry Kressel, Bogart Leashore, Edward Overstreet, and Harold Weissman were much more than colleagues. Their loss is daily felt. Nor was this sabbatical as reposeful and contemplative as I had anticipated. Life intruded. Those who supported me personally during this unexpectedly turbulent year included Jim Agioli, Ted Benjamin, Michael Bramwell, Bill Cabin, Wallace Chan, S.J. Dodd, George Downs, Ros Giles, Harriet Goodman, Daria Hanssen, Craig Hodges, Dana Holman, Richard Joelson, Sarah Jones, Lynette and Jacques Joubert, Marina Lalayants, Bruce Lord, Harry Lund, Emily Ma, Jane Miller, David Nilsson, Rosalie Pockett, Alicia Pon, Leonard Quart, Andrea Savage, Penny Schwartz, Maryanne Sea, Chris Tanti, Sandra Tsang, Darrell Wheeler and, of course, my dear family.

Finally, special thanks must go to Tony Tripodi. Tony and I have been friends and research colleagues since we were graduate students together at Columbia University. As editor of this Oxford University Press series, he encouraged me to write this book, giving me a chance to "showcase" CDM alongside other, more accepted and institutionalized research methods. For that and for his continuing friendship, I am deeply grateful.

Irwin Epstein, PhD
New York City

Contents

Clinical Data-Mining

Introduction

The purpose of this book is to introduce social work practitioners, students, agency evaluators, and research academics to the knowledge-generating possibilities inherent in what I call *Clinical Data-Mining* (CDM). Although these terms may connote other things in medicine or marketing, in my simplest definition, CDM is *the practitioners' use of available agency data for practice-based research purposes* (Epstein, 2001).

In this context "clinical" is used in the broadest possible sense, echoing its usage in Vonk, Tripodi and Epstein's (2006) text entitled *Research Techniques for Clinical Social Workers*. In that book, we define clinical social work practice as follows:

> By this last term we refer to the efforts of social workers to help individuals, families and groups of clients to resolve their psychosocial problems. These efforts may involve changing the clients, changing others in the clients' environment, or both. They take place in a range of organizational settings and are rooted in a variety of theoretical perspectives. (Vonk, Tripodi & Epstein, 2007, p.1).

Because the majority of my early experiences in developing and refining CDM took place in health and mental health settings with direct-service practitioners, it would be very easy to employ a narrower use of the term "clinical." However, my more recent experience in employing CDM suggests that it is applicable to any human service setting where there are paper, computerized, electronic and even unintended physical "data" routinely available.

By "data-mining," I refer to the full range of analytic possibilities that might be applied to existing data for research purposes. Unlike most marketing uses of data-mining, which are limited to large quantitative data-sets and complex statistical manipulations (Rexer, K., Gearan, P. & Allen, H.N., 2007), my use of the term "data-mining" embraces all appropriate applications of quantitative *and* qualitative analysis—from simple descriptive and/or phenomenological studies with small samples to complex multivariate, quantitative studies with large samples or total client populations. In this book, CDM exemplars of each are offered.

WHY SHOULD PRACTITIONERS CONDUCT CDM STUDIES?

In our research text, Vonk, Tripodi, and I assume that the application of "research concepts and techniques can facilitate the rational use of information by social workers engaged in direct practice with individuals, families or groups" (2007, p.1). Furthermore, we point out that the NASW Code of Ethics requires that "[s]ocial workers must possess research knowledge and skills that enable them to utilize existing research to inform practice as well as to engage in research in order to evaluate practice and build practice knowledge" (p.3). These assumptions and justifications apply here as well.

Similarly, the Educational Policy and Accreditation Standards 2.1.6 of the Council on Social Work Education require that schools of social work prepare their students to "engage in research-informed practice and practice-informed research (http://www.humboldt.edu/~swp/docs/EPAS)." CDM facilitates both.

In accordance with these professional mandates, Vonk, Tripodi, and Epstein describe a range of research designs and methodologies for social workers to employ routinely in their practice. Though we conclude with a very brief section on CDM, that book emphasizes the collection and analysis of *original* rather than *available* data. The current book is an attempt to fill that gap, and it assumes that unlike research methods that rely on original data collection, CDM makes practice research easier, less costly, and more profitable for social workers to fulfill their professional knowledge-building obligations. Plus, it can be enjoyable as well as enlightening.

THE BOOK'S INTENDED AUDIENCES

Broadly, the book is targeted at several audiences within social work but has applicability to other health and helping professions. More specifically, and within social work, the book is intended to be read by

- academics who teach research in schools of social work and are looking for something new to try pedagogically;
- research consultants who conduct and facilitate research in social work settings and are seeking a way to engage practitioners in a more meaningful, collaborative experience;
- evaluation researchers in social work settings who work in isolation from their fellow practitioners and seek a more satisfying partnership;
- research-oriented practitioners who are interested in systematically reflecting on their practice in a manner that does not compromise their service commitment to clients;
- social work master's degree students who want to conduct meaningful and do-able research in their field placements;
- social work doctoral students contemplating their dissertation research projects.

More broadly, CDM can be used by allied health professionals within their disciplines and in multidisciplinary teams. Though the majority of CDM studies cited in this book are conducted by social workers, significant multidisciplinary exemplars are presented as well.

THE THESIS OF THE BOOK

I first employed the term CDM in a keynote address given in 1998 at the 2nd International Conference on Social Work in Health and

Mental Health held in Melbourne, Australia. My talk was dedicated to Helen Rehr and was inspired by her many research publications with agency-based practitioners (Rehr & Rosenberg, 2006). For Rehr, practice and research are inextricably linked (Rehr, 2001). For me, CDM was a practice-research "breakthrough."

Only now, I realize that the method I was describing was so heavily influenced by the paper written four decades before by Shyne (1960). With characteristic understatement, Shyne titled her paper "Use of Available Material." Like my own, Shyne's paper focused on the research potential of available agency data. Unlike mine, Shyne's target audience was fellow researchers. In contrast, my primary audience was composed of social work practitioners and academics seeking research partnership with them. However, because most social work researchers prefer original data collection and standardized instruments (Epstein, 2001), Shyne's paper is rarely cited in research texts. Until now, I've repeated the oversight.

Benefiting from decades of advancement in computer technology and a more research-friendly climate within social work than Shyne enjoyed, my paper proposed that with truly collaborative research consultation, minimal financial and adequate administrative support, social work practitioners could conduct meaningful, practice-relevant research. They could do this most easily, I argued, by directly retrieving, computerizing, and systematically analyzing the clinical data that they routinely generated in the course of their work. The results in knowledge generated and professional reflection are highly valuable. That, in short, is the thesis of this book.

Since I gave that keynote presentation and published that paper, well over a decade's experience in helping American, Australian, Chilean, Hong Kong, Israeli, Singaporean, and Swedish social work practitioners conceptualize and conduct CDM studies has provided considerable "empirical evidence" to support my thesis in the form of peer-reviewed, practitioner-initiated research publications. Many of these will be cited throughout this book.

More recently, on the strength of my positive experience with practitioners, I began encouraging my doctoral students at Hunter College School of Social Work—many of whom were themselves practitioners—to consider CDM as a possible dissertation research strategy. Some decided to do so together with other more conventional research approaches that made use of original data collection. Others completed dissertations based *entirely* on available clinical information. For several, CDM dissertations generated peer-reviewed publications as well and became stepping stones to academic careers. One published hers as a book.

Most recently, a presentation on this subject at the University of Hong Kong involved four local CDM dissertation co-presenters—three of whom had completed their dissertations and one who was well on his way. What distinguished these dissertations was their remarkable combination of methodological rigor and clinical sophistication. For someone promoting CDM, this experience was extremely gratifying as well as suggestive of new analytic possibilities for employing available data. These studies are cited here as well.

Whether with direct-service practitioners or with doctoral students, my somewhat serendipitous "discovery" of CDM was made all the more surprising because practitioners and social work students are commonly characterized by social work academics as *inherently* antagonistic to research (Epstein, 1987). Even at the doctoral level, some have recently suggested that the principle obstacle to more practitioners' going on for their PhD's is the fearsome prospect of *magnum opus* research dissertation looming ahead (Robb, 2005). On the contrary, my experience is that the prospect and possibility of a CDM dissertation has quite the opposite effect.

Consequently, one chapter in this book is devoted to practitioner-initiated CDM studies and another to CDM doctoral dissertations. Though I offer no exemplars of CDM studies conducted by BSW or MSW students, there is no reason to assume that the method is beyond the capacity of such students. The simple explanation for the absence of BSW and MSW exemplars is that I do not teach research at those levels. Nonetheless, some of my Hunter School of Social Work academic colleagues do and find the approach quite congenial.

In this book then, I am following the time-honored editorial advice to write about what one knows best, and for me, that's doing research consultation with practitioners and supervising doctoral dissertations. In fact, for me, these represent my form of "practice." For research students and teachers at the undergraduate or Master's degree level, I suggest that CDM research principles and pedagogical applications can easily be extrapolated.

Reflecting back on my own 40-year journey of discovery (as well as failures) in teaching research in social work Master's and PhD programs and consulting in social work agencies, I see that most of my career has been devoted to disproving the proposition that practitioners hate research: Or, to put it more positively, seeking ways to successfully engage practitioners in research studies, research consumption, research ways of thinking, and ultimately, research utilization (Grasso & Epstein, 1992). In that long and possibly quixotic quest, it is especially pleasing to have, at this late stage of the journey, finally found a strategy of practitioner involvement in knowledge development that really works. CDM is that strategy.

THE STYLE OF THE BOOK

In writing about my circuitous path to CDM and my evolving experience with it, this book combines aspects of a personal memoir and a research text. For that reason, I write in the first person. Additionally, I acknowledge strategic mistakes I've made in my efforts to integrate social work practice and research. Some readers may find the former self-indulgent and the latter a waste of their time. To those who find the first person objectionable in a research text, I can only apologize for my stylistic choice. To those uninterested in the blind paths I've followed, I fervently believe there are things to be learned from one's mistakes that are worth sharing. Or, if a more research-friendly and less "touchy-feely" metaphor is required, think of it as rejecting the null hypothesis.

Though I may occasionally lapse into humor (for which I won't apologize) or into irreverence towards research shibboleths (for which I won't apologize), it should be clear that I am seriously committed to adding CDM to the standard repertoire of social work and allied health practice-research methods. In that respect, both the book and the method are part of a serious scholarly enterprise and purposeful trajectory. Though I may not convince all readers—particularly some of my academic research colleagues—I have chosen a writing style that resembles the way I teach, hoping to maintain a proper balance between accessibility and authority.

MY ULTIMATE EPISTEMOLOGICAL FANTASY

As a social worker and a sociologist, I confess that in my most grandiose academic fantasy, this book will resemble in style and impact Glaser and Strauss's sociological classic, *The Discovery of Grounded Theory* (1967). Though I couldn't possibly achieve their brilliance or their book's ultimate influence, at least to me, both books share two important similarities. First, each book employs an a-theoretical starting point and places emphasis on inductively deriving theory from empirical findings.

Second, both books present both quantitative *and* qualitative uses of their central methodology. So while Glaser and Strauss are clearly committed to championing qualitative research methods, they devote an entire chapter to "Theoretical Elaboration of Quantitative Data" (Glaser & Strauss, 1967, Chapter VIII). That chapter considers the grounded-theory generating potential in both original and "secondary" quantitative data. In the spate of qualitative research texts that their work has spawned, that pathway is routinely ignored though it parallels some of my own CDM thinking.

Similarly, whereas conventional applications of data-mining are entirely *quantitative*, my book devotes a good deal of attention to *qualitative* CDM. Consequently, it would be just as much a mistake to equate "grounded theory" with qualitative research as to think of CDM as solely quantitative. In spirit, at least I maintain that both books are methodologically pluralist.

WRITING ABOUT CDM AS A RESEARCH METHODOLOGY

In my 2001 paper, I acknowledged that even under the best of circumstances, CDM produces less than perfect "gold-standard" research studies—if by that term one means randomized, controlled experiments. Instead, I offered some modest early examples of practitioner-initiated CDM studies. These generated valuable research knowledge for the social workers doing the data-mining and informed decision-making in the programs in which they were conducted. Later, if presented at conferences or published, they might make research-based knowledge contributions for the field. In 2001, I was just beginning to appreciate CDM's potential.

These fledgling CDM exemplars supported Rehr et al.'s contention that practitioners could play an active and significant role in research and knowledge production (Rehr, Rosenberg, Showers & Blumenfield, 1998). With both the weaknesses and strengths of CDM studies in mind, I subtitled that original paper "Mining for silver while dreaming of gold."

The implication of the subtitle's conjoint metaphors was that while I acknowledged and accepted the methodological limitations of CDM studies, in conducting them, I still relied on the *logic* of "gold-standard" experimental inquiry. In other words, while CDM studies offer only *approximations* to cause-effect statements, such statements remained the ultimate, if unreachable, objective of much CDM research. Notwithstanding their limitations, however, I noted that CDM was far more appealing and acceptable to practitioners than the RCT's that the "gold-standard" relies upon. This is because CDM is neither disruptive of practice nor ethically objectionable to practitioners.

Because metaphors often communicate more effectively and efficiently to practitioners than academic research jargon, those practitioners and even some academics that have read and liked my paper invariably refer to it by its subtitle. Rarely does anyone remember the blandly descriptive title that preceded it, that is, "Using Available Clinical Information in Practice-Based Research." Even I have to look it up each time I cite it. But for good reasons, the subtitle stuck.

Since then, "Mining for silver" has been enthusiastically read by "countless" (only because I have no idea how many) practitioners and, of course, by all of my doctoral students. They have no choice. A few academics have responded favorably—maybe three.

In addition, the article has enjoyed translation into Hebrew and Japanese. Because I neither read nor speak Hebrew or Japanese, I have no idea how my international colleagues have responded to it, if indeed they have. I am aware of having received a blog attack from one of Japan's pre-eminent Evidence-Based Practice (EBP) advocates. However, I subsequently began an intense, e-mail epistemological exchange with the blogger who graciously came to Hong Kong to attend my CDM workshops and presentations at the 5th International Conference on Social Work in Health and Mental Health in 2007. In the process, we became friends. At least I think we did. I can't read his web site.

In Israel, at another presentation, one academic researcher accused me of being "unethical" for promoting the "myth" that practitioners could do research, when only academics were qualified to do so. In fact, when the audience suddenly seemed uncomfortable, my simultaneous translator whispered that the respondent to my plenary had called me a "liar." We never became friends. Of that I am sure.

But friendships and international travel aside, this is the era of EBP, with the placement of "gold standard" randomized-controlled trial studies (RCT's) and RCT-based meta-analyses at the pinnacle of the research hierarchy (McNeece & Thyer, 2004). Surely, if CDM ever gets ranked, it will be low on the existing EBP hierarchy, possibly even lower than "silver." But we'll return to CDM's relation to EBP elsewhere in this book. For now, the "Mining for Silver" metaphor should suffice to convey my intention.

CDM AND SECONDARY ANALYSIS

Despite my positive experience with CDM and its increasing methodological refinement, honesty compels me to say that as an approach to research, CDM is neither widely known nor richly funded. Frankly, one of its appeals to me and its utility for practitioners is that it can be done on the cheap. Naturally, this does not endear it to grant-seeking academic researchers or overhead-lusting academic administrators.

The closest social work academics come to doing anything like CDM is in "secondary analysis" (SA) (Sales et al., 2007). And, there are some marvelous, grant-funded SA research studies in social work based on large available data-sets (see, for example, Pottick et al., 2007).

But SA is not CDM. The former generally relies upon quantitative databases that were originally amassed by researchers for *research* purposes. The "secondary" part of SA refers to the fact that the databases are now being used for research purposes other than those for which they were originally intended. Often, generated by academics who serve as Principal Investigators, once these databases serve their original research purposes, they are turned over to doctoral students to support their dissertation research projects.

In contrast, CDM makes use of information that is *not* originally generated for research purposes. It may seem like a small distinction but because CDM studies are conducted by practitioners, are driven by practice-questions, and make use of practitioner-generated information, their primary purpose is to inform clinical, programmatic, or administrative decision-making. In other words, their primary research purpose is to enhance practice decision-making. Hence, the information that CDM studies rely upon was never intended for research purposes, nor to inform practice through research. This renders CDM uniquely challenging. Nonetheless, while CDM studies begin with practice-questions in mind and make use of available practice information, they can make significant contributions to research knowledge. In this context, practice and research are not incompatible. In fact, CDM brings them closer together.

Equally remarkable, practitioners enjoy doing CDM. And if I am to take them at their word, some even love it (Ciro & Nembhard, 2005; Hutson & Lichtiger, 2001). Many with whom I've worked have conducted CDM studies on their own time and some have even completed studies in services or in agencies in which they no longer work. One brought her new-born baby to data-extraction meetings. But there I go getting anecdotal.

CDM AND ITS PERSONAL ATTRACTIONS

At the risk of mixing my metaphors, elsewhere in describing my own personal attraction to CDM, I have used the analogy of cooking with leftovers (Epstein, 2007). Given my taste for CDM, it is perhaps not surprising that as an amateur cook, I love the challenge and the economy of cooking with whatever I happen to find in the refrigerator or the cupboard. While I recognize that what I produce is highly dependent on the quality of what is left in the fridge from the day before or stored and forgotten in the cupboard for years, I can still rely on well-established cooking principles and basic slicing and dicing techniques in what I create today. I enjoy reading recipes but rarely, faithfully follow them. Instead, I apply "classic" cooking principles and newly suggested ingredient combinations to what is already at hand. Sometimes the results are quite spectacular, sometimes quotidian. But always a useful meal is produced. When things don't quite work out as expected, it's an opportunity to learn about what was missing, what techniques needed refinement, and what ingredients just didn't go well together.

So it is with CDM. Sometimes the studies are quite spectacular in what they produce. Sometimes what they produce is not ideal, but for reasons of cost, ethics, or intrusiveness, the study could be done in no other way. Sometimes the findings are predictable and extremely simple but equally satisfying. At their least elaborate and most descriptive, CDM studies produce invaluable information about client profiles, services received, and outcomes achieved. For program planning and other forms of practice decision-making, this knowledge is extremely valuable. And, how much better are these decisions for having been made on the basis of data-informed reflection? More specifically, every CDM study that I have ever facilitated has

- produced findings of interest to the practitioners who conducted the studies;
- enhanced the research skills and appreciation of research on the part of the practitioners involved;
- acquainted the practitioners with the prior research literature on the topic;
- helped practitioners to meaningfully articulate what it is they are trying to do;
- helped them evaluate how well they were doing it.

In many instances, these studies have led as well to practitioners' first conference presentations and/or publications. Conducted in multidisciplinary settings, CDM studies have raised social workers' profile as professionals as well as their own self-confidence and pride in professionalism.

The prize that my eye is always on, however, is the integration of practice and research, not for its own sake or to enhance the status of social work, but in the interest of those we serve and should be serving. To me, that is the essence of professionalism.

CDM AND ITS DETRACTORS

Despite its appeal to practitioners and to me, when most of my fellow academic researchers refer to "using available information" or CDM, they tend to do so dismissively, as the antithesis of "real" research. In so doing, they often emphasize the limitations of research based on agency information (Kagle, 1996; Reamer, 1998). Informally, some researchers with whom I am acquainted have disparaged my efforts as "plumbing," "data-dredging," "cherry-picking," "data-trawling," "fishing," and/or "hunting expeditions." Implicit in the foregoing stream of research pejoratives and disparaging metaphors are implications that CDM studies are based on flawed information, attend only to pleasing findings, are aimless, do not test explicitly stated hypotheses and ultimately, depart from established research canons, and so forth. In other words, they do not meet generally accepted notions of what is "science." Some have even accused me of having "gone native," by which they mean that I identify too closely with the interests of practitioners, suggesting that I am pandering to them rather than bringing the religion of "science," the discipline of critical thinking or the manna of valid and reliable "evidence" to the primitives (aka "practitioners"). Similarly, I recently heard a researcher colleague refer to practice wisdom as "pre-evidentiary."

Well, I'm proud to say I did marry a practitioner and (dare I say it?) some of my closest friends are practitioners as well. Though I'm not proposing marriage or even friendship as the solution to the practice/research divide, it has given me an enormous respect for what practitioners do on a daily basis and caused me to seriously doubt whether I could. I happily admit that I even publish with practitioners and facilitate their publishing on their own.

Speaking of practitioner-research more generally, Shaw (2005) has described the way practitioner inquiry is often treated as a "street market" version of "mainstream research." In response, he proposes a "transformative agenda" to refashion the interface between practice and research. Elsewhere, in a study of the experience of British practitioner-researchers, Shaw and Faulkner (2006) describe their marginalization from *without* as well as *within* the organizations in which these remarkable practitioner-researchers work.

Along with Shaw and Faulkner, I'm suggesting that we *blur* rather than *sharpen* the borderlines between practice and research and provide practitioners with "somewhat more sophisticated evaluation methodologies" that would promote: (1) more collaboration between practitioners and researchers; (2) more computer-assisted data-analysis; (3) utilization of practitioner evaluation outside the practitioner-researcher's particular work setting; and (4) publications (Shaw & Faulkner, 2006, p.60). CDM is one such "somewhat more sophisticated" methodology. In response to its critics and potential critics, I would argue that CDM research consultants can effectively collaborate with practitioners without shedding their business suits and throwing rigor or fundamental research principles to the winds, unless of course they want to. Clothed or unclothed, readers of this book can judge for themselves, but I am absolutely convinced that, at the very least, CDM is an extremely effective strategy for engaging practitioners in describing client needs, for documenting social work interventions, and for evaluating social work outcomes.

HOW IS THIS BOOK DIFFERENT FROM OTHER BOOKS IN THIS SERIES?

That stated, aside from its singular focus on CDM, this book is probably different from other books in this series in that it is promoting the reader's exploration of a relatively new and evolving research methodology rather than one that is established and widely legitimated in social work research circles.

This book is based on a set of interrelated propositions. The first is that the integration of practice and research in social work is essential to social work's effectiveness and survival as a profession. I think it would be safe to say that every academic author of every book in this series would agree.

There is likely to be less consensus among my Oxford co-authors, however, about the propositions that follow. My second proposition is that in order for practice-research integration to be successfully achieved in social work, practitioners as well as academic researchers need to be *active* participants in the research enterprise. In this book and elsewhere, I refer to research initiated and implemented by practitioners as Practice-Based Research (PBR) (Epstein, 1995; 1996; 2001).

A third and possibly more contentious proposition is that EBP, the prevailing paradigm of practice-research integration, treats practitioners primarily as "consumers" rather than as potential "producers" of knowledge. In so doing, EBP excessively privileges what I have called Research-Based Practice (RBP), that is, practice based on a hierarchy of research methodologies as well as a hierarchy of research role-relationships (Epstein, 2001).

In the book, I advocate a more methodologically inclusive, pragmatic, and pluralistic practice-research paradigm that includes both PBR and RBP. Expanding on the work of MacNeill (2006) but borrowing his terminology, I refer to this expanded paradigm as Evidence-Informed Practice (EIP).

Whether they agree or not with any or all of the foregoing propositions, readers are likely to agree that engaging practitioners in research is no easy matter. The reasons given are legion. Forty years in the trenches as a research teacher and PBR consultant has taught me that as well. However, based on the very positive experience of my last decade's teaching and consulting, my final proposition is that CDM is a remarkably effective and efficient way of doing just that—that is, engaging practitioners in research. And it works as well with agency-based practitioners as it does with practitioners seeking their doctorates.

Forging ahead, I'll assume that we all agree on the value of practice-research integration and on the difficulty of engaging practitioners in research. Through (1) epistemological persuasion; (2) description of CDM practices and principles; and (3) practice-research exemplars drawn from published practitioner-initiated CDM studies and recently completed CDM doctoral dissertations, I hope to make a convincing case for all the propositions presented above.

DATA-MINING ELSEWHERE

Though I would be honored to share a place in social work research history with Shyne, it is for me alone to receive credit or cudgels for naming and promoting CDM within social work. Clearly, however, I did not originate the idea of using available information for retrospective research purposes. Historians do it all the time. It is the essence of the historical method (Danto, 2008). Some historians even do it quantitatively. Likewise, practitioners have conducted simple, descriptive "case-record reviews" over the years to describe the number of clients who fell into particular categories for accountability purposes or other very basic quality assurance functions.

Nor did I invent the term "data-mining." The ubiquity of data-mining and its metaphorical trappings are amply illustrated in a sampling of *New York Times* headlines I've collected over the past two decades:

The Health Care Debate: Finding What Work; New Frontier in Research: Mining Patient Records (*NYT*, 8/9/1994).
Digging for Nuggets of Wisdom (*NYT*, 10/16/2003).
Taking spying to higher level, Agencies look for more ways to mine data (*NYT*, 2/25/2006).
Bright Ideas; Reaping Results: Data-Mining Goes Mainstream (*NYT*, 5/20/2007).
Mining of Data Prompted Fight Over U.S. Spying (*NYT*, 7/29/2007).
FBI Data Mining Reached Beyond Initial Targets (*NYT*, 9/9/2007).

And, though it focuses on Dow-Jones industrials, most apposite of all:

Strategies; In the Data Mine, There Is Seldom a Pot of Gold (*NYT*, 8/13/2007).

So, long before I began using the term or conducting CDM studies, market researchers, pharmaceutical houses, banks, and credit-card companies were already employing extremely sophisticated and occasionally surreptitious techniques of data-acquisition, storage, and analysis for making empirically-based decisions about product-placement in supermarkets, for pushing drugs to doctors based on their "prescription profiles," and for identifying characteristics of high-risk mortgage applicants and credit-card holders. And, they called it "data-mining." And, it was profitable.

Thus, for example, Salford Systems www.salfordsystems.com a San Diego-based consulting firm regularly offers online training seminars and "new generation" data mining and choice modeling software that they have applied to "direct marketing, fraud detection, credit scoring, risk management, biomedical research, and manufacturing quality control." Their web site claims they have provided data-mining products and consultation services to industries, including "telecommunications, transportation, banking, financial services, insurance, health care, manufacturing, retail and catalog sales, and education. Salford Systems software is installed at more than 3,500 sites worldwide, including 300 major universities. Key customers include AT&T Universal Card Services, Pfizer Pharmaceuticals, General Motors, Sears, Roebuck and Co.

Working less hygienically in the back alleys of corporations as well as residential condominiums, "dumpster-divers" are equally aware of the value of "available" information for stealing identities and for their fraudulent use. At a much higher level, perhaps, I take little comfort in reading front page headlines in the July 27, 2007, edition of the *New York Times* such as "Mining of Data Prompted Fight over U.S. Spying" describing secret surveillance by the National Security Agency of phone calls and e-mail messages of millions of Americans.

Admittedly, some of the foregoing examples do not put me in great company. However, something that I do admit sharing with identity thieves, CIA agents, bankers, pharmaceutical executives, and supermarket managers is recognition of the potential of systematic use of available data for informing decision-making. What sets CDM apart from all of the above is that it can be used ethically, unobtrusively, and economically in the interest of improving practice and service directly to social work consumers.

CLOSE COUSINS TO CDM

Some equally intriguing but less egregious analogs to CDM outside of social work involve consumer and advocacy groups. An example of the former is the international online group called PatientsLikeMe. Members of this group—patients diagnosed with serious health problems such as Lou Gehrig's Disease, multiple sclerosis, and Parkinson's disease—post their own diagnostic information and test scores, treatment data, and effects and side-effects for analysis and feedback. In so doing, they have the opportunity to consider the effects of "alternative" or "complementary" interventions that they may be trying but their doctors are not recommending. Likewise, they have access to databases and results that are not "massaged" by pharmaceutical companies. Rightly or wrongly, neither physicians nor drug companies are pleased about the power that access and control over this information places in the hands of "Practicing Patients" (*NYT* 2008a). PatientsLikeMe is like CDM if it were conducted by social work clients rather than by practitioners.

Also displeased is the New York City Police Department about a suit brought against it by the American Civil Liberty's union "to release an internal database of hundreds of thousands of street stops of pedestrians to civil rights advocates who want to analyze it for evidence of racial bias." (*NYT* 2008b). In challenging advocacy groups who want to "mine" these data, police officials cite a report they commissioned by the RAND Corporation that the data on hundreds of thousands of "stop and frisk" interventions distort the picture of racial bias in police practices. Information such as this is routinely analyzed for its policy and practice implications within the department's Comstat program.

Coincidentally, the closest organizational analog I know of to CDM in social work had its origins in Comstat. Thus in 2006, New York's Administration for Children's Services (ACS) implemented Childstat, a weekly administrative review of internally generated data concerning child-protection and placement patterns in an effort to improve outcomes and reduce child fatalities. In the Childstat program, statistical analysis is combined with individual case reviews, making use of both extensive quantitative data and purposively selected, single-case qualitative information to reflect on child-protection policy and practices within the agency (ACS Press Release, December 11, 2006).

What differentiates the Childstat process from CDM is that the former is initiated and is controlled by management. In this regard, it also parallels the police use of Comstat. In contrast, CDM places the data collection, analysis, and interpretive functions in the hands of practitioners at *every* level in the organization. Hence, most of my CDM consultations have been to direct-service practitioners and supervisors rather than to top administrators. Nonetheless, it is important to point out that for CDM to work at any level it requires administrative approval and support.

Perhaps the closest academically conducted research to CDM is a study conducted in Israel by Zeira and Rosen (1999, 2000). That study empirically demonstrates the range and differentiation of the practice wisdom of 61 social workers in treating 141 clients in 6 public family agency settings based on a predetermined conceptual framework provided by the researchers. While the database is drawn directly from practitioners' case information, Zeira and Rosen's approach is different from CDM in several important ways. The differences and similarities are quite instructive and will be discussed in greater detail in Chapter 3 of the book.

Suffice it to say at this point, other than providing them with "raw data," Zeira and Rosen's practitioners remained uninvolved in the research process itself. Probably the only conceptual tools they might have picked up along the way were indirectly associated with the Systematic Planned Practice framework they were taught for structuring the practice records they submitted for research purposes. From the authors, however, we learn nothing about whether practitioners applied this framework to their future case recording or about any impact of the study on their practice decision-making. Those objectives appear to be outside their agenda. Although Zeira and Rosen have made an important contribution to knowledge, for the practitioners to learn anything about practice-research in general or, more particularly about their own practice, they would have had to read Zeira and Rosen's publications or possibly attend a presentation that they gave somewhere.

Despite the differences, what CDM shares with Zeira and Rosen's work is a respect for the value of practice wisdom and a belief in the possibility of testing it with available clinical data. In fact, in the concluding paragraph of their *Social Service Review* article, they comment:

> Although our sample was relatively large for this type of research and participating cases were assigned nonselectively, the practice sample, and hence the repertoire of outcomes and interventions that we studied, obviously be viewed as representing other practice domains. However, in this study we sought to demonstrate the feasibility and value of 'mining' workers' practice wisdom as reflected in their actual activities with clients.... (p.121)

Unintentionally, taking the mining metaphor one step further, they describe the records of "naturally occurring practice decisions" as a "treasure trove" of opportunities to formulate and empirically test practice hypotheses. The major differences between our approaches involve who is doing and disseminating the research? In other words, who is "mining," who is "owning" and who is "enriched" by the resultant knowledge?

Although this book is largely about social work practitioners as clinical data-miners, I should add that my CDM consulting experience in Australia with Lynette Joubert of the University of Melbourne School of Social Work with allied health practitioners has shown CDM to be of remarkable utility to music therapists, nurses, occupational therapists, physicians, physiotherapists, play therapists, and speech pathologists as well (Joubert & Epstein, 2005).

Although some social work practitioners and academics concerned about the competition over "turf" with allied health professions have been less than enthusiastic about my transdisciplinary consultations, to me, providing them with the tools of CDM and seeing how readily and creatively they use them has been something of a revelation. Whatever their professional stripe, these research-oriented practitioners are what my Aussie friends refer to as "good value." Their purpose is clearly patient health. Teaching them the principles of CDM and moving them through the CDM process have proven to be enormously informative, productive, and gratifying for them as well as for Lynette and me. Ultimately, I am confident that the knowledge they produce is translated into better patient care. That is a "gold standard" we all share.

CDM has been successfully employed at all levels in social work settings—that is , by social work supervisors, managers, and administrators—as well as by those working directly at what my Australian colleagues refer to as the "coal face" with clients or patients. More broadly, as I indicated above, CDM can be used by all types of allied health practitioners, physicians, and any other professionals who have *legitimate* access to information about their own and their colleagues' practice and wish to learn from this information.

In using the term "data," I am referring to facts, observations, descriptions, or measurements that are routinely available in case records, minutes of meetings, electronic charts, and so forth. When these data are accurately retrieved and converted into reliable and valid form, they can be analyzed and interpreted as information that enhances our understanding and facilitates decision-making (Grinnell & Unrau, 2008). The information may be qualitative or quantitative or some combination of the two. Its analysis may be simple or complex and the product may be highly refined or relatively crude. The point here is that it has informative value greater than the raw data alone and that value is a product of systematic inquiry.

After all, "mining" is only a metaphor for how the data are acquired and processed. Unlike real mining, CDM is rarely dangerous or even troubling, unless, of course, one discovers that cherished beliefs about who one is serving, what services they are receiving, and what happens to them afterwards are unsupported by one's findings. However, when such things occur (and they sometimes do), it has been my experience that because of their respectful involvement in every stage of the research process, practitioners' ethical commitments to those they serve lead them to make positive and constructive use of even "negative" findings.

In its uses to date, CDM is not nearly as statistically complex nor as methodologically sophisticated as business or intelligence data-mining approaches (see for example, Olson & Shi, 2007). However, it requires a high level of clinical attunement and a willingness and capacity to work collaboratively across the boundaries of research and practice. That involves a different kind of sophistication: one that combines grounding in basic research principles and an empathic appreciation of what practitioners are about. Consequently, CDM does represent a unique practice-research strategy and a unique model of research consultation. This book is about both.

Finally, it should be stated that the intention of CDM is neither to disprove nor to prove the soundness of clinical judgment or practice wisdom. And it's not about who's a better practitioner or academic. Its ultimate purpose is to enhance clinical awareness and to improve clinical and programmatic decision-making based on a reflective process of research inquiry.

ORGANIZATION OF THE BOOK

Without question, CDM is the most productive, transformational and generative practice-research strategy I have ever tried. Because my own career history has been heavily involved in the research-integration enterprise, I begin the book by locating CDM in a long but not especially glorious history of efforts to integrate research into social work practice.

Thus, Chapter 1 situates CDM specifically as a "practice-based research" strategy rather than as an example of "research-based practice." The latter more closely approximates EBP. In making this distinction, I describe the underlying epistemological assumptions of each. In this context, I briefly review some of my own less successful prior practice-research integration efforts and how they prepared the ground for CDM. More broadly, I locate CDM in the context of the current EBP movement and introduce the idea of a less hierarchical "evidence-informed" model of practice-research integration. Working the same claim as my Canadian practitioner-researcher colleague Ted McNeill (2006) but extending its boundaries, I also call this more inclusive practice-research integration paradigm "Evidence-Informed Practice" (EIP) (Epstein, 2009).

Chapter 2 describes my "discovery" of CDM as a research method and the study that was in many ways the prototype for all future CDM studies. The Mount Sinai "liver transplant study" helped me articulate research and consultation principles and procedures that have served me well in all subsequent CDM studies.

These principles are described in greater detail in Chapter 3. Like social work practice, CDM has elements of both "science" and "art" in its implementation. The scientific principles underlying CDM are well known to any researcher. The "art" involves knowing when and how to "strategically compromise" those principles in the conduct of CDM. Here again, the distinction between the "gold-standard" ideals of research and what data are available, accessible, and ethically attainable is relevant. CDM tries to make the best informational use of what is already available. As mundane as they might sound to the academic researcher, to the practitioner, CDM studies of client needs, services delivered, and outcomes attained can be extremely valuable for practice decision-making purposes.

Basing that assertion on the "evidence" that is most available, Chapter 4 presents several published exemplars of practitioner-initiated, quantitative CDM studies on which I have consulted. Statistically straightforward and, in that sense, not very complex, often they demonstrate the complexity of practice. These studies were all conducted by practicing social workers, occasionally in collaboration with other professionals from health, mental health, and child welfare settings. The studies as well as the authors are meant to serve as models for research-minded practitioners to consider doing CDM studies. Likewise, they are meant to encourage research consultants to consider working alongside their practitioner colleagues.

As stated earlier, it has been several years since I have taught master's level social work research courses. Although some of my teaching colleagues at Hunter have successfully introduced CDM into their courses, my pedagogic experience with it has been entirely at the doctoral level.

Staying with what I know most directly, Chapter 5 discusses and illustrates the use of quantitative CDM methodology in recently completed social work doctoral dissertations with which I have been associated. Although these doctoral dissertations are more methodologically sophisticated and inventive than the studies presented in the previous chapter, they are no less practice-relevant than those conducted by practitioners in practice settings. Indeed, most were done by practitioners going on for doctoral degrees with a desire to return to practice or to bring what they know about practice to teaching. All are interested in contributing to the knowledge-base of the profession and have found CDM an especially congenial way of doing that.

Though it further demonstrates the methodological and knowledge-generating possibilities of CDM, Chapter 5 is especially targeted at current doctoral students who are planning their dissertations, their academic instructors, as well as practitioners who are considering entry into doctoral programs but fearing that they would have to sacrifice their clinical and/or practice interests in conducting their dissertation research. Exemplars are drawn from completed quantitative CDM doctoral studies conducted in Australia, Chile, Hong Kong, and the United States.

Chapter 6 offers the fewest study exemplars because it describes the rarest form of data-mining that I know—*qualitative* CDM. In this chapter, two qualitative CDM doctoral dissertations as well as a single qualitative CDM study initiated by a practitioner are discussed . The unique methodological requirements and potential contributions of qualitative CDM are discussed. However, the point is made that both qualitative and quantitative CDM doctoral dissertations as well as practitioner-initiated studies require rigor and adherence to scientific principles.

Chapter 7, the final chapter, is CDM "futures-oriented." It briefly describes some practitioner-initiated, multidisciplinary CDM studies, and some CDM doctoral dissertations that I know are currently in the works. Then it discusses prior efforts to create experimental analogs with available data that most closely approximate the RCT research ideal. Next, a promising new data-analytic tool (Propensity Score Matching) is introduced that carries with it exciting data-mining possibilities. Finally, Chapter 7 becomes even more speculative. Returning to the "gold-standard" metaphor and the EBP movement, I stake a final claim for a model of social work research that includes CDM in particular and practitioner-research more generally. Whether one calls it EBP or EIP (gold, silver or bronze?), is less important than the recognition that such a change would increase the value of what we know about what we do as social workers.

CONCLUSION

Let me end this lengthy introduction with a few more words about my previously unacknowledged inspiration. As clear-sighted as Shyne was about the practicality of research using existing data, she was candid about its not being especially popular among her fellow researchers. That hasn't changed very much. But, for all her pragmatism and candor, Shyne could not have known how much more conducive the future agency environment would become to the possibilities for exploiting these informational sources.

So while "use of available material" still carries something of a paradigmatic stigma among researchers, what *has* changed is (1) the increased availability of available information and, in some instances, routine use of standardized research measures in clinical assessment; (2) the advent of agency computerization; (3) the introduction of electronic records in health settings; (4) the availability of personal computers to practitioners as well as researchers; (5) the new generations of computer-savvy social work students; and (6) the development of user-friendly, data-analytic software, some programs specifically designed for data-mining.

Reflecting on the future implications of these contextual changes and the practice-based research exemplars cited in this book, it is hoped that my audience—researchers, academics, practitioners and students alike—will seriously consider incorporating CDM into their practice-research and consultation repertoires.

1

Terminology and Defining Concepts

For more than half a century, social work academics have ardently advocated for the incorporation of research into practice (Polansky, 1960). No one disagrees with the objective. The question has always been how to do it? More than 40 years of my career has been devoted to various hopeful pathways and subsequent blind alleys in this elusive quest. The challenge continues today and remains a preoccupation of aspiring researchers (Mendenhall, 2007) as well as seasoned academic researchers like myself and others (Rubin, 2006; Vonk, Tripodi & Epstein, 2006).

Clearly, the integration of practice and research has always been easier to justify than to achieve. The justifications have not changed very much over the years. They remain as follows: (1) accountability pressures; (2) the need to show that "scientific" or "evidence-based" knowledge rather than ideology guides our practice; (3) competition with more "research-based" professions; (4) ethical imperatives to demonstrate that we do no harm; and, ultimately, (5) the presumption that practitioners who rely on research knowledge are more effective and efficient (Krysik & Finn, 2007; Vonk, Tripodi & Epstein, 2006). Every new research text begins with a similar litany.

Notwithstanding these justifications, social work students and practitioners alike have been notoriously and historically labeled as unenthusiastic and unresponsive to the academic muezzin's call to the ivory tower of research. This probably explains why one of my most persistently cited articles is entitled "Pedagogy of the perturbed: Teaching research to the reluctants" (Epstein, 1987). That article begins as follows:

No other part of the social work curriculum has been so consistently received by students with as much groaning, moaning, eye-rolling, bad-mouthing, hyperventilation and waiver-strategizing as the research courses. (Epstein, 1987, p. 71)

There is no reason to assume that the historic aversion to research is any less formidable today than when Polansky wrote that first social work research text. Over the course of our history as an aspiring profession, undaunted by student grumbling and practitioner indifference, academics have championed various social work research "movements" on behalf of practice-research integration (Kirk & Reid, 2002; Tripodi & Lalayants, 2008). These movements included, but were not limited to, the "Empirical Practice movement" (Reid, 1994), the "Scientist–Practitioner movement" (Briar, 1979), the "Single-system design" movement (Thyer & Thyer, 1992), the "Social R & D movement" (Rothman, 1980), the "Intervention Design & Development" movement (Thomas, 1984), and the like—none achieving notable success.

Most recently, proponents of the "Evidence-based practice movement" (EBP) have taken up the cause. And while EBP promoters are fervent and occasionally even doctrinaire in their exhortations to practitioners that they are ethically bound to choose interventions based on the "best available evidence" or follow practice guidelines that are "evidence-based" (Gambrill, 2006), some EBP advocates are already showing signs of pessimism (Rubin & Parrish, 2007). Thus, in a recent evaluation of the impact of an EBP-infused research curriculum, MSW students were shown to have improved their "subjective attitude" toward research but not their ability to critically appraise research evidence (Smith, Cohen-Callow, Hall & Hayward, 2007). Clearly, learning to say you like research is not the same as learning to use it.

Elsewhere, I have argued that the underlying explanation for this most recent expression of practitioner resistance resides in the fact that EBP places practitioners in roles as critical consumers and implementers of research-based interventions generated by others (Epstein, 2009). EBP proponents who consider practitioners more than mere consumers and appliers of evidence-based interventions still advocate single-system designs as devices for only "monitoring client progress" (McCracken & Marsh, 2008; Rubin, 2008). However, the implementation of single-system designs often ends when practitioners leave the classroom (Kirk & Reid, 2002; Mullen & Bacon, 2004; Mullen, Shlonsky, Bledsoe & Bellamy, 2005).

In the less idealized, "real life" of current agency practice, administers of EBP programs have been known to treat practitioners as mere bureaucratic implementers of "manualized" practice guidelines and treatment protocols. These rigid applications are denied by EBP activists and are never written about. But they certainly are resentfully talked about by practitioners at my Practice-based Research (PBR) and Clinical Data-Mining (CDM) workshops.

None of the foregoing EBP versions involves envisioning practitioners as potential *contributors* to practice knowledge development. More commonly, practitioners are portrayed as stubborn and malevolent obstacles to research-based practice (Epstein, 2009; Rubin, 2006). The future of EBP in social work is yet to be determined. Looking back at other practice-research integration movements, however, I suspect that the reason they have failed and EBP is facing so much practitioner opposition is that they all approach the practice-research integration challenge from a researcher's, rather than from a practitioner's, point of view.

Whether correct or incorrect, I think there is something to be learned from reflecting on various practice-research integration paradigms and their underlying assumptions. More specifically, the purpose of this chapter is (1) to introduce and contrast research-based practice (RBP) and PBR as alternative practice-research integration paradigms; (2) to introduce the notion of evidence-informed practice (EIP) as a more inclusive and pluralistic alternative; (3) to briefly describe various PBR strategies that my colleagues and I have developed and tried over the years; and finally, (4) to situate CDM as a new and potentially effective PBR strategy for engaging even "reluctant" practitioners in the actual *conduct* of practitioner-research and knowledge development. For the reluctant reader, I hasten to add that after this conceptual exploration things will get less murky in the data-mines.

Before spelunking our way into a warren of epistemological caves and corners, let me confess that to all but research academics that the conceptual distinctions and sets of initials that lie ahead in this chapter are likely to be seen as cumbersome and potentially boring. However, they are offered as *heuristic* devices to help understand fundamental differences in practice-research integration approaches. Accordingly, they are intended to clarify things that might have been previously obscure. Though anticipation of them may be off-putting, my students and the practitioners with whom I have consulted have been remarkably responsive to them. In short, they have reported that these conceptual distinctions and categorizations have been extremely helpful in sorting through the maze of different research approaches and strategies that academics like me have placed before them.

As with all such conceptual devices, however, they inevitably oversimplify and distort reality and frequently rely on dichotomous distinctions, that is, this *versus* that (Epstein, 2009). Playing on a familiar dichotomy, a former student of mine began every research paper he wrote for me with "In research as in real life." To paraphrase him, in the "real life" of actually conducting research, treating each of these dichotomies as though they represent opposite points on a *continuum* is more useful, but it makes communication more complex. That's why teachers and students alike prefer dichotomies. They make multiple-choice questions so much easier to devise and so much easier to study for.

Despite these acknowledged obstacles to more subtle forms of communication, the remainder of the chapter briefly describes three decades of planful efforts at practice-research integration that brought me to the location where I stumbled upon CDM, not quite as dramatic as the donkey that stepped in a hole in the Egyptian desert leading to the discovery of a Pharaoh's tomb, but for me, pretty big.

RESEARCH-BASED PRACTICE VERSUS PRACTICE-BASED RESEARCH?

To understand and make clear to students and practitioners what is perhaps the fundamental difference between the two dominant practice-research integration paradigms, I have found it helpful to distinguish between RBP and PBR (Epstein, 2001). (See Table 1.1.) Others might see it more as the difference between "basic" and "applied" research, respectively, but really, we are talking about different ways of promoting practice-research integration. In that sense, they are both intended to be "applied" to practice.

RBP integration approaches are generally derived deductively from social science research or "privileged" social work theory that is considered to be empirically validated. As a result, it favors "gold-standard" randomized-controlled trial studies (RCTs) and meta-analyses based upon these experiments; emphasizes use of standardized, quantitative data-gathering instruments; and seeks generalized knowledge about cause-effect relations between interventions and outcomes. This is what Scriven has termed "summative knowledge" (Scriven, 1995). Ultimately and much like EBP, RBP is a *research-driven* model of practice.

Put simply, RBP is focused on establishing cause-effect relations between social work interventions and outcomes. In turn, EBP is about employing only those interventions where that relationship has been empirically validated. In this context, EBP may be considered as only the most recent expression of an RBP strategy that moves from research to practice, but there have been others before it. For example, the Doctoral Program in Social Work and Social Science at the University of Michigan and in other so-called tier-1 research universities are organized on the assumption that social work practice should be rooted in social science and social work theories and research testing of those theories.

In contrast, PBR seeks to integrate practice and research but attempts to do so in a manner more compatible with practice norms.

Table 1.1 Research-based practice versus practice-based research

• Deductive (theory-based)	• Inductive (practice-based)
• Favors RCTs	• Rejects RCTs
• Standardized instruments	• Qualitative & quantitative
• Summative	• Formative
• Research-driven implementation	• Practice-driven implementation

Consequently, it derives its questions inductively, that is, from the requirements of practice itself and/or from "practice wisdom" (Klein & Bloom, 1995). And while practitioners are certainly interested in knowing about the impact of their interventions, they are generally unwilling to randomly assign service recipients to interventions or to withhold interventions in order to *prove* that their interventions have a desired outcome.

Moreover, practitioners are often confronted with individuals, families, groups, and communities with complex and pressing problems that do not allow for parsing or prioritizing into single problems that can be experimentally approached to the exclusion of all others. Their informational needs can be both *quantitative* and/or *qualitative,* but they do not have the luxury of being able to ethically impose standardized information-gathering instruments on their clients. More likely, the best we academics can hope for is that they can employ research to inform their practice decision-making in ways that are a bit more systematic than they would otherwise employ.

Consequently, PBR is more about *improving* what we know and do, rather than about *proving* its effectiveness or ineffectiveness. In Scriven's terminology, this is "formative knowledge" (Scriven, 1995). In my research lexicon, both formative and summative knowledge have a place. And, obviously EBP proponents are interested in improving and making practice more responsive to client differences. Similarly, all practitioners are interested in knowing whether their interventions work or not. Here, however, we *are* talking about priorities. And to practitioners, proof is not the highest priority. Nor should it be. Service is.

EVIDENCE-INFORMED PRACTICE

Although making conceptual distinctions and emphasizing the conflicts between RBP and PBR have made for a useful didactic device, this dichotomous characterization has never reflected my own commitment to a full range of practice knowledge–generating strategies. So, for example, under certain conditions, when we have good reason to suspect that intervention might do harm or when we simply don't know which intervention of a number of reasonable interventions works best and when multiple interventions might conceivably undermine each other, RCTs make sense to me. But it comes as no surprise that EBP activists emphasize the possibility of harmful interventions with such alacrity in order to claim the higher moral ground (Gambrill, 2003). Labeling social workers who are resistant to EBP as "charlatans" and "quacks" or ethical violators is no way to win friends among practitioners (Myers & Thyer, 1997). And no amount of browbeating about the need for proven effectiveness or the possibility that they might be doing harm will persuade them about the value of research.

Moreover there are contexts in which RCTs are simply unthinkable (well almost) no matter how valuable the knowledge they produce might be. Borrowing from the field of corrections, a recent article in the *New York Times* dealing with the thorny question of whether "the death penalty saves lives?" makes the point quite effectively. After a lengthy discussion of the limitations of existing studies based on available state and national statistics, a noted Stanford University academic is quoted as saying that the answer to the foregoing question is

> not unknowable in the abstract… [i]f I was allowed 1,000 executions and 1,000 exonerations, and I was allowed to do it in a random, focused way… I could probably give you an answer (Liptak, 2007, p.32).

Clearly, there are occasions when the price of "gold" is higher than we should be willing to pay. Instead, we need to be both humane and practical. Correctly or incorrectly, social work practitioners believe that their interventions are at worst benign, but at best, what clients need, want, and benefit from: that more interventions are better than fewer; and that a very important component of their expertise involves matching the clients to interventions. Given this set of assumptions and perceptions, the use of standardized research instruments to assess clients' needs or evaluate outcomes, client randomization, withholding of interventions to create "control" conditions, or rationing interventions in order to generate "gold standard" knowledge about intervention effectiveness is anathema to most practitioners. Nonetheless, research academics and RBP-oriented consultants continue in vain to preach the "gold standard" gospel, to which very few practitioners have been converted.

In an attempt to more effectively reconcile the RBP/PBR distinction and to provide a more holistic and harmonious paradigm for integrating practice and research, I recently followed McNeill's (2006) lead in employing the concept of *evidence-informed practice (EIP)*, which embraces all forms of knowledge generation and communication as a paradigm of practice-research integration in social work. Here, EIP is meant to be both methodologically and structurally pluralistic in that it views practitioners as both consumers and producers of qualitative and/or quantitative knowledge (Epstein, 2009). Finally, it is intended to be culturally pluralist in equally valuing knowledge that is specific to different client populations in different settings rather than "universal" truths that social science and, by implication, EBP seek for all clients in all settings. Writing about an analogous issue in evidence-based medicine, the late John Eisenberg, former director of the Agency for Healthcare Research and Quality, wrote:

> The use of evidence is most successful when local differences are factored into the decision-making process, whether at the clinical, system of policy level. (Eisenberg, 2002, p.166).

Thus, EIP has the potential to be more inclusive, flexible, and less perfectionist than EBP and more empowering to practitioners. But it values all forms of practice-relevant research, RBP as well as PBR.

My assumption, which has been supported by lots of unsolicited practitioner testimony, is that by teaching practitioners research *ways of thinking* as well as ways of engaging them in systematic information-gathering, analysis, and interpretation of information from their *own* practice helps practitioners become more mindful about what they actually do and about the outcomes they do and do not achieve. However, as a more formative approach to knowledge generation, EIP is rarely about *proving* whether an intervention works. And it certainly isn't driven by a desire to prove that it doesn't.

Instead, it is about trying to *improve* practice and helping the practitioner to become more *reflective* in doing so (Schön, 1983). This approach does differ from the "reflective practitioner" model proposed by Schön, however, in that, like McNeill's earlier conception of EIP (2006), it accepts as useful both quantitative, post-positivist as well as qualitative, interpretivist strategies for knowledge generation and reflection. In contrast, Schön's version of the "reflective practitioner" rejected the "technical rationality" that he associated with all forms of quantitative research. Alternatively, my conception of a "reflective practitioner" who employs data-mining, for example, makes relatively systematic use of quantitative case information as well as qualitative case observation. But like Schön's practitioner, by making use of research ways of thinking, clinical information and prior research, practice is raised to a somewhat higher level than would otherwise be the case.

Borrowing as well from positivist principles of hypothesis testing and rejection, EIP in general and CDM in particular also open practitioners to unanticipated discoveries—both positive and negative—and encourage them to greet negative findings less defensively and with a greater openness to change or revision. In short, by empowering practitioners as knowledge generators as well as appliers, CDM helps practitioners take ownership of what they do, why they do it, and of the correlates if not the proven consequences of their actions.

Assumptions within EIP

Although EIP is motivated more by an openness to various approaches to practice-research integration rather than a single one such as EBP, its inclusiveness is intended to be more congenial to practitioners (see Table 1.2). Thus, in its methodological, structural, and cultural pluralism, it values all ways of knowing and seeking useful knowledge—everything from RCTs to qualitative case studies. Like Zeira & Rosen's writings (1999, 2000), it values practice wisdom as well as research-based knowledge, but unlike them, it positions practitioners as knowledge producers alongside academic researchers.

Consequently, EIP rests on a full range of possible collaborative relationships between researchers and practitioners. These would

Table 1.2 Evidence-informed practice principles

- Methodologically, structurally & culturally pluralist
- Honors practice-wisdom as well as research-based knowledge
- Supports practitioner-researchers & academic researchers alike
- Full continuum of collaborative relationships
- Promotes both practice-driven research & research-driven practice
- Empowers practitioners as co-creators of social work knowledge

include everything from studies in which practitioners are functioning as the "principal investigators" with researchers serving as consultants to studies in which practitioners function essentially as subject recruiters, information gatherers, and attrition preventers.

Ultimately, whether the model of EIP is considered a conflicting alternative to EBP or a corrective to EBP, or gets incorporated into EBP is less important than that practitioners become more valued participants in knowledge production. PBR is a route to that, and CDM is one strategy for getting there.

PREVIOUS PBR STRATEGIES I HAVE TRIED

Although trained at Columbia University both as a social work researcher (MSW) and as an academic sociologist (PhD) in the post-positivist tradition, with the exception of my dissertation research, I have generally walked on the PBR side of the street (Epstein, 2007). In so doing, along with a handful of academic colleagues and many practitioner colleagues, I have attempted and applied various research-practice integration strategies in my teaching, research consultations, conference presentations, and workshops. A few of these are described briefly below.

DIFFERENTIAL SOCIAL PROGRAM EVALUATION

My dissertation research—a formal hypothesis-testing study of social worker professionalization and its political consequences—was later replicated by Reeser, resulting in a historical, quantitative comparison of social work in the 60's and the 80's (Reeser & Epstein, 1990). Though positively reviewed, that book which was written for a nonresearch audience and my earlier dissertation-based articles, as far as I could tell, had little impact on practice or the profession. The findings were too complex and did not fit the political agendas of any of the prevailing ideological camps. They still don't.

As a consequence, I turned my attention to what I now call PBR in collaboration with Tony Tripodi and Phillip Fellin. Working in the early 70's at the University of Michigan, we developed a program-level, practitioner-friendly guide to program evaluation that linked a stage model of program development with basic evaluation research logic and simple research methodology (Tripodi, Fellin & Epstein, 1971). The idea for the book emerged from the enthusiastic response to a paper that Tripodi, Mac Murray, and I had written on the evaluation of planned social action programs and given at a multidisciplinary health conference (Tripodi, Epstein & MacMurray, 1970). We called it "Social Program Evaluation" (SPE—sorry, I can't help myself).

We wrote the paper in one day, and having just spent four years finishing my PhD in sociology of professions and organizations, I thought the paper was so simplistic that I was too embarrassed to go to the conference. Fortunately, Tripodi did attend and was besieged by requests from physicians, pharmacists, and other health professionals for copies of the paper. It offered them a clear conceptual framework for linking program development and the logic of evaluation and taught me that practitioners of all kinds wanted simple, directly applicable material concerning practice research. Whether the target audience was nurses, pharmacists, physicians, or social workers, the complexities, ambiguities, and multiply-qualified, contingent statements that I had learned to love in my PhD program were unsuited to applied research pedagogy.

In the SPE book that eventuated, program development was conceptualized as a three-stage process, moving from program initiation to client contact to program implementation—each with their unique informational questions concerning *program efforts, effectiveness, and efficiency,* and administrative problems to be solved through simple research methods that we proposed administrators could employ. Two years later, we revised the book, demonstrating how various research strategies, for example, survey methods, audits, case studies, and so forth could be used to assess program efforts, effectiveness, and efficiency at each stage of development (Tripodi, Fellin & Epstein, 1978). We referred to this as *differential social program evaluation* (DSPE).

What made DSPE "differential" was the idea of matching the most appropriate and least intrusive research method with the decision-making questions that were necessary to be answered to move the program successfully to the next stage of development. Bielawski and I extended the stage model to include *program stabilization*, an issue that became much more problematic in the conservative, early 80's (Bielawski & Epstein, 1984). By then, Tripodi and I had published a research text for macro-level practitioners that encouraged their use of research techniques for decision-making regarding program planning, monitoring, and evaluation (Epstein & Tripodi, 1978).

The early more conceptual writings and the latter more "hands-on" textbook encouraged program-level practitioners and macro-level students to employ research concepts and techniques themselves in collecting *original data* to enhance their programmatic decision-making. In that sense, our writings generally maintained the prevailing bias against using *available* information. Nonetheless, they were pragmatic and well received by both practitioners and students but not paid much attention to by academic researchers.

In addition, they were published a few years before the proliferation of evaluation texts and, more generally, before the "program evaluation movement" took hold. Practitioner-oriented, they gave scant attention to the randomized controlled experiments that promised "proof" of program effectiveness and efficacy to grant-funders and the research academics that courted them. Finally, our books predated the development of computerized clinical and management information systems in social agencies and the advent of the personal computer on social workers' desks and in their home offices. Conceptually and technologically premature, DSPE did not capture the imaginations of macro-level practitioners or academic research educators who might have employed these as texts.

DIFFERENTIAL CLINICAL EVALUATION

Recognizing that most social agency administrators began their careers as direct services workers and that the majority of social work students were (and still are) microlevel students, Tripodi and I turned our attention to writing a parallel PBR text for "clinical" social workers, that is, those in direct practice with individual clients, families, or groups (Tripodi & Epstein, 1980). Similar to the aforementioned administrative text, we conceptualized clinical social work in terms of stages—that is, *diagnostic assessment, treatment formulation and implementation,* and *treatment evaluation*. In this more clinically- oriented text, research concepts, methods and techniques were illustrated and *differentially* applied to the decision-making issues facing direct service practitioners at each of the foregoing stages.

In some ways anticipating the EBP movement, this *differential clinical evaluation* (DCE) included everything from critical assessment of prior research literature to questionnaire construction, observational research, as well as single-system designs (SSD's). Throughout, however, we maintained the assumption that if given the technical tools, the research logic, and the administrative support, clinical practitioners could routinely incorporate *their own research* as well as that of academic researchers into their practice.

The book had some limited success as a text but probably missed the mark because it was published in the height of academic enthusiasm about single-system designs and before the EBP movement took hold. Also, it offered a wider repertoire of approaches to practice-research integration than either SSDs or EBP. Since then, the SSD movement has enjoyed limited utilization by practitioners despite the pedagogical investment that some EBP advocates have made in it (McCracken & Marsh, 2008; McNeece & Thyer, 2004).

Still, with the encouragement of its publishers, a second updated edition was recently published (Vonk, Tripodi & Epstein, 2006) on the basis of similar utilization assumptions as the first. The timeliness and impact of this update is yet to be determined. Needless to say, it is not an Oprah selection.

CLINICAL INFORMATION SYSTEM DESIGN AND UTILIZATION

Another path to PBR that I tried involved promoting research utilization by practitioners at *all* levels in the agency through the development and implementation of computerized clinical information systems. The notion was akin to what are now called "decision-support" systems (Kirk & Reid, 2002). This new turn was suggested to me by Tony Grasso with whom I spent a decade exploring the potential uses of information technology in agency settings.

Our work in this emerging field was largely conducted at Boysville of Michigan, where with Boysville's backing we hosted a national conference on research utilization. Within the agency, we sought structural ways to bring the agency and academy together in a true partnership, rather providing a "laboratory" for academic exploitation (Grasso & Epstein, 1992). Enlisting the ongoing intellectual input of a number of prominent social work researchers and the unflagging ideological, emotional, and financial support of Edward Overstreet, our efforts were only partially successful. More specifically, we produced practice-related research publications—some even co-authored by Boysville practitioners—but the aspiration to use the Boysville Information System (BOMIS) in all aspects of practice decision-making outdistanced the available computer technology and the agency's infrastructural support possibilities (Grasso & Epstein, 1993).

At Boysville, the ideas arrived too soon for the available technology and existing administrative resources. In short, we had too much client data for the system to feedback to practitioners in a timely manner. Moreover, training practitioners to employ research findings in their ongoing clinical decision-making was too labor intensive, too complicated, and too costly for the agency to continue to support. After Grasso left Boysville for an academic career, a revision of the information system got mired in problematic external software consultation.

Tragically, my dear friends and Boysville colleagues Grasso and Overstreet departed much too soon to see our computerized vision of practice-research integration realized. Inspired by Overstreet's vision for the agency and informed by the cumulative experience of Grasso, Steve Kapp, Paul Neitman, Sue Ann Savas, and other former agency staff as well as academic researchers, a practice-oriented research and consultation center named after Edward Overstreet is currently in the planning stage at Boysville.

CDM AND "FUZZY LOGIC"

While at Boysville, I co-authored two articles linking available Boysville data with publicly accessible adult imprisonment data (Collins, Schwartz & Epstein, 2001; Kapp, Schwartz & Epstein, 1994). The purpose of those articles was to identify adolescent client risk factors that might predict adult imprisonment. Strictly speaking, these articles fall somewhere between secondary analysis (SA) and CDM because they use available agency data but were conducted by researchers. However these studies are classified, they did move me in the direction of CDM.

Since then, Schwartz's research took a different turn, albeit with available information. Most recently, he has advocated the use of "smart" software with available client information to "support" practitioner decision-making in child welfare and other practice and policy arenas (Schwartz et al., 2008). Here it might be instructive to consider the differences between what he is proposing and CDM.

In contrast with CDM, Schwartz's use of highly sophisticated data-analytic software represents a *direct* application of data-mining as it is commonly employed in other industries. Thus, in discussing Schwartz's "neural network" approach to practice-research integration, Whitehurst (2007) remarks that the same computational strategy

> is being used to make predictions in areas as diverse as dog racing, airfare costs and the success of Hollywood movies. Credit card companies monitor their customers' purchasing habits to identify patterns and project trends. The National Security Administration analyzes millions of bits of information to identify potential terrorists. (p.1).

It should be clear, however, that neither Schwartz's nor the NSA's research approach is what I am calling clinical data-mining. What sets CDM apart is neither the use nor nonuse of highly sophisticated forms of number-crunching. As the reader will see in Chapters 4, 5, and 6, CDM studies have been successfully and productively implemented with very simple as well as very complex forms of quantitative as well as qualitative data analysis. The complexity of analysis depends upon the study question, the quality and quantity of data available, and the level of sophistication and/or aspiration of the practitioner-researchers. Instead, what sets CDM apart is that it involves practitioner-researchers in every aspect of the study's problem formulation, available data collection, analysis, and interpretation.

In contrast, in Schwartz's approach, the researcher conceptualizes the problem, collects the data, and hands it over to the "fuzzy logic and evolutionary algorithms" of a neural network in order to come up with a practice-relevant, statistical prediction. Schwartz and his colleagues proudly quote Einstein in declaring "as far as the laws of mathematics refer to reality, they are not certain, and as far as they are certain, they do not refer to reality." They go on to suggest that the difference between perfect mathematics and imperfect reality compels us to apply mathematical logic to our imperfect decision-making (Schwartz, Kaufman & Schwartz, 2004, p. 1090).

In their exemplar study, what is predicted is the likelihood of meeting the most extreme "harm standard" of child abuse, given a set of client risk indicators extracted from case files in a large population of clients (N = 1767). They acknowledge that their prediction is not perfect, but with a large enough N and an extreme outcome, it is not that difficult to come up with statistically significant predictors. Nevertheless, their findings *are* in two uses of the phrase, "empirically-based." First, they are subject to replication and rejection by future researchers. Second, they are completely atheoretical. However, rather than *supporting* practitioners decision-making, the spirit behind computational intelligence comes closer to *supplanting* it. Simply stated, they make their case by attempting to demonstrate that the computer can outperform the practitioner.

As indicated earlier, CDM studies are no less empirical, but they are informed by practice wisdom (Klein & Bloom, 1995) and the theory that is implicit in practice (Schön, 1972). Moreover, in the process of implementing CDM studies, practitioners are encouraged to participate in, reflect upon, and learn from every aspect of the study process. In so doing they are helped to

• surface and articulate often tacit practice theories;
• comprehend research concepts as practice-research analogs;
• acquire or revivify research skills;
• apply these to a practice context in which they and their clients have a vital interest.

At each step in the process, practitioners consider what they know and what they don't know. Ultimately, their findings, just as Schwartz's, are open to replication and rejection in other practice settings.

As important as replication is for knowledge accumulation, it is important to point out that in CDM, practitioners learn from their own knowledge imperfections as well as from what they can demonstrate to be empirically true. In that sense, it may be fair to say that CDM seeks a higher standard than the often idealized RCT "gold-standard" or Schwartz's mathematical ideal of predictive perfection. This is what I was trying to say when I subtitled that first CDM paper "Mining for silver while dreaming of gold" (Epstein, 2001). I could go on, but I fear that this discussion is getting too abstract for a CDM handbook. So, let's return to the data-mines.

THE "MINING" METAPHOR

In my original paper on the subject, I spoke of why the "mining" metaphor seemed so appropriate to what was involved in doing CDM. The following listing broadly summarizes the steps in the process and the reasons why the metaphor applies so well:

• Each project begins with *prospecting* by *surveying* all available data sources that are relevant to the context of practice and the initial objective that is driving the search.
• The work is often dirty and tedious and occasionally involves rummaging about in subterranean and unhealthy places.
• The work is labor intensive, and there are frequent false leads about where the *pay dirt* is.
• Once located, the informational *ore* must go through several stages of refinement and analysis before its value can be determined.
• The *findings* can be frustrating and/or rewarding, often in unexpected ways, sometimes raising only more questions that whet the appetite for more *mining*. However, to date, there are no reported and confirmed cases of "CDM fever."
• Ultimately, *fool's gold* is always a possibility if one loses sight of the practice context and the agency history and makes claims beyond what the methodology warrants and what the strength of the findings justify (Epstein, 2001, p. 19).

Obviously, the last point is subject to debate and depends on the standards used to assess the "truth value" of CDM findings.

As indicated earlier, in Australia, which has a proud history of both real gold and coal mining, the metaphor is even more apposite because direct service social workers are often referred to as working at the "coal face." Perhaps this, combined with Aussie irreverence toward academic as well as other forms of authority, explains the alacrity with which Australian practitioners have embraced CDM (Joubert & Epstein, 2005).

In New Zealand, the highly successful, rigorously conceptualized and modestly funded Growing Research in Practice (GRIP) program (Lunt, Fouche & Yates, 2008) exemplifies a broader PBR effort to promote practitioner research and a "culture of enquiry" in nine different community-based Auckland agencies. Beginning in 2004 and concluding in 2007, GRIP trained and facilitated practice-research teams from agencies and programs that included hospitals, mental health settings, parenting support, male sex offender, youth at-risk, and domestic violence programs.

GRIP provided teams of practitioners with skills in questionnaire construction, research interviewing, and the conduct of focus groups as well as data-mining of administrative and clinical information. The approach to research consultation was based on a "collaborative" and "grass-roots" model of enquiry, with the intention of promoting reflective practitioners who are research minded. Particular attention was given to compatibility between research methods chosen and the cultural group that the agencies or programs serve—that is, Maori, Pacific Island, or Chinese. Different practice-research teams made use of different methods, but all were encouraged to develop a sense of "custodianship" whereby the team had "ownership" of the project from start to finish (p.48). Eight of the nine research projects were completed. Only two of the eight made use of data-mining, but all incorporated one or more research method into their practice inquiry. None were experimental, nor did they employ single-system designs.

In evaluating the overall impact of GRIP, the authors of the final report—a group of Massey University and University of Auckland partners—concluded that the projects resulted in the following:

- Direct changes from program delivery (including changes to policy or funding).
- Changes to recording processes.
- Reconceptualization of practice areas.
- Changes to or affirmation of practice models.
- Critical reflection on practice. (p.45).

Wherever PBR or CDM studies are implemented, academic research-converts and neophyte practitioner-researchers alike are reminded that even the most rigorous PBR or CDM studies are only *approximations* to experiments. As such, they are never truly *summative* and can never definitively *prove* that an intervention is the cause of a treatment outcome or that a program intervention is the complete explanation for achieving a particular programmatic objective. Nonetheless, I believe that the "evidence-informed" knowledge they produce is superior to practitioners "going with their guts"—how superior is again open to debate. This debate will be taken up again in the final chapter where—audacious as it might sound—I consider conditions under which CDM studies might even be considered in some sense superior to prospective RCTs.

CONCLUSION

Returning to more practical matters, however, each of the preceding PBR strategies that my research collaborators, colleagues, and I have tried over the previous three decades seems to have led me inexorably to finding CDM—as much by their failures as by their achievements. Although congenial with practitioner's ways of thinking, rarely did any of these prior approaches produce a significant body of practitioner-generated research studies or publications to be read, applied, and possibly replicated by those outside. Then, I got lucky. The following chapter describes my fortuitous "discovery" of CDM, defines what it is instead of dwelling on what it isn't, and sets out some basic elements of the CDM process.

2

On the "Discovery" of Clinical Data-Mining, and Why Practitioners Should Do It

Decades before PCs and management information system software became accessible to social work administrators and researchers, Shyne recognized the enormous potential for programmatic decision-making inchoate in available agency information. Likewise, she recognized the reluctance that both practitioners and researchers might have toward using it. In her characteristically understated way, she averred that studies based on available administrative data were "not very popular with social work practitioners or with social work researchers" (Shyne, 1960, p. 107). They weren't then and they aren't now, although I would submit that there are different reasons for this. Academic researchers tend to object to its use on epistemological grounds, although I suspect that it has as much to do with yielding power and authority.

In my clinical data-mining (CDM) experience, practitioners are quite willing to use available data; they just haven't been taught that it is a "legitimate" research strategy. Elsewhere, Blumenfield and I make use of Veblen's ironic and iconic concept of "trained incapacity" to describe how practitioners are persuaded that research is beyond their skill set. In my opinion, the messages contained within the evidence-based practice (EBP) movement add to the problem. Alternatively, CDM represents a potential corrective to practitioner alienation from research. As one neophyte CDM practitioner-researcher recently put it, "I think it's great. I just didn't know it was O.K. to do that."

Writing from the vantage point of the fine researcher that she was, Shyne anticipated every methodological limitation, every epistemological headache, and every practical advantage associated with the research use of available data that I will discuss in this and subsequent chapters. Three decades later, I resurrected Shyne's methodological approach and now routinely start each of my practice-based research (PBR) agency consultations by exploring the CDM possibilities (Epstein, 2007). Clearly as well, my disappointment with prior practice-research integration efforts created the personal platform for this "new," and at least by my standards, highly successful practice-research strategy.

Although I indicated that my original research use of available agency information characterized my first social work publication, this chapter describes my personal "discovery" and conscious consideration of CDM as a distinct research method. In it, I discuss in detail the study that has served as a prototype for all succeeding CDM studies. I begin the chapter, however, by broadly describing the many possible sources of CDM data in making the case for using available information in PBR studies. Then I describe some other early PBR efforts based on available information that led to my self-conscious articulation of CDM within the context of that prototypical study. Next, in building my case for the legitimacy of CDM, I indicate why I think social work practitioners should do PBR studies in general and CDM in particular. Finally, I discuss the various benefits as well as the limitations of using available data for research purposes. Predictably, unlike other researchers, and possibly even Shyne on the subject, my list of positives outweighs the negatives.

THE SOURCES OF CDM DATA

In the course of their work with individuals, families, groups, organizations, and communities, social work practitioners routinely generate and store enormous quantities of data. These data sources may include anything from handwritten case notes to word-processed and computerized case records, minutes of meetings, tape-recorded or video-taped interviews, administrative spreadsheet data, numerical scores on standardized quantitative assessment or outcome instruments, client satisfaction questionnaires, and electronic records. Data may be stored in personal diaries, file cabinets, personal computers, clinical and/or management information systems, and so forth.

Although collected for administrative or training purposes or just to create a clinical or organizational "memory" of events, they are rarely collected with a research purpose in mind. Consequently, they are infrequently retrieved, aggregated, and systematically analyzed. When they are, as in the case of management information systems data, they are generally analyzed for external accountability purposes alone. In cybernetic terms, while practitioners may "input" these data, they do not participate in the "throughput," and the informational "output" does not get shared with them. Thus they become structurally disconnected (some might say "alienated") from the very data that they themselves have created in the routine course of their work. What sets CDM apart is that it provides practitioners with an opportunity to recapture, analyze, and interpret these data for their own knowledge-generation and/or decision-making purposes. Thus, CDM completes the cybernetic loop.

Historically, voluminous case-recording was seen as a vehicle for social work supervision, education, and practitioner self-reflection. In today's managed care environment, this in depth, discursive use of practitioner-generated information is viewed as unproductive and much too costly. In contrast, however, many settings do require extensive, systematic, and standardized documentation for reimbursement and accreditation purposes or for protection against liability. Future social workers in health and mental health settings, in particular, are likely to be required to contribute to an "electronic record" describing patient characteristics, practitioner interventions, and patient outcomes along with physicians, nurses, and allied health professionals. For all members of the health team, electronic recording is likely to become mandatory.

Ultimately, whether these data will be used by practitioners for research purposes or not is an entirely different and, possibly, a "political" question. In the latter sense, returning data and the information contained within to practitioners for the purposes of their own collective reflection has powerful professional and organizational implications. In my "Mining for Silver" paper, however, I argued for the consideration of CDM from a purely research perspective:

> Despite the amount, accessibility, and unintrusiveness of available clinical information, social work researchers generally have rejected the conduct of studies based on it claiming that this information is unreliable.... As a result...the research potential of retrospective studies based on available clinical information has been relatively unexplored and untested. (Epstein, 2001, p. 16)

Not knowing that I would spend the next decade of my career exploring the practice-research potential of varied sources of available agency data, I went on to adumbrate what was to become the central premise and metaphorical underpinning of this book:

> Nonetheless, although not originally intended for research purposes, available clinical information can be 'mined' and converted into valuable retrospective, quantitative data-bases for practice-research studies. (Epstein, 2001, p. 16)

Today, with the empirical evidence and personal experience of many completed and published CDM studies, I would modify that original premise as follows:

Although not originally intended for research purposes, available clinical data can be 'mined' and converted into valuable retrospective, quantitative *and qualitative databases for practitioner-research studies as well as for doctoral dissertation research.*

The remainder of this book is intended to demonstrate the validity of this proposition and to encourage the reader to consider CDM as a legitimate and robust methodological option, despite its acknowledged "silver standard" limitations.

SOME EARLY CDM EFFORTS

In Weissman's book entitled *Serious Play: Creativity and Innovation in Social Work,* Grasso and I published a paper about the nonroutine use of routinely available agency data in promoting program innovation (Epstein & Grasso, 1990). Although written a decade before I called it CDM, several of our exemplars involved practitioner-conducted quantitative studies based on available data—some computerized, some in handwritten case records and one, quite literally rescued from a garbage can.

Perhaps the most elegant and dramatic of these early CDM efforts was a study that involved practitioners making use of computerized family and individual client intake data as well as clinical case records. Beginning with standardized, quantitative, adolescent and family coping scores that the agency routinely collected for assessment purposes and moving on to qualitative client self-disclosures, the study employed what was basically a CDM approach to documenting the prevalence of sexual abuse among children and adolescents placed at Boysville of Michigan. The study, conducted with extensive help from Boysville practitioners empirically tested a commonly held element of their "tacit knowledge" (Imre, 1985) that adolescent crime and delinquency was associated with, if not caused by, early childhood sexual abuse. This "practice wisdom" (Klein & Bloom, 1995) was widely believed by practitioners working "in the trenches" with adolescents at Boysville and, in my experience, at many other youth-serving agencies. Certainly, it had never been empirically tested *within* the Boysville client population.

Remarkably, despite the prevalence of the belief among its practitioners, the agency had no special sexual abuse treatment program for young people placed there and provided no special sexual abuse training for social workers providing care for these youngsters. In that sense, it came closer to what Hartman referred to as "subjugated knowledge" (Hartman, 1992) in that while it was a pervasive belief it enjoyed no programmatic expression. The absence of such training and such a treatment program, left practitioners feeling ill-equipped to address a serious issue confronting an unknown percentage of Boysville residents. It also contributed to a sense of professional dissatisfaction and frustration that was occasionally, if ineffectively, expressed.

In our paper, Grasso and I described how:

A systematic survey of qualitative case-record data conducted by treatment staff validated this perception. That survey, which reviewed intake information as well as information revealed through client careers in the agency, indicated that nearly 60 percent of the males and 93 percent of the females in placement had been involved in sexual abuse before placement at the agency. (Epstein & Grasso, 1990, p. 34)

Admittedly, the study did not demonstrate a *causal* link between sexual abuse and juvenile delinquency in the Boysville client population. Nonetheless, it validated staff perceptions that prior sexual abuse was endemic to the majority of Boysville's client population—massively so to the young women—which led to the development of a sexual abuse training program for staff and a treatment program for young persons in placement.

In this study, for reasons of confidentiality, practitioners extracted client data from their own case recordings and Grasso and I accessed Boysville's Computerized Clinical Information System (BOMIS). Although through research training and by setting rules about data-extraction and coding, we ensured that practitioners who were extracting data were maintaining confidentiality of their records regarding sexual abuse, contemporary critics of CDM have argued that their findings were the result of a self-fulfilling prophecy.In other words, academic research critics might contend that practitioner-researchers cannot be trusted to fairly test and to possibly refute their cherished clinical theories or practice wisdom.

As a counterfactual to that argument, in the same paper but from other agencies, we offer three less than elegant exemplars of practitioner-conducted studies based on available information. In these CDM studies, however, the findings *negated* the workers' beliefs and expectations. So, for example, in a study conducted in family-service agency in which too many potential clients were lost because of time delays in the intake process, the central unanticipated finding was that part-time intake workers who worked largely at home completed the intake process more efficiently than full-time workers located in the agency (Epstein & Grasso, 1990, p. 34). This came as a complete and unwelcome surprise to the full-time workers who conducted the study.

Another study we cited was conducted in a family treatment training program for psychiatrists that had never been evaluated. The purpose of that program was to encourage psychiatric residents to provide family treatment where appropriate rather than limiting themselves to one-on-one treatment. Although the training director was loathe to conduct a study based on the "simplistic" and "crude" quantitative notion that family treatment could only be done when more than one member of the family were present, her reluctant review of psychiatric residents' case records revealed that 80% of their treatment interviews were conducted with only one patient (Epstein & Grasso, 1990, p. 35). This simple finding had complex implications and led to a complete and more comprehensive reevaluation of the program.

A final, though certainly least elegant, exemplar comes uncomfortably close to "dumpster-diving." In a senior citizen breakfast program, the program director was troubled by the amount of breakfast food that was being discarded, despite her well-intentioned effort to introduce variety into the morning menu. Her practice theory, of course, was that the more variety, the greater the consumer satisfaction. With an understandable reluctance, the program director followed our inelegant suggestion.

> Encouraged to count the types of food and the quantity thrown away, she inferred that program participants preferred the same daily menu rather than variety. A return to daily bagels from trendier muffins saved money and reduced waste. (Epstein & Grasso, 1990, p 34)

Of course the original research-oriented reader might respond that she could have simply asked the seniors what they wanted for breakfast. But several were disabled and when offered the more time-consuming PBR alternatives of a client satisfaction questionnaire or a focus group involving *original* data collection, dumpster data-mining was actually her methodology of choice. The most important point here, however, is that her findings ran counter to her expectations. Elegant or inelegant, that's why we do research—to discover that we might be wrong. What makes it "applied research" is that we do something different based upon what we found.

"DISCOVERING" CDM

Despite these nascent examples and formative experiences, my first impulse to self-consciously reflect on CDM as a distinct PBR consultation methodology came as a result of my work on a liver-transplant project at Mt. Sinai Medical Center in New York city. Until then, the methodology itself and my approach to engaging practitioners in the CDM process remained largely inchoate. The impetus to articulate CDM was precipitated by two conference-presentation invitations. The basis for both invitations was a single study however.

In a sense, my "discovery" of CDM came as a result of a highly successful, two-year PBR consultation experience with a team of four social workers and two psychiatrists who conducted psychosocial assessments of candidates for liver transplant at Mt. Sinai.

After patients with life-threatening liver disease were identified as suitable transplant candidates on purely medical grounds, the assessment team bore the heavy responsibility of determining which patients were suitable candidates on psychosocial grounds. As in all transplant settings, donor livers represented a scarce resource. For patients, a low rating on a psychosocial assessment could be tantamount to a death sentence. This was without question a far cry from decisions about bagels versus muffins, but I take all practitioner decision-making quite seriously.

What made the assessment team's task even more onerous was that because donor livers were so scarce they could only accept about half of patient requests. Patient candidates came to Mt. Sinai from all over the world hoping for a transplant. Some were very poor, others quite wealthy.

Consequently, the work was highly stressful for the team, and while they had done an unsystematic research literature review, they sought a more local "evidence-base" for their decision-making. Uncomfortable about making potentially life-and-death decisions based on studies done with other patients in other settings, they hoped to do a practice-based study of their *own* patient population. Since I was already a research consultant on several Mt. Sinai social work and multidisciplinary research projects, the consultation began with a request for me to help them design a *prospective* study of patient risk factors associated with liver-transplant outcomes.

Trained as a "gold-standard" researcher, my first thought naturally was a randomized, controlled experiment in which half of the patients who were medically approved would receive the transplant and half would not. Then, after a suitable period of time, we could look at "outcomes" of various kinds, including the ultimate liver-transplant outcomes—did the patient survive the operation and, if so, for how long? Then, I thought, we might look at psychosocial assessments as a way of explaining outcome differences.

Before I even got the words "randomly assign" out of my mouth, however, the team vociferously and collectively rejected my suggestion. First, it implied that they had no accumulated clinical expertise. Doing so would mean systematically ignoring the practice wisdom they had accumulated while they awaited the results of their "gold-standard" study. My suggestion would also require gathering follow-up data about each transplant and nontransplant patient for at least one year post-transplant or denial of transplant. Some patients who were denied transplants at Mt. Sinai might secure them elsewhere, and would they be willing to even talk to us after we turned them down? Finally, it might take three years to accumulate enough patients to make a reasonable inference about predictive factors. Despite the acknowledged epistemological benefits and logistical limitations of the experimental approach, the team clearly found my first study suggestion ethically intolerable and professionally abhorrent. Quite honestly, I was surprised at the intensity of their negative response.

By now, I was convinced that they were sincerely interested in conducting research, but I needed to come up with an acceptable design alternative. Before getting to this point, I should have remembered Shyne's injunction to consider all "available materials." However, returning to the team and understanding more about liver-transplant, practitioner-based study objectives, and design constraints than I did when we started, I went on to ask the assessment team two additional questions. The answers to these and my opening question led to my first, self-consciously named and implemented "CDM" project and the prototype for many succeeding projects. Accordingly, the three questions that I asked the liver-transplant assessment team became the starting questions for all future CDM enquiries.

The first and foremost question was "What are you interested in knowing?" After lengthy discussion with the team, I already knew the answer to that. In researchable terms, they wanted to know what psychosocial characteristics were associated with positive and negative liver-transplant outcomes?

Agreeing upon the question that would drive the study, my second question was "What data do you already have about these patients?" Their answer was astonishing.

Team members said they routinely collected data about patient demographics, support system, life stresses, functional status, mental health symptoms, past and present diagnosed mental disorders, cognitive deficits, past and present mental health treatment, suicidality, substance abuse history, medical history, history of medical compliance, and acuity of need for a transplant (Epstein, Zilberfein & Snyder, 1997, pp. 229–230). Some of these data sources came from patient interviews; some from standardized, self-administered instruments; some from psychiatrists' and social workers' clinical assessments; and some from the medical record. Wow!

As far as potential patient "outcome" measures were concerned, I learned that it was relatively easy for the team to access the hospital database indicating whether the patient was still alive or not, and if the patient had died, when that had occurred. This database could be linked to the assessment data via patient ID numbers, which could then be de-identified. This was getting even better.

My third question was "How many transplants have you already done with patients for whom you have all this information?

The answer was "Probably around 500." With this imprecise response, I sensed that I had struck "paydirt." Until then, it had never occurred to me that we might conduct a *retrospective* study of patient psychosocial risk factors and liver-transplant mortality. Nor did it occur to the assessment team. In response, I proposed that together we conduct a quantitative study based entirely on available data that they would extract from patient records and from hospital statistics. Once I was able to assure them that research based on available data was "legitimate," they all enthusiastically signed on. In fact, they loved the idea; so much for practitioner resistance to research.

In a relatively short time and with relatively little money, the practitioners' study became the largest, longest follow-up study of psychosocial factors and liver-transplant outcomes done to date both *within* Mt. Sinai and the published liver-transplant literature. An intramural grant of $ 5,000 covered all of the costs of data-entry and data-analysis. The rest was CDM history. My original definition of CDM and many of the principles and practices that emerged in the course of the liver-transplant study were the basis of my own guidelines for all future CDM consultations and studies.

STAKING THE CLAIM FOR THE LEGITIMACY OF CDM

As indicated above, I began presenting on the topic of CDM and writing about it as a response to invitations to present at two major conferences. The first was the National Symposium on Outcomes Measurement in the Human Services held at Columbia University School of Social Work in 1995. In the paper presented at that conference, which emphasized the use of quantitative outcome measures in health research, my Mt. Sinai colleagues and I discussed some of the methodological and ethical limitations of RCTs and "suggested that rather than be obsessed with failures to achieve the 'gold standard' of RCT social work research, more PBR should be conducted with available health information" (Epstein, Zilberfein & Snyder, 1997, p. 224). The liver-transplant study was used as an exemplar and potential prototype although no research findings were at that time ready to be presented. Perhaps it was a gamble, but it seemed worth taking.

In the Columbia Symposium paper, we also cited an article on measuring effects without using randomized trails published in the journal *Medical Care* (Moses, 1995) in which the physician who authored it boldly posited "the idea of information routinely generated in the course of health care delivery for assessing the effectiveness of alternative therapies has an undeniable attraction." He modestly concluded that research based on available data calls for "imaginative thinking, experimentation, and patience, but it is an idea deserving much effort" (Moses, 1995, p. 8). That effort is represented in the various exemplars that populate this book.

As indicated earlier, the first time I actually used the term "datamining" was a year after the Columbia Symposium in the "Mining for Silver" paper at the Melbourne Conference. That paper did not focus solely on the limitations of RCTs in practitioner-initiated research. In addition, it challenged the conventional academic assumption that the use of *standardized* instruments for measuring patient or client psychosocial variables is *always* preferable in social work research studies. More specifically, for PBR purposes, I irreverently argued that even in *prospective* studies based on *original data*, standardized, self-administered patient instruments

1. are often too long and cumbersome to allow for inclusion of more than only a few dimensions;
2. have been standardized on very different populations;
3. are not closely linked to practice concepts or practice theory;
4. employ language that is middle-class biased;
5. require relatively high literacy levels;
6. are, for all their 'psychometric robustness,' rarely shown to be predictive of setting-relevant, behavioral outcomes (Epstein, 2001, p. 20).

Since then, studies in diabetic medicine suggest that in some situations, well-documented patient records are *superior* to both patient and health professional recall of treatment based upon questionnaire responses (Parkin & Skinner, 2003; Skinner, Bernard Cradock & Parkin, 2007). Likewise, a recent single-system analysis of the effectiveness of an exercise intervention with Hispanic breast cancer patients indicated that of the 48 who volunteered to participate, only 25 (52%) completed the three sets of standardized baseline measurements and physical assessment required by the researchers and the single-system methodology, even though Spanish or English versions of the instruments were available (Hughes, Leung & Naus, 2008). And some of the measures involved "short form" versions of standardized measures.

Other than the practical, ethical, and clinical obstacles presented by the baseline research requirement of asking patients to repeatedly complete assessment instruments prior to intervention, it should also be noted that in this study, it was the researchers themselves who provided the highly standardized intervention. Perhaps that added to the problem.

For the most part, however, I believe that when standardized instruments (e.g., Rapid Assessment Instruments) are effectively and routinely used by practitioners alongside other more traditional and interpretive techniques, such as interviewing and observation for assessment as well as evaluation research purposes, the combination is ideal (Corcoran, 1997; Hudson, 1997). The use of standardized research instruments can more easily be incorporated into *prospective* research studies. But, in *retrospective* studies based on available clinical data, we rarely have that opportunity. Instead, we frequently must rely solely on the clinical information and professional judgments placed in the record by practitioners. For some researchers, however, that automatically disqualifies available clinical data sources from inclusion in research studies.

So, for example, in dismissing the possibilities of conducting research based on available records, Kagle (1996) cautions us that "...information that is accessible is not necessarily suitable for research. Although information that can be easily quantified may appear appropriate for research, it may actually be neither reliable nor valid" (p. 162).

Alternatively, I would argue that the clinical data that practitioners gather from service recipients and the clinical judgments that practitioners make are central to their professional expertise. This is what they are paid for. Moreover, we rely on these judgments in their practice decision-making. Why not incorporate them and their judgments *systematically* into the research process? This is precisely what CDM does, and beyond generating useful findings, it requires that practitioners reflect on their theories, purposes, assessment, and outcome criteria as well as on the available evidence of what they do and what they accomplish. Finally, research-based logic, procedures, and statistical methods can be used to assess the validity and reliability of available as well as original data. These are discussed in the following chapter and employed in some degree in every CDM study described in this book.

Regardless of how extensively they use these statistically based techniques, practitioners stand to benefit greatly from the opportunity that the consideration of the research concepts of validity and reliability gives them to reflect on the meanings of (1) their key practice concepts; (2) the observable indicators that they employ to make clinical judgments about them; (3) how consistently they use them; and (4) how much consensus there is about them among team members. These issues inevitably surface in CDM when we are developing data-extraction and coding instruments using case record and other practitioner-generated data.

As a PBR consultant and as someone who is extremely respectful of what practitioners do, I see this as an opportunity to collaboratively raise both theirs and my level of consciousness about their practice decision-making rather than as an opportunity to disparage them for their lack of clarity or consistency. The latter approach, which is so often used in the research classroom, can only have negative consequences for practitioner attitude formation about research (Epstein, 1987). That's where the "trained incapacity" often begins.

WHY SHOULD PRACTITIONERS DO RESEARCH?

While EBP proponents exhort practitioners to be sophisticated and critical consumers of research, their model of practice-research integration is silent about practitioners conducting their *own* research studies other than on a case by case, single-system design basis (McCracken & Marsh, 2008). Unlike academics or agency-based researchers, practitioners are not paid to produce research. Why should they?

Clearly, I believe that practitioners have a responsibility to constantly refine, test, and enhance their practice wisdom and to do that with their *own* "best available evidence" as well as with what the research literature provides. CDM does both in that it combines *local* empirical evidence with systematic research literature review. In fact, it "incentivizes" the latter because of the former. In other words, practitioners are much more likely to want to read and reflect upon other people's research when it has implications for their own. Consequently, CDM provides a more comprehensive and potentially richer knowledge base than either an EBP-prescribed systematic review or Schön's less systematic but more interpretive model of reflective practice alone would. Certainly, CDM does not ignore published studies. However, it brings them in at a slightly later stage in the research process. More will be said about literature review in the following chapter. Suffice it to say at this point, bringing together these two information streams and running them through the dual filters of agency constraints and professional values yields the more highly refined "evidence-informed" practice knowledge that I spoke of in the previous chapter.

Thinking about it this way, perhaps a more appropriate metaphor for CDM should be "panning for gold". Whatever the metaphor, CDM requires neither the use of standardized assessment instruments, the denial of service until a "stable baseline" can be achieved, nor the imposition of a standardized, evidence-based "practice manual" for practitioner research to take place.

More generally, a career's experience of trying to engage Master's and Doctoral students and practitioners in research has convinced me that it is only through their own "hands-on" experience with the research process that they can become both critical and *appreciative* consumers of prior research. By this, I mean having the capacity to recognize the inevitable flaws in every existing research effort as well as their own research and the capacity to learn what there is to learn from both. That includes the imperfections *within* each and the contradictions *between* them. Indeed, as I frequently remind my practitioner-researcher colleagues and my doctoral dissertation students, we benefit most from (1) the findings that are inconsistent with our expectations; and (2) the contradictions among our findings. That's where the real learning begins.

For the reader, a moment's reflection should reveal that as a practice-research integration strategy, CDM is more ambitious as well as more respectful of the capacities of practitioners than is the case with most interpretations of EBP.

WHY SHOULD PRACTITIONERS DO CDM?

If you agree that practitioners should play an active role in the research process, let me suggest that CDM is the most effective way of promoting that. There are several reasons why.

First and most important, it begins with "ore" that is rich, familiar, and often easily accessible to the practitioners. Though retrieval may require new organizational arrangements, for the most part, this is information that practitioners themselves have generated. As a result, they have a professional stake in its value and utility. Remarkably, CDM provides an opportunity for many social workers to read their own case materials from start to finish—often for the first time. As several practitioner-data-miners have attested, this, in itself, can constitute a revelatory learning process.

Second, CDM is entirely *unintrusive* and *naturalistic*. In other words, data-gathering does not intrude in any way into the practice context since the practice that is being studied has already been completed. Closely related to this is the fact that the process of information gathering is relatively *nonreactive*. Unlike practice-research studies that introduce some kind of data-gathering instrument into the treatment process primarily for research purposes, the data gathered by practitioners through questions or observation is intrinsic to the practice. Consequently, there is less reason to be concerned that respondents will react negatively or fabricate responses to please the practitioner than if they were completing a standardized research instrument. Of course, issues of transference or desires to influence or manipulate service outcomes are never completely eliminated though practitioners are trained to deal with them. However, these potential biases can be respectfully considered during the data-collection process. Most importantly, in CDM, they are not further obscured or confounded by an overlay of externally imposed research requirements.

Third, CDM studies do not require manipulation of practice for knowledge-generation purposes. Although we may employ *experimental logic*, CDM never makes use of control groups, random assignment to various intervention options, withholding or withdrawal of treatment interventions, or the like, for the purpose of inferring the impact of practice. As discussed earlier, design variations of these kinds are ethically objectionable to most practitioners. In addition, it is relatively easy to *de-identify* CDM data so that client anonymity is protected.

Finally, CDM studies are relatively inexpensive to conduct and offer the possibility of efficient sampling of large numbers of cases. In some instances, whole patient or client populations are studied, precluding the need for sampling. In large, quantitative studies, CDM allows for the use of various sampling procedures as well as fairly sophisticated and robust multivariate analyses if the data satisfy their analytic requirements, and the practitioner-researchers are statistically sophisticated and sufficiently robust. If not, a great deal can be learned from small-scale descriptive studies that are based on the total client population and make use of only percentages and univariate analyses or via qualitative analysis And, as will be seen in Chapter 5 on the CDM dissertation, some doctoral students have conducted their studies with quite sizable samples depending upon the availability and the extent to which the information is already computerized. Naturally, with the advent of electronic records, the potential for CDM studies with large samples will only be increased.

Writing before computerization of agency records, the ever-practical Ann Shyne made multiple references to the efficiencies achieved by researchers working with available information:

> Data collection is very expensive in time and money. It is obviously inefficient to engage in such a costly process if available data will serve the purpose just as well. (Shyne, 1960, p. 108)

> Not only does collection of original data tend to be costly, but it may so prolong a study that the question at issue may have ceased to be important by the time the study is completed. (Shyne, 1960, p. 109)

> Another practical consideration is the effect on agency operation of carrying out a research project. Collection of new data frequently necessitates the participation of the service staff. If this participation consists merely of noting a few factual items that are ordinarily known to service personnel, it will not be seriously disruptive to service. If, However, it involves additional recording beyond that usually expected, then the time available for service is reduced." (Shyne, 1960, p. 109)

Looking at the larger picture, how much better is it if evaluative studies are conducted by practitioners who have a direct investment in the practice and program implications of the studies they are doing? Some would respond that it is precisely their stake in the process that represents an insurmountable obstacle to practitioner research. For example, a program officer from a major federal research funding agency who attended my first CDM presentation in Australia was impressed by the obvious enthusiasm in response to my talk. The international audience was largely made up of practitioners.

Speaking with me afterwards, his interest seemed to flag when he realized that I was talking about practitioners doing the research. Our conversation ended with his rhetorical question, "How can you expect practitioners to be objective enough to evaluate their own practice?" Without waiting for an answer, he shook his head and walked away.

From my perspective, the investment of practitioners in their own practice is a strength and/or an issue to be productively explored through the research consultation process, rather than a deficit. Consequently, this book is as much about research *in* practice as it is about research *on* practice. But perhaps I have been hanging around with practitioners too long.

THE "PITFALLS" OF CDM STUDIES

After all this overt advocacy, candor requires that I also acknowledge that like any research methodology, CDM has some serious drawbacks and potential pitfalls.

First and foremost, CDM is, more often than not, labor-intensive, tedious, and occasionally dirty work. It's one thing if we are working with electronic records and all the information is computerized; it's quite another if the central sources of data must be retrieved from handwritten files, stored in ancient file cabinets or in cardboard boxes in roach-populated closets. Practitioners with dust allergies beware. CDM can be bad for your health: though it can't compare with being mortally threatened and physically thrown out of places by community residents that you are supposed to be interviewing. Or, having a co-interviewer robbed and stabbed on the first day of a study after all the safety-training sessions had been completed. As a veteran applied researcher, I've survived all of the above.

In CDM, perhaps the closest equivalent to the "canary in the mines" is the wheezing and sneezing that occasionally afflict practitioner-researchers in the process. Rarely life-threatening, when it happens, it's still a good time to come up for air.

Another problem ironically emerges from one of CDM's great advantages. It's too cheap. For academics who are seeking large research grants and academic administrators hankering for overhead, it is not especially lucrative. Although I have had some success with securing relatively small intramural or external foundation ($5,000–30,000) grants that supplied adequate resources for the proposed studies, few academic or agency funding sources are willing to finance CDM studies—either because funders assume that meaningful research can only be done with original, research-intended data or that they should be conducted by academic researchers rather than by practitioners. In addition to questioning the objectivity of practitioner-researchers, another common potential funder response is " if you already have the data, why do you need a grant to study it?"

Then there are the problems with the data. Oftentimes, the variables that are of greatest interest are simply not available. Simply stated, *missing data is the bane of the CDM researcher.* Always was and always will be. Although "heavy-duty" business data-miners are coming up with elaborate statistical techniques to compensate for missing data, for example, www.salford-systems.com, a half a century ago, Shyne alerted us to the problem:

> This point may seem too obvious or elementary to mention; however, it is easy to be trapped into assuming that data important to one's study plan will be available simply because the agency has intended that such a record be kept. (Shyne, 1960, p. 112)

Obvious and elementary perhaps, but each time one encounters the variable void, it's as though it's the first time. No "discovery" requires more rethinking than the realization that the dimensions you are most interested in studying and that were supposed to be there just ain't there. One example that immediately comes to mind is a CDM project wherein practitioners were well versed in the "strength-perspective" theory and rhetoric.

Much effort was expended developing an instrument that would extract from patient records data reflecting patient strengths and family supports as well as patient risks and family deficits. When we completed the data-extraction phase and conducted our analysis, what came as quite a shock to all of us was how little data were available concerning patient strengths and family supports in patient records. No amount of statistical manipulation could make up for that.

Nonetheless, from a practice standpoint, this disappointing finding led to an extremely productive discussion of why these data were missing and how they should be reflected in future case-recording. What became clear from this discussion was that despite their rhetoric practitioners were still viewing patients and their families through a risk and deficit "lens," which was reinforced by the organizational context in which they practiced. Likewise, the process of operationalizing relevant indicators of patient strengths and family supports increased workers' sensitivity to these important dimensions and the degree to which they fell short of their own rhetoric in their practice. More generally, reflection on these contradictions was enormously helpful and produced a much more refined conception of what a strength perspective could mean in a hospital setting. At the very least, however, it led to an improvement in the quality of their case recording.

Other ambiguities inherent within CDM are apparent in the prior study as well. Do all workers mean the same thing when they employ a key concept such as patient strengths? Do all workers rely on the same indicators in making their clinical judgments about family supports? Does each worker rely on the same indicators in making judgments over time? Does the absence of a comment about a particular dimension (e.g., patient adherence) imply the absence of that phenomenon (i.e., the patient is following medical recommendations)? Applying these research-based validity and reliability questions with these workers to their practice was wonderfully productive and led to a clearer understanding and greater consistency of the team's purpose and intervention approach.

Just as with every other research approach, problems of validity and reliability confront every CDM study. With regard to studies based on available data, Shyne's brief paper devotes two full pages to strategies for dealing with validity and reliability problems; her introduction to this section captures the essence of this CDM quandary.

> Assuming that the necessary data appear to be available with sufficient consistency to permit their use in addressing oneself to the problem at hand, there remains the more difficult question of whether the data are what they seem to be. (Shyne, 1960, p. 113)

A final problem that I have encountered but Shyne did not mention is the way CDM can surface political and organizational conflicts in complex bureaucratic settings where different departments have responsibility for maintaining accurate and accessible information systems. Hospitals are such settings in which Information Technology, Hospital Records, Quality Assurance, Human Resources Departments, and so forth are expected to maintain and sustain consistently trustworthy databases.

In more than one CDM study in more than one organization, major gaps and inconsistencies in data systems became obvious only by virtue of trying to conduct studies that required the integration of multiple sources of available data. So, for example, in conducting a CDM study of employee turnover, there was something definitely wrong when the same employees were listed as "no longer employed" on one organizational database and "employed" on another. And, no matter how postmodernist, social constructionist, or phenomenological one chooses to be, there is something wrong when several patients are "alive" on one database and simultaneously listed as "deceased" on another.

Neither of these examples is hypothetical. Separate from the research implications, such discoveries are politically disruptive and potentially embarrassing though one can argue that it is better to identify these problems and correct them than to make organizational decisions based on the assumption that both contradictory "facts" are true.

Even when information systems are accurate and reliable, they are not always compatible. Often they have been created at different points in time, at different stages in the development of information technology, by different consultants wed to different software preferences. As a result, integration of data from multiple systems and sources may be much more costly than anticipated and too costly to consider.

Writing before the advent of computerized clinical and management information systems, Shyne could not possibly anticipate these intraorganizational, information systems problems. But in making the case *for* studies using available information, she deserves the final words of support in this chapter for such studies.

> Although no one would gainsay the desirability of the projected experimental study with the researcher in full control of data collection, the difficulty of attaining this ideal should not be underestimated, nor should the social work researcher underestimate the results to be derived from, nor the wisdom and skills required in analysis of the wealth of material already available to him. (Shyne, 1960, p. 123)

CONCLUSION

In concluding this chapter, I address my final comments to my fellow academics who maintain a hard and fast distinction between those who do research and those who apply it. Likewise, I want to direct some comments to those who categorically reject available clinical data, a potential research resource.

Clearly and emphatically, in this chapter, I have argued that RCTs, Single-Systems Designs, and standardized research instruments have serious limitations for practitioner-research but that practitioners should be actively engaged in PBR. This handbook is based on my "strongly agreeing" with the foregoing sentence. (Of course I agree with it; I wrote it.) From the standpoint of practitioner engagement, research productivity, and application to practice, CDM is the most effective and efficient PBR strategy that I know of. But that, in turn, assumes that practitioner-generated data can serve as legitimate basis for meaningful research.

It goes without saying that many of my research colleagues "strongly disagree" with all of the above. However, with regard to the concern about the validity and reliability of practitioner-generated information, let me make one final point.

If practitioners' files and case-record entries concerning client psychosocial attributes, social work interventions, and client outcomes are essentially and intrinsically unreliable and invalid, what justification is there for practitioners to work with and make intervention decisions about patients or clients in the first place? This is what they are paid to do. If they had to wait for "evidence-based" researchers and research studies to generate sufficient knowledge to eliminate all the uncertainty and complexity that practitioners deal with on a daily basis, it would be disastrous for the individuals, families, and communities that social workers serve.

The often-heard EBP claim that practitioners should only employ interventions that are *proven* to be effective and if not should be accompanied by a disclaimer is based on a fundamental distrust of practitioners. Alternatively, a recent article by Aisenberg (2008) concerning the premature and inappropriate application of "evidence-based" mental health interventions to ethnic minority patients raises question about the extent to which we can trust EBP claims to universality.

CDM, in particular, and PBR, in general, are built on *trust* rather than *distrust* of practitioners. Trust that practitioners are committed to best interests of the clients they serve and trust that they are interested in knowing who they are serving and how to serve them best. CDM can help them answer those questions. However, because CDM makes use of sound research concepts and principles such as validity and reliability and because it promotes articulation and empirical testing of practice wisdom and/or program theory, it does not imply *blind trust*.

Indeed, it encourages practitioners to be self-reflective, self-critical, and open to learning from even those research findings that do not support their prior expectations. Starting with a foundation of mutual trust, CDM consultation offers practitioners an opportunity to contribute the knowledge base and to learn about both research and practice in doing so.

Before I called it CDM, my prototype liver-transplant study was cumbersomely described as a "retrospective, quasi-experimental outcomes study of psychosocial selection based on routinely available information" (Epstein, Zilberfein & Snyder, 1997, p. 227). In the "Mining for Silver" paper, the Mt. Sinai liver transplant study joined other CDM studies facilitated by me but conducted by practitioners in an agency serving the homeless, a VA Hospital, and at Mt. Sinai's Adolescent Health Center as case examples intended to demonstrate its potential as a PBR strategy.

In the first book on the subject, the former Director of Social Work Services at Mount Sinai and I co-edited a collection of six, peer-reviewed CDM studies that were conducted by practitioners and researchers working collaboratively with me and with less than a handful of other like-minded academic researchers in Australia, Israel, and the United States—places in which I had conducted CDM workshops (Blumenfield & Epstein, 2001).

In Peake, Epstein & Medeiros (2005) is presented a subsequent collection of 10 quantitative, peer-reviewed CDM studies co-authored by adolescent mental health social workers who had never before conducted and/or published research studies. Also, in 2005, was published a special issue of the *Journal of Social Work Research & Evaluation*, entirely devoted to a multidisciplinary quantitative and qualitative CDM articles by Australian allied health practitioners working by themselves or in collaboration with me or with Lynette Joubert from the University of Melbourne.

These collections and an increasing number of individually published CDM articles and completed CDM doctoral dissertations that are referred to in Chapters 4, 5, and 6 are offered as "evidence" of the utility of CDM as distinct research and PBR consultation methodology, of the contribution it can make to practice knowledge development, and of its effectiveness as a strategy for engaging practitioners in the coproduction of useful practice knowledge.

The next chapter attempts to convey both the "science" and "art" of CDM. In so doing, it presents a working definition of CDM, describes in greater detail the purposes of CDM, the steps in the CDM process and the infrastructural resources and supports necessary to sustain it. The chapter concludes with principles that govern effective CDM consultation.

3

The "Science" of CDM and the "Art" of Strategic Compromise

In the previous chapter, I indicated that the premise of this book, which has emerged out of a decade's experience exploring the potential of clinical data-mining (CDM) is that available clinical data can be "mined" and converted into valuable retrospective, quantitative, and qualitative databases for practice-based research (PBR) studies as well as for doctoral dissertation research. Just as this premise has evolved, so have the working definition of CDM, the basic steps involved in the CDM process, and the principles of CDM research consultation. While the principles of CDM are rooted in firmly established social research methods, their application inevitably requires what I have called "strategic compromise." The research methods are consistent with what we call "science"; their application comes closer to an "art."

Comfort and skill with *strategic compromise* are essential to effective CDM consultation. It entails knowing when ideal research approaches must be modified or adapted to the limitations of available data (or the absence of desired data) and how to maximize the knowledge-generating potential of the study despite its informational shortcomings. However, experienced researchers know that virtually all agency or community-based research studies—even prospective studies based on original data collection—require making compromises in their implementation and taking these compromises into account in their interpretation (Alexander & Solomon, 2006). The "real world" studies that require no compromises are the rare exceptions rather than the rule. In fact, I can't think of any.

Just as practitioners refine their skills over the years, I believe that my own mastery of the art of strategic compromise evolves with each new CDM study. In the introduction, I offered a simple *nominal* definition of CDM. However, with each new application of CDM, its *operational* definition evolves. And, while I like to think I become more graceful in my CDM artistry over time, my current working definition of CDM looks more like a dancing bear than a Baryshnikov.

Nonetheless, this chapter begins with my most recent and graceless operational definition of CDM. It then describes the steps that must be taken to successfully embark on a CDM expedition. Next are described various infrastructural arrangements that have been employed in support of successful CDM efforts. Finally, for aspiring practice-research consultants, I describe the consultation principles that have guided me in my conjoint CDM expeditions. In doing so, I remind the reader that none of the foregoing is static and immutable like the formula for the "classical" experimental design. Much has been modified and refined with each new CDM study. Indeed, in the final chapter, I describe some future CDM studies that are already underway and promising methodological advances that might be incorporated into CDM.

Perhaps the reminder is gratuitous, however. For "high-minded" audience members who judge a work by its location on the evidence-based practice (EBP) hierarchy, my departures from evidentiary ideals may be all-too-obvious and none-too-acceptable. Some even view my work as "pre-evidentiary." But, while CDM critics might dwell of its limitations, CDM practitioners have been understandably occupied with the findings of their studies, and doctoral students have been adding methodological refinements with each new dissertation application.

WORKING DEFINITION OF CDM

After this lengthy overture, it is about time that I operationally defined CDM. As indicated above, the definition has been changing and expanding with each new use. For now, the following working definition will do:

> Clinical data-mining is a practice-based, retrospective research strategy whereby practitioner-researchers, alone or with the assistance of a research consultant, systematically retrieve, codify, analyze and interpret available qualitative and/or quantitative data from their own and other agency records in order to reflect on the practice, program and/or policy implications of their findings.

In this context, it is important to say something about the use of the word "clinical" in CDM. Because my initial CDM efforts took place primarily in medical settings and were focused on patient needs, services received, and patient outcomes, I chose the adjective "clinical" in its literal sense as the best descriptor of the purpose for which and context in which these studies took place. The term was also intended to differentiate what I was doing from more conventional, business, and/or governmental antiterrorist uses of data-mining.

With subsequent applications, CDM has been employed in studies of service recipients in nonmedical settings, such as child welfare and for nonpatient populations, such as family members who provide informal patient care. In addition, CDM methodology has been used to study or make inferences about units of analysis other than individuals. Thus, CDM has been used to seek generalizations about families, social programs, social agencies, aggregates of agencies, and in one recent doctoral dissertation, the impact of an antipoverty program on an entire nation including unintended as well as intended service recipients. As a result, some have suggested that I refer to it as "practitioner data-mining." Perhaps this more inclusive and less "clinical" label is more descriptive of its potential use. For the purposes of this book, I prefer to stick with CDM. In truth, however, I'm less concerned with what it is called than with convincing researchers and practitioners alike that studies based on available data have a legitimate place in the social work and allied health practice-research repertoire.

Webster's first definition of "clinical" is "of, relating to, or conducted in or as if in a clinic" (1970, p. 135). That's where CDM began. Since then, I have admittedly stretched the definition beyond its literal meaning. However, what "clinically" links all of these horizontal and vertical applications of CDM is that they all involve social workers and/or other health care professionals in making research use of available data in human service settings with the intention of improving practice effectiveness and efficiency.

Some skeptics have asked whether I could "prove" that CDM does these things, to which I acknowledge that, at this point, these are more like "hypotheses" for which I have an increasing amount of supportive personal experience and "empirical evidence" in the form of peer-reviewed publications and completed doctoral dissertations supervised by me and by like-minded academic research colleagues. Admittedly, however, these are testable propositions. Although I have no "proof" that would satisfy die-hard experimentalists, it would be possible to design meta-evaluative studies that compared CDM with other PBR and EBP practice-research integration strategies. Admittedly, I haven't tried because my full attention has been given to both the challenges and the valuable yields that have come from each new CDM operation. Perhaps it's me who has the social work research equivalent of "mining fever."

SECURING ADMINISTRATIVE SUPPORT AND ORGANIZATIONAL LEGITIMATION

Whether CDM-crazed or not, there is little question in my mind that the success of every prior CDM project has depended on the financial, structural, and symbolic support that program administrators, managers, and supervisors have provided. Although the financial and structural resources required are relatively low (i.e., my consulting fees, some released time for participating social workers, and costs of data-entry and processing), the symbolic support of organizational administration for practitioner-research is crucial. Securing such support is not easy because many social work program administrators do not think of research and knowledge-production as a legitimate role for practitioners. Others think of it as a distraction from practice. Unfortunately, such views are quite common and probably reinforced by some interpretations of the EBP movement.

So, for the majority of administrators, what I am advocating is at best seen as a "luxury item" and at worst, an inappropriate expectation. Rarer still are those visionary administrators who see PBR as a necessary element in staff development and in promoting reflective practice

(Blumenfield & Epstein, 2001; Peake, Epstein & Medeiros, 2005; Rehr, 1992). These are the leaders who provide an infrastructure and maintain an organizational culture that is required for PBR to flourish and CDM to be successfully implemented. Inherent in such an infrastructure is a reward system that encourages practitioner-initiated research, conference presentation, publication, and so on. I've been blessed to know a few such leaders.

BEGINNING PBR AND CDM QUESTIONS

Once permission has been granted and access to research-oriented staff has been provided, some very basic ground is gone over. Before even contemplating a CDM study, I begin with some rather obvious PBR consultation questions. The first is "What is your service or treatment program trying to achieve?" Once there is some consensus on program objectives, I generally ask "How do you go about achieving this?" The answer to that question gives me an initial understanding of the treatment or organizational technology that is employed and the "program theory" that drives the work. Next, I ask "Who are you trying to serve?" This tells me about the intended target population. The answer to "How well do you do with this?" gives me a general sense of their perceived level of success in engaging the target population and their perceived effectiveness. "How do you know when you've done a really good job?" provides information about the indicators that they use to evaluate their own performance. Finally, responses to "What are the things that get in the way?" tell me about the perceived obstacles and problems that they experience.

In asking these questions and *positively* probing the answers I receive, I never challenge practitioners about their inability to articulate treatment or program goals and objectives or when each of them says different things. As surprising or disappointing as it may sound to research academics, practitioners often have considerable difficulty in responding to these questions. Frequently, they disagree among themselves when they do answer. Rather than suggest that this reveals their lack of evaluation acumen or that this reflects a supervisory problem, I accept it nonjudgmentally. In fact, I treat it as "normal" and, in an empirical sense, it is. I've come to expect it.

Whatever the reasons for it, in my experience, difficulty in articulating treatment or program objectives or inability to state the explanatory linkage between the two is endemic among practitioners. However, if a positive working relationship is to be established, it is extremely damaging to disparage practitioners' difficulties in giving clear and consistent answers to these questions or to fault their supervisors or program administrators. Such disparaging comments can scuttle a PBR or CDM operation before it even begins. Instead, I use this as an opportunity to help practitioners inform me as well as themselves about the work they do and why. My being nonjudgmental and accepting of this "organizational irrationality" is as well a part of building trust and promoting collaboration.

As I learned from the liver transplant study discussed in the previous chapter, once I feel oriented and there is a general consensus among the workers, I begin exploring the CDM possibilities with the following questions:

- What are you interested in knowing?
- What data are currently available in your agency that is in any way related to your interest?
- How much of these data is currently accessible to you?

In sorting through their responses to the first question, I gently but extensively probe so that we arrive at a consensual understanding of what they are interested in learning rather than what they would like to *prove*. Often the latter is about justifying their work but it gets expressed in the form of "wouldn't it be interesting to know" statements. Occasionally, people tell me that their research interest emerges from a school assignment they once had or some similar research that they recently became aware of or that their program has never been researched or evaluated or that they want to "prove" how successful their program is.

Here, I make it clear that applied research is neither about justifying a program or definitely proving that interventions work. Nor is it sufficient to generate "interesting" findings. Instead, PBR, in general, and CDM, in particular, are about making discoveries that are useful for practice and program decision-making. This is only possible if the research is done with an awareness of how the questions that drive the research are at least potentially linked to treatment or programmatic decisions. In addition, I make it clear that it requires openness to making *negative* as well as *positive* practice findings, in other words, discovering that you are wrong. Alternatively, coming up with "interesting" findings is not enough if there are no practice implications. And, while PBR, in general, and CDM, in particular, are intended to answer practice-relevant questions, their primary purpose is not practice justification.

METHODOLOGICAL CHOICES

From a methodological standpoint, there are only three basic types of CDM studies. I can't imagine the types changing, though in the future the frequency of their use might. Some begin with available *quantitative* data that is directly convertible into a quantitative database that can be statistically analyzed. These studies closely approximate "secondary analyses" (SA). However, as I indicated earlier, what sets these CDM studies apart from SAs is that the latter make use of existing databases that have been generated for research purposes to begin with. Moreover, SAs often make use of standardized research instruments with established reliability and validity as well as statistical norms. They may or may not involve large amounts of missing data.

By contrast, in CDM studies of this type, available quantitative agency databases are likely to have been originated for purely program account-ability and monitoring functions. As a result, their research potential has rarely been explored or exploited. However, CDM findings are more likely to be directly practice relevant than is the case with SAs.

A second type of CDM study is based upon available information that originates in narrative form, but is then converted *from qualitative data to quantitative databases* and analyzed statistically as well. Examples are studies that make use of social workers' clinical case records. In such instances, the databases may include variables reflecting clinical assessments, practitioner interventions, and client outcomes that offer significant coding challenges as well as the more easily codified client demographics.

A final methodological possibility involves available *qualitative data* that are converted into a database for subsequent *qualitative* analysis. At this point in CDM developmental history, this is a far more rare occurrence than the prior two options.

Several CDM practitioner-initiated studies have combined Type 1 and Type 2. So, for example, the liver transplant study was entirely quantitative but involved conversion of qualitative case-information into a quantitative database that was linked to the hospital database that measured outcome variables such as whether the patient survived the transplant and for how long. Studies such as these will be discussed in Chapter 4.

In principle and in some instances (particularly in doctoral dissertations), CDM studies may combine different types of data-extraction, conversion, and analysis. For the CDM consultant or the dissertation advisor as well as the practitioner-researcher, such studies require a wide research repertoire, paradigmatic flexibility, and, above all, imagination and inventiveness. Some "mixed-method" studies have combined CDM with *original* data-collection. Others have broken ground in doing purely qualitative CDM. It should come as no surprise that in my experience such ground-breaking studies are most likely to be conducted by doctoral students who are less methodologically hidebound than many of their professors. Their innovative work is discussed in Chapter 5 on the CDM doctoral dissertation and in Chapter 6 on qualitative CDM.

I've yet to crack the problem of converting available quantitative information into qualitative data though there are many times that I wish I could. But who knows? Who could have imagined a telephone that takes pictures and receives e-mails? Certainly not me. Anyway, I'll leave that conversion problem to my more technologically sophisticated compeers.

As with any applied research study, however, the decision about which methodological paradigm to employ is determined by the question that is driving the study as well as the more pragmatic and ethical issues, such as resources, access, cost, and the importance of not doing harm to research subjects (and for that matter, to the practice-researchers).

Pragmatically speaking, CDM studies begin with what data are currently available and how these can inform our practice understanding? Consequently, CDM studies are more heavily influenced by practical considerations than are those based on original data-collection. The creative challenge to the CDM consultant, the practitioner-researcher, and the doctoral student is to envision what is potentially precious in the available data, to extract, refine, interpret, and apply it.

Often, before there is even a research question, the process begins with prospecting all available data-sources. Such is the case when practitioners know that they want to do some evaluation research on their practice but can't articulate a research question. In such instances, as a practice-research consultant, I find it extremely helpful to begin with what data are available and then suggest the research possibilities that exist within the available data.

STEPS IN THE CDM PROCESS

Prospecting Potential Data-Sources

Using the most basic evaluative algorithm, the starting place for every CDM study is the collection of data regarding three basic informational categories—data about clients, about interventions, and about outcomes. With these categories in mind, we conduct a *prospecting survey* and assessment of *all* available data-sources that might yield information about these. At this point in the process, it is extremely important that the survey be as broad as possible, including *all routinely available data-sources that have anything to do with service recipients, interventions, and outcomes.* In more complex studies, we may include data about family members, organizational and community context, and even about practitioners, for example, practice orientation, years of experience, ethnicity, and so forth. Whatever the range of variables to be included, the potential sources of information should entail everything from computerized data to handwritten chart entries, diaries, logs, and so forth.

Equally important at this early stage of the process is to not to limit our attention to social work data even if the study is to be conducted entirely by social workers. So, for example, working in a palliative care unit of a hospital, one doctoral student whose study will be discussed later and at greater length, started and prematurely stopped his CDM exploration when he limited his clinical data-sources to social work records. By extending his boundaries to include nursing records, an enormously rich "vein" of data concerning patient psychosocial characteristics became accessible to him.

In such instances, however, it is extremely important to work through the *political* issues of access as well as the technical issues of *connectivity*. By the former is meant the kinds of formal and informal organizational barriers to accessing data that can arise in relation to authority, territoriality, competitiveness, and defensiveness in multidisciplinary bureaucratic settings such as hospitals, schools, and so forth. These problems can be ameliorated through some form of positive co-optation, for example, creating a multidisciplinary research team or advisory panel. When such obstacles arise, one can base an appeal on "contribution to knowledge" grounds but more often than not, the incentive of coauthorship on a publication or inclusion in a conference presentation is enough to do the trick, even in nonacademic settings.

It's one thing to secure permission to access computerized records; it's quite another thing to link them in an integrated database. At the very least, one hopes for a numerical identifier, such as a patient or client ID number or a social security number that allows us to connect client information from multiple sources. However, more often than I'd like to admit, there are problems with different computer languages and formats that render easy data-integration only a number-cruncher's dream. In this regard, sometimes organizational IT people are enormously helpful in achieving the dream. At other times, it is "virtually" possible, but practically impossible. In working through these intramural political and technical issues, as an outside consultant or as a doctoral dissertation advisor, I generally stay out of the way and let the practitioners or doctoral students sort out these difficulties. Here an organizational "outsider" such as myself would only confound the problem.

Descending from the ethereal heights of IT systems and executive offices to basement closets and file cabinets, CDM prospectors may have to contend with burrowing for data in unhealthy environments as well as the distinct possibility that the informational "gold" or "silver" or possibly "nickel" that was supposed to be stored and for which you've secured permission to mine, just isn't there.

Just as practitioners and (dare I say it?) research academics are not always paragons of rationality, claims about organizational rationality are frequently overstated. In contrast with certain governmental organizations, profit-making corporations, and the occasional former president or vice president, my experience is that when files are lost or shredded or thrown out in human service organizations, it's rarely for nefarious reasons. Still, as I indicated earlier, the bane of the CDM researcher is missing data, and that can apply to particular cases as well as data concerning all service recipients from a particular source or during a particular period.

But think about it. Historians (Danto, 2008) and archeologists confront such problems all the time. Yet they carry on. So, for the clinical data-miner, the disappointing "discovery" that important data are missing or inaccessible does not imply that the "canary has died" and the CDM study is "kaput". It simply means that this source of potential information is unavailable. Like our fellow field researchers, when this occurs, CDM researchers are obliged to dust themselves off, acknowledge that it's a bummer, and make do with whatever data *are* available. And if that sounds grim, compare CDM in social work to the labors of those intrepid archeologists who study the contents of available prehistoric "coprolites" (aka human turds) and make dramatic discoveries in the process (Zorich, 2009).

When the desired social work data are there but in handwritten form, CDM researchers have it easier than archeologists. Other than practice jargon, we needn't learn arcane ancient languages or wait for a Rosetta stone to appear. But we do have to deal with the practical issue of *legibility*. Because practitioners are best suited to reading their *own* handwriting and knowing what it is that they intended to say with their own conceptual "shorthand," whenever information takes this form, I find it best to have practitioners extract data from their *own* treatment or service records. To conventional researchers, this is at best counterintuitive and at worst shockingly "unscientific." However, for reasons that I will enumerate below, I think it improves both the quality and the quantity of study data.

Here again, however, steps can and should be taken to assure both the validity and reliability of the data. These will be discussed subsequently. Likewise, an evenhanded and open-minded approach to data-analysis and interpretation can increase confidence in inferences that are made from study findings.

Inventory Study Variables

Once potential data-sources have been identified and initially assessed, I find it valuable to rather crudely conceptualize, inventory, and sort *all* the available variable dimensions about which there are usable data. Practitioners are quick to comprehend my simple, three-fold categorization of (1) *client characteristics,* for example, demographics, psychosocial factors, diagnostic assessments, service needs and requests, and so forth; (2) *practice interventions,* for example, types, frequency and intensity of social work, and nonsocial work services; and (3) *treatment or service outcomes,* for example, both short and long-term indicators of quality of life, psychosocial factors, morbidity, mortality, and so forth. To researchers and practitioners alike with experience in logic modeling (Unrau, Gabor & Grinnell, 2006), this categorization is likely to be familiar.

For those who are initially conversant with traditional research lingo and over the course of working with practitioner-researchers, client characteristics and interventions are reconceptualized as potential *independent variables* and/or *intervening variables* in the data-analyses to follow. Outcome data generally serve as *dependent variables* in many CDM studies but, of course, so can intervention data, for example, in looking at relationships between client characteristics and services received. For practitioners, however, at the starting point in the process, I find that *keeping the categories I employ as descriptive and devoid of research jargon as possible at the early stages of a project is extremely important.* I can't tell you the number of times I've heard practitioners equate interventions with intervening variables and watch their eyes glaze over when I've tried to explain the distinction. Now is not the time.

More important than getting the terminology correct is to be sure that you collect as much data as possible that will shed some light into what Bickman (1987) has referred to as the "black box" of intervention. In other words, all possible data concerning the services clients and patients receive from social work as well as from other related professions should be included whenever possible. Sometimes, this is provided retrospectively by practitioners via their general program descriptions. Ideally, however, there are records of *types of services* received, their *frequency, intensity,* and possibly even indicators of *quality.* These can be used later for program description, for assessing "program fidelity" (Hanssen & Epstein, 2007), and for more rigorous evaluation in the context of quasi-experimental studies and experimental analogs (Sainz & Epstein, 2001). For a discussion of the former, see Chapter 5 and for the latter, see Chapter 7.

Deciding on the Unit of Analysis

Once a decision is made about the general type of data-collection and analysis, and the potential variables have been inventoried, it is important to decide on the *unit of analysis* for the study. In principle, CDM studies can vary from those in which a single case, an aggregate of cases, single groups, aggregates of groups, single programs, aggregates of programs, single agencies, and aggregates of agencies represent the central analytic unit of the study. This is the study unit about which one wants to make generalizations.

The decision about unit of analysis is based upon a combination of how the data themselves are organized and the research question that is driving the study. In studies that rely on original data-collection, one is free to choose a data-collection strategy that is most consistent with the central research question and the unit of analysis. Here, however, as in many other aspects of CDM studies, one often has to strike a strategic compromise between the ideal and what is pragmatically possible. In CDM, the unit of analysis is frequently determined by the way data are routinely conceptualized and collected.

Because most of the CDM projects that I have consulted on with practitioners have relied heavily on multiple case records from multiple social workers, the studies have generally described aggregates of individual clients or patients. To a lesser degree, however, I have had experience as a dissertation advisor with studies that focus on single programs, one on a total agency, one on a single program for an entire country, and another on a collection of over 100 agencies. Clearly, the potential involves some combination of what is available and the imagination of the CDM researcher.

Selecting a Time Frame

In addition to the unit of analysis, one has to choose a *time frame* or *window* within which to collect data and if sampling is necessary, a *sampling strategy*. Since CDM studies are primarily retrospective, an important question is, how far back to go in the data-collection? However, this question can't be answered unless one knows how far forward one needs to collect data to make inferences about short-term and long-term outcomes? As with other aspects of these retrospective studies, determining the sampling window for data-collection may require thinking that is the *reverse* of conventional research decision-making.

So, for example, in the liver transplant study (Zilberfein, Hutson, Snyder & Epstein, 2001), the determination of how far back to go began with asking about what the most appropriate time span would be to assess the effectiveness of the procedure? With the primary outcome measure being patient mortality, I learned from the practitioners that too short a time span, for example, three months, would have yielded insufficient variation on the dependent variable to assess differences in outcome. From a clinical standpoint, one year was considered the minimum time span within which to measure success. It was also helpful to learn that the one-year cut-off point was generally used in prior medical research studies on liver transplant outcomes. This was one of the uses of the preliminary literature review that we did early in our study. Similarly, in studies related to mental hospitalization, juvenile justice, and adult criminology, one year is a common cut-off point for assessing recidivism in retrospective SA studies as well as in randomized-controlled trial studies (RCTs). But, liver transplant clinic patients at Mt. Sinai were not enrolled in an RCT nor did they come for transplants based on our research protocol. Moreover, the transplant assessment team did not begin generating systematic data concerning applicants until well after the transplant program began offering this medical procedure. Consequently, the window established needed to include all those for whom the desired data concerning psychosocial risk factors were available *and* who had their transplants at least one year prior to the data-collection. Finally, by collecting data on how long patients survived post-transplant, we arrived at a time span of two-and-a-half years that included patients who had lived up to three years post-transplant and were still alive. This yielded a total population of 286 patients who had full assessments for the study. Once the window was established, the remaining number and the cost of collecting data on all these patients were sufficiently small that further sampling was unnecessary.

Clearly, the process of arriving at the correct sampling window for data-collection can be complex and somewhat tedious for the practitioners as well as for the consultant. But in the process, I learned a good deal about the practice being studied in the course of thinking it through together. Likewise, they seem quite happy to use this opportunity to teach me about what they do. Finally, from a research perspective, at the rate of one or two transplants a week, think of how long it would have taken to accumulate such a sample if the study was going to be done *prospectively*.

Similar issues with different solutions might arise in studies of recidivism. At Boysville of Michigan, for example, an unpublished, prospective, follow-up study using original data demonstrated that delinquent adolescents released to their home communities were most likely to recidivate between 6 and 12 months post release. Knowing that, a subsequent retrospective CDM study of recidivism required a window of at least 6 and 12 months post release. In this instance, relying on more universal operational definitions of recidivism, that is, 12 months or more, would be insensitive to local, programmatic variations. However, by combining these data with available data from Michigan's adult prison system, we were able to identify predictors of adult imprisonment as well as variations in risk that occurred prior to 12 months (Collins, Schwartz & Epstein, 2001).

From a broad research perspective, it is always advantageous to set the window in a manner that conforms to research conventions in the published literature. This promotes comparison of findings with prior studies as well as future contributions to knowledge from the current study. However, at the very least, the window should be broad enough to allow for analyses that serve the needs of *both* local programmatic decisions as well as contribute to the more universal body of research. After all, as a PBR strategy, the primary purpose of CDM is to inform programmatic decision-making. The real possibility of contributing to knowledge beyond the agency as evidenced in the growing body of CDM publications makes CDM that much more valuable as a research methodology.

Another design consideration related to the window is whether the CDM study is attempting to capture a *longitudinal* clinical process, a *cross-sectional* representation of a longitudinal process, or a single, *dichotomous outcome* of one kind or another. For example, in a study of end-stage renal disease patients' responses to dialysis (Dobrof, Dolinko, Lichtiger, Uribarri & Epstein, 2001), a decision was made to collect information on 100 patients reflecting patient characteristics, social work services received, level of depression, and other more administrative and medical outcomes such as missed appointments, hospitalization, use of the emergency room, and so forth, every three months over the course of their first year on dialysis.

The first year on dialysis was chosen because it is seen as the critical time in patient adjustment to the process; but because it takes approximately two months to know whether a patient can even tolerate dialysis, the window included those 100 most recent patients who were in dialysis for at least 2 months and remained in dialysis for at least one year. Here, the number of cases that the CDM team was willing to study combined with what they knew about practice allowed them to study when in the dialysis process, patients were most vulnerable to different kinds of negative outcomes as well as how patterns of service varied from quarter to quarter (Dobrof et al., 2001).

Thus, setting the window properly also requires a sound knowledge of the programmatic and clinical context. This can only come from the practitioners. Consequently, it is important to establish that the program environment was relatively stable during the time period under study. Consequently, one needs to know that there weren't major changes in intervention approaches, staffing, programmatic resources, and so forth. To the research-sophisticated reader, it is obvious that here, as elsewhere in CDM studies, we are applying basic *cause-effect thinking* and *experimental logic* to retrospectively collected information. To the extent possible, we are trying to keep all potentially confounding variables constant during the data-collection window.

Choosing a Sampling Strategy and Sample Size

Although we would always prefer to not have to sample, as with conventional research studies, CDM *sampling strategies* are likely to be determined as much by practical resource considerations of time and money as by "gold standard" power analyses.

In principle, there is no reason why a power analysis could not inform the sampling strategy and sample size of a CDM study as well. However, since in my experience these studies have been either funded by the agency itself or supported by relatively small foundation or dissertation grants and because they rely on the voluntary involvement and participation of staff, a more practitioner-driven or agency-determined sampling strategy is generally chosen. Consequently, in most CDM studies, a combination of ideal research principles, data availability, practitioner willingness to commit their own time and resources, and/or agency tolerance serve as the basis for the decision.

Most practitioner-driven CDM studies make use of no sampling at all or *systematic* sampling if the available case records are too numerous to include them all. This is a particularly useful sampling strategy if the records are in file drawers somewhere. Taking every third case for example is much more efficient than generating a list of random ID numbers and opening and closing drawers to try to find them. From the standpoint of *external* validity, if the sample size is large enough, the result will probably be equivalent. And if no sampling is required, then at the very least one can say that on the variables that are available, the population enumerated, we have a *complete* description

One relatively sophisticated CDM doctoral dissertation (Kochkine, 2006) employed a stratified random sampling technique to study cultural and gender differences in adolescent depression and school performance. Using a computer-generated listing of client ID numbers, that study randomly selected 50 males and 50 females from 8 different cultural groups that were served by a single agency. Of course, this level of CDM commitment and research sophistication can be reasonably asked of doctoral students but not of practitioners who are full-time clinicians who aren't paid to be researchers.

Critical to the sampling strategy is also an early awareness of the *counter-factuals* that are driving the study at the start. Because his was a doctoral dissertation, Kochkine structured his inquiry and sampling strategy based on a literature review that emphasized issues of gender and cultural difference in depression and school performance. Because he had available data that allowed for so many comparisons, these could be built into his sampling strategy. However, as will be seen in the more detailed discussion of his dissertation in Chapter 5, his original practice-driven focus was on gender differences within the Russian immigrant population alone. It was only through a dialogue between us (with me serving as his dissertation advisor) that he came to see the greater knowledge-generating potential of including other ethnic groups and comparisons in his study.

In many CDM studies, the most fruitful comparisons may not be anticipated and may only emerge through the data-analysis. In the liver transplant study, for example, the most powerful finding involved the comparison between patients with a history of substance abuse and those without. When we began the study, we had no idea that this would be a central comparison and therefore did not build it into the sampling strategy. Moreover, it was only through a dialogue with the practitioners that I came to comprehend the significance of what we found. The point is that it wasn't built into the sampling strategy. Though here again, PBR consultation departs significantly but strategically from the "gold-standard" research ideal, most practitioner-based CDM studies involve a sampling strategy based on an honest and direct answer to "How many do you think you can manage?" And while for researchers this may seem too far from perfection, combined with missing data and missing variables, CDM researchers never have to apologize or adjust for low response rates or large numbers of respondents who didn't complete standardized scales.

Developing Preliminary Strategies and Forms for Data-Extraction

Once there is a window and a sampling strategy is arrived at, one can begin thinking about strategies for data-extraction and collection. In qualitative studies, it might mean photocopying whole records or portions of records. These can be directly transcribed or transcribed and coded using qualitative data-analytic software. This will be discussed in greater detail in Chapter 6 in which *qualitative* CDM studies are introduced.

Most frequently, however, practitioner-initiated studies have involved converting qualitative case-information into quantitative data. This requires an intermediary step of reading the qualitative case entries and coding them in an approximation to a structured, forced-choice questionnaire that, in effect, queries the qualitative record. These data-extraction forms look quite like a self-administered questionnaire with an ID number and all the variables and forced-choice responses listed below. The major difference, however, is that the practitioner is essentially completing the form for the client based on what has transpired through the case history.

The form itself follows the conventions of questionnaire construction—that is each variable covers a single dimension, response categories should be mutually exclusive and exhaustive, always have an "other (write in)" category for observations that fall outside the anticipated categories, and so forth. One difference, however, is that the order of the questions should comport with *where the data are likely to appear in the case records* rather than the logical flow of the information, which is more important in original questionnaire construction. Once the form has been developed and the data extracted and recoded, the newly developed quantitative data-set can be entered into a quantitative database for analysis using Excel, SAS, or SPSS, or some other comparable quantitative data-analytic software.

Although I have lots of experience with questionnaire construction, practitioners rarely have. In collaboratively putting together the data-extraction instrument, I learn more about their practice thinking, and they learn more about basic research principles. Perhaps, more importantly, the exercise requires them to conceptualize their practice and to surface their practice theories in ways they have rarely done before. This is one of the many points in the process where I often find myself wondering whether they get as much or more from the CDM process than they will from the actual study findings.

In other CDM studies, the available data have already been computerized but were intended and used for other purposes. In principle, this could save a good deal of time and grief but unfortunately, that is not always the case. So, for example, in one proposed CDM study of the effectiveness of employee assistance interventions in job-jeopardy cases in a large organizational setting, it was assumed that different departments used the same categories and operational definitions in coding staff absenteeism and job performance. Human Resources said they did, but we found out too late that several units were noncompliant. As a result, all of our outcome measures were blown. We scrambled and the fall-back position was a very useful descriptive study of who was being served and what services they received (Hughes, Elkin & Epstein, 2004), but even within the limited context of CDM possibilities, it wasn't what we had originally planned.

I never said this was easy. Going into the clinical data-mines requires methodological agility and flexibility as well as physical fortitude.

Securing Human Subjects, Institutional Review Board, or Ethics Committee Approval

Perhaps, one of the most ambiguous issues in CDM research concerns the ethics of doing it. Because of the negative press about various forms of national security justified data-mining, critics are justifiably wary about the ethical legitimacy of conducting such research focused on identifying individuals who might be engaged in subversive activities. Here both the violation of First Amendment rights of privacy and the operational definition of subversive behaviors are particularly troubling.

Less concern has been voiced about private industrial use of data-mining although, as indicated earlier, drug company data-mining of physicians' prescription patterns has raised some health-provider hackles.

Surprisingly, my experience with Institutional Review Boards (IRBs), Human Subject's Committees and Ethics' Committees in various hospitals, universities, and other social agencies in the United States and abroad has been remarkably varied. The influence of data-mining exposes has palpably influenced responses to CDM research proposals at various times. Some have "rubber stamped" CDM evaluative studies treating them as "administrative" or "programmatic" research and wondering why we are even submitting the study for approval. Others only wanted to see the final product if there was to be external dissemination of the study to be assured that confidentiality was maintained.

Naturally, the outer limits of what is acceptable from the standpoint of information access and utilization in the United States are governed by the privacy and research regulations promulgated by the Health Insurance Portability & Accountability Act (HIPAA) of 1996 that went into effect in 2001. That was the year of publication of my "Mining for silver" paper. As more and more health and social work settings embraced HIPAA regulations to protect themselves from lawsuits and research grant denial as well as study subjects, I feared that my golden dreams would be short lived and my modest silver mining activities would be totally extinguished. However, because so much medical and public health research relies on available health information, with proper safeguards, much of this work falls comfortably into the "exempt" category.

So, after the initial flurry of frightened IRB responses to HIPAA, things settled down in both health and university settings. Now, generally speaking, committees want assurance that the data will be "de-identified" and that there are no names or identifying numbers attached or retained. If ID numbers were necessary to link diverse data-sets, assurances are provided that the numbers and their identifiers would be kept in a locked file and ultimately destroyed. More commonly, new and unique ID numbers are provided that free the data-set from the identities of the subjects.

In extreme cases at extreme times, when doctoral students were conducting dissertation research with patient data other than their own, relevant available data had to be photocopied by agency staff and separated from any identifiers before the student could have access to the data. In the rarest instances, where distrust reached its peak, a few academic researchers (never actual ethicists) began from the point of asking that subjects be recontacted to consent to this *particular* use of their data. Generally, if they held to this position, it would have rendered the study impossible to do either because the cost of locating study subjects would be prohibitive or because they were deceased. In my experience, however, committee objections were generally negotiable and when it became clear that the study presented little risk and offered significant contributions to practice knowledge the CDM proposal was approved. And after some considerable "agita," the study went forward.

I suspect however that on those few occasions when individual committee members have challenged the "ethics" of CDM studies, the opposition was really on methodological grounds. This has happened most often in hospital settings where RCTs represented the only acceptable scientific knowledge-generating paradigm. But in these settings, I've encountered difficulty about the conduct of qualitative research for the same reasons. When I encounter such resistance, I look for informal guidance and support from more flexible committee members and have found that toning down the "science" jargon and "reframing" the study as "services research," "program evaluation," or "program monitoring" generally does the job.

In one hospital setting that is a "Federally Designated Cancer Center" where anything called "research" required approval by both an ethics committee and a scientific review committee, a CDM proposal was rejected on "scientific" grounds—that is "no control group." Once it was redefined as "quality assurance," it was approved by the Quality Assurance Committee.

Although this makes me somewhat cynical about IRBs, ethics committees, and the approval process, it should in no way suggest that I am cavalier about client and patient protections. I am not. But I do think that when people raise objections to CDM studies, these objections have less to do with human subjects' issues *per se* and more to do with epistemological biases in favor of original data-collection, standardized instruments, or experimental designs in opposition to research conducted by practitioners and/or out of concern about protecting the scientific image of the institution. When the potential for or the existence of grant-funding accompanies the request, these objections are frequently jettisoned. Alternatively, when a completed study is ready for publication and it becomes obvious that patients have not been identified nor their interests abrogated, IRB/ethics committee members have, on more than one occasion, wondered why they were even asked for an opinion.

Responses to CDM proposals have ranged from unquestioning approval based on pre-existing patient or client agreement to absolute rejection unless each intended subject signs a new consent form specific to the proposed use of the data. This is virtually impossible when subjects have relocated and extremely costly and inefficient when people have not. In such situations, the benefit of using available data is rapidly extinguished. Maybe that's the point. When subjects are no longer alive, the prospects of "re-consenting" them are even worse. However, by the simple process of *de-identifying* the database, that is, detaching it from any identifying information, the ethical problem is, in my opinion, negated. If multiple databases are employed, new identifying codes may be employed to link individuals in more than one database, but once this is accomplished, original ID listings can be destroyed.

As annoying to me as the approval process can be, I sometimes benefit from suggestions made by very smart people on the committees who become intrigued with the methodological approach. More universally, however, I must acknowledge that for the practitioner as well as the doctoral student, writing the approval submission itself is an extremely useful exercise in further conceptualizing and "owning" the study.

Promoting Validity and Reliability

Once available data-sources are cleared for research purposes, we can begin collecting data in earnest and doing everything that is pragmatically possible to promote its validity and reliability. This applies whether this is going to be a quantitative, qualitative, or a mixed-method CDM study. Here, as in other aspects of CDM consultation, it is important to strike an artful balance between scientific principles and what one can reasonably expect from practitioner-researchers. Of course, with doctoral students, as an advisor, one may require greater investment in establishing validity and reliability. In consulting with practitioners, I have to always be aware of the need to sustain their forward movement. Consequently, the procedures that I use represent yet another strategic compromise.

As with any study employing original data, in CDM, issues of validity and reliability of the data must be taken into account. Often, however, as with other methodological aspects of CDM, basic research principles and logic are applied retrospectively and *in reverse* rather than prospectively or in a conventional research sequence. So, for example, in original data-collection, we try to promote as high a response-rate as possible to assure external validity of the data and take steps to establish the internal validity and reliability of the data-collection instruments we are using through pretesting before the data-collection process actually begins.

In CDM, in contrast, the data are already there, and we must determine, often variable by variable, whether it is adequately represented (external validity), measures what we claim it measures (internal validity), and does so consistently (reliability). The data is already collected, but whether we can use it or not is determined by how much confidence we can place in it. As was the case with the liver transplant study, if we are lucky enough, some of the key variables in the study are clinically assessed using standardized instruments for which validity, reliability, and population norms have been established. Even here, to be on the safe side, we can compute *alpha* scores to determine whether the reliability of the clinical information we are working with is consistent with that reported by prior studies and established scale ranges, distributions, and so forth.

More typically, we are working with quantitative data drawn from qualitative case records or self-administered *ad hoc* questionnaires that practitioners have designed and clients have completed.

In their prospective study of practitioner's "tacit knowledge," Zeira & Rosen (1999) promoted the validity and reliability of clinical data extracted from case records by training 69 practitioners in 6 social agencies to record client problems, clinical interventions, and short- and long-term outcomes according to a conceptual framework that the researchers provided. Next, using content analytic techniques and Strauss & Corbin's (1990) "open-coding" procedures, they trained two seasoned practitioners to serve as external raters to categorize qualitative case entries and ultimately convert the information into quantitative variables for which they, Zeira and Rosen, computed inter-rater reliability scores (pp. 107–109).

While their approach to assuring the reliability and validity of their data is much more rigorous than mine, these authors and I draw on similar research principles. However, because CDM engages practitioners in every step of the research process, the research consultant must take into account the burden that labor-intensive reliability checks would place upon practitioners.

Alternatively, helping practitioners develop their own data-extraction forms on which they will enter their own case data has distinct advantages. Though by the conventional RBP standards employed by Zeira and Rosen (1999, 2000) it is less rigorous and "objective," from a PBR standpoint, it gives practitioners an opportunity to

- articulate their own conceptual and theoretical frameworks;
- establish the *face validity* of key concepts that they routinely employ;
- test the *intra-* and *inter-rater reliability* of their own ratings;
- determine why they disagree on variables where agreement scores are too low;
- reflect on their practice interventions and theories in ways they had never done before.

By following these procedures, key concepts and tacit practice theories are derived as *inductively* as possible from practitioners rather than imposed upon them deductively from "privileged theory" or from myself as an outside research consultant. It also gives me an opportunity to reteach long-forgotten research concepts and principles in a context that is so much more meaningful and salient than the classroom in which they learned research as students. Here, I see my task as helping practitioners surface and test their own ideas with data that they themselves have generated—but to do so in an evenhanded and more or less objective manner.

More specifically, I usually begin by having each practitioner choose about 10 closed cases with no other preestablished criteria. Although strictly speaking this is not *random* selection, I suggest that they choose the cases so we can get the greatest possible variation for data-extraction instrument construction purposes, but no truly random process is used. Instead, I usually have them select cases "blindly" from different locations in their file drawers. This often becomes an occasion to discuss what random sampling is, how it compares to accidental or convenience sampling, why it is desirable, but how it is preferable to not sample at all.

Once practitioners have selected their cases, we begin identifying potential variables and categories within variables. This becomes an occasion for discussing different kinds of scales (i.e., nominal, ordinal, and interval) and key concepts in instrument construction (e.g., the importance of having mutually exclusive and exhaustive categories). Originally arrived at through a process akin to "open-coding," ultimately the data-extraction instrument constitutes a structured questionnaire for "interrogating" the available data-source.

As with more conventional self-administered questionnaires, spaces are left for open-ended qualitative entries or quotes that are especially rich and evocative. These may be positive or negative, and I make it clear to the practitioners that we are not seeking "testimonials" about how helpful they have been. Rather, we are trying to understand the client's "true" experience through quantitative and/or qualitative data. Here, I also instruct practitioners about the value of the metaphors that clients employ and the importance of gathering these. But, here again, I emphasize the importance of seeing and recording *both* the positive and negative outcomes.

Once the instrument is constructed, we usually select 10 cases and have all the participating practitioners code all 10 cases. Then, we tally up the percentage agreement and note the variables on which their scores indicate less than 80% agreement. On those variables that do not achieve this desired level of agreement, we collectively look at the cases on which the practitioners disagree and see whether they can establish why. Often, when they do, we either develop new code categories to accommodate the differences or sharpen the rules for coding the variable. If we cannot arrive at agreement, we exclude the variable.

Using similar principles, if there is only one practitioner doing the study or, more likely, a doctoral student, I encourage the practice-researcher to have a social worker friend code the 10 cases with identifying information obscured or separated from the case. Or, if that is not possible, I suggest a *test/re-test* approach by which the single practitioner waits a sufficient amount of time (say a month) and then re-codes the cases to see whether adequate *intra-rater reliability* has been achieved on all key variables. If not, we go through a similar process of considering why and problem-solving to improve the data-extraction instrument. For variables that remain unreliably coded, we exclude them from the study.

Once we have sufficient confidence in the instrument and the data-extraction process, practitioners code their own cases on blank instruments, and we usually have paid data-entry people on staff or pay research students to enter the data on SPSS databases for analysis. Naturally, we do regular spot-checks to determine that the data have been entered accurately. But, to the extent possible, we try to protect practitioners from *unnecessary* drudge work in moving the study forward. There have been instances in which practitioners wanted to do the data-entry themselves and, of course, this was an opportunity to teach them to do so as well as to create an SPSS database. Sometimes, only one member of a team is interested in doing that. Clearly, I take my cues from them and each team develops its own unique division of labor. My task as a CDM consultant is to keep the process moving forward based on my knowledge of research principles and awareness of the various elements in the research process.

In qualitative CDM, analogous processes are engaged to assure the validity and reliability of the qualitative data and the inferences that are drawn from them. However, since most of the CDM studies I have consulted upon or supervised have been quantitative, this is an area of my own "consultation practice" skill development that I need to work on.

Perhaps, most valuable in this process, however, is the way it helps practitioners *conceptualize* what they are doing, why they are doing it, and how they know when it works. In other words, what *observable indicators* they rely on in making practice decisions and decision about their practice? Along similar lines, in a recent two-year follow-up survey of clinical research utilization by former MSW students, Staudt (2007) shows that the research skills that remain most useful to them are those having to do with conceptualization of problems, interventions, and desired outcomes rather than critical assessment of research literature or evaluation of data-collection and analysis.

Establishing a Plan for Analysis

Now comes the fun part. Like with any quantitative research using original data, in quantitative CDM, we begin with a run of the *frequencies, percentages*, and where appropriate, *measures of central tendency* on all variables and have practitioners fill them in on a blank data-extraction instrument. This gives us a picture of where we have *missing data, incorrect entries*, and *ambiguous data*. This is an opportunity to *clean* the data-set and correct the incorrect entries by going back to the original cases. More importantly, it provides an opportunity to see which items have sufficient variability to be included in bivariate and multivariate analyses and which lend themselves only to a univariate, descriptive statement.

Now, the two dread problems endemic to CDM arise again. First is *missing data*. Looking at the frequency distributions, we often find that key variables have fairly high percentages of "no answer." Here, it is important to distinguish between a "no" (meaning the phenomenon that the variable intended to measure was not present) versus a "no answer" that is clinically relevant. Thus, in our CDM study of adolescent sexuality, a client's leaving a question blank about sexual orientation was found to be clinically significant when correlated with other variables such as risk behaviors (Peake, Mirabito, Epstein & Giannoni, (2005). Equally problematic are the *ambiguous* "blanks" in case records when practitioners don't bother to list psychological symptoms that are not present. Thus, for example, in CDM studies that focus on client depression, no mention of depressed symptoms often implies that the client is not depressed. Of course, such an inference needs to be explored with the practitioners involved in the study.

As a consequence of the missing or ambiguous data, once the data-set is *cleaned* of incorrect or ambiguous entries, we exercise a high tolerance for missing data but at various steps in the research process may need to reflect again on its meaning. This as well represents an issue in writing up findings in a manner as "close to the data" as possible—a principle that I learned to exercise early in my research career.

The next step is to collectively arrive at a *plan for analysis*. This is an opportunity to reteach practitioners about causal relations and rethink which variables will serve as *predictors, intervening variables* and *dependent variables*. The challenge here is to rethink the original study plans in the light of what is now possible given the actual empirical distributions, psychometrics, and so forth. Some variables may have to be recoded into dichotomous categories. Others may drop out entirely if there are inadequate distributions. But this is no different from what one does with original quantitative data collected via a self-administered questionnaire.

What is always striking at this point in CDM studies is how excited the practitioners become by these most basic and initial data-runs and how much they make clinically of seeing the frequency distributions alone. In addition, they are frequently struck by areas in which there is missing data and provoked to critically think about their own case recording, that is, what is routinely recorded and what is routinely left out. This is a time for productive reflection about their informal information systems. It is also a time for me to register the inferences they make from the preliminary data; to reign in their inferences, hunches, and flights of fancy that are released by having some data; to show how we can use the data to test some of them, and so forth.

But first, we must re-inventory the variables to see what we have to work with. Then we must come up with a plan for the first sets of cross-tabulations or other bivariate analyses that we might do. This is based on which variables are considered *independent, intervening, dependent,* and possible *control* variables. And while I generally do not press for formal hypotheses and predictions, I do ask practitioners to say what they would expect to find. In doing so, I make it clear that this process is a disciplined one in which sets of practice relationships are being tested. Here again, I discourage analyses that are driven by statements such as "wouldn't it be interesting to look at this or that?" My standard response is to say that "interesting" is not enough and that we need a rationale (if not a theory) for why we are looking at that particular relationship. I say this because there are usually so many possible pairings to look at that "interesting" alone is the road to data-analytic chaos.

Finally, we discuss the types of bivariate analyses that will be run and why, with some beginning discussion of statistical measures, we will employ them. Here I go lightly because I am preparing the practitioners for meaningfully considering the next set of findings. By this point in the process, however, they can tolerate a good deal of research teaching and deferred gratification until the next, more complicated set of findings arrives.

Data-analysis and Interpretation

Once we have a clear sense of which relationships we will be looking at, which variables serve what functions, and essentially what the analysis will tell us, I either run the bivariate analyses or, if practitioners wish to acquire these skills, teach them to do it for themselves. More frequently than not, I do it for them and bring them the output.

This is a time to go through the bivariate findings, to reflect on their possible meanings and to consider, if possible, multivariate analyses through which we can test possible explanations or rule out spurious relationships. From my point of view and theirs, this is the most exciting time of all. It's when we discover what we have found, where the surprises are, where the ambiguities for further analysis are, and so forth. More likely than not, this is a time when I learn the most about the complexity of practice thinking and of the organizational context that affects practice in so many subtle and not-so-subtle ways. This learning provides an opportunity to positively and respectfully reflect the complexity of what they do back to practitioners.

Finally, it is extremely important that we review the research results thoroughly and together so that practitioners are clear about what the empirical findings tell them and what they do not. Here, it is important to guard against the natural desire to attend to only positive findings. I don't view this as an opportunity to "confront" practitioners with findings that are disappointing to them. In addition, I look for ambiguous and seemingly contradictory sets of findings. Here again, I make the point that we learn much more from the negative and contradictory findings than from those that please us. And learning about practice is why we do practice-research.

This is when a trusting dialogue between researcher and practitioners is most important and most fully realized. It's also when I learn the most about the contextual influences that practitioners face and the complexity of their thinking about what it is that they do. Here both the dialogue between researcher and practitioner and between their empirical findings and their subjective experience are enormously productive and often revelatory. It represents a unique experience for both sets of actors that I find humbling and practitioners seem to find empowering.

The CDM Literature Review: The First Shall Be Last?

Although it may seem like an afterthought, this is the time for me to say something about when and where the research literature review fits in the CDM tool bag. Like everything else in CDM, the timing and functions of the literature review are different from its location in conventional research studies. To research academics it may seem anathema to begin a serious study without first conducting a comprehensive review of available research literature. In the clinical data-mines, however, starting with a literature review can occasion the "canary's" last chirp. In my experience with CDM and other PBR projects, *a literature review conducted too soon and too comprehensively can be the death knell to any practice-research project.*

Here we're talking about the TMRI (i.e., too much research information) syndrome. In many practice contexts, the overwhelming number of potentially relevant studies (especially if the key concepts are framed too broadly) or discouragingly few studies (if chosen too narrowly) can both constitute major obstacles to moving forward—especially when sufficient CDM "traction" hasn't been achieved. However, this in no way implies that literature review does not play a major role in CDM studies—especially if practitioners hope to publish their results. Of course, doctoral dissertations are another matter, and we can expect a comprehensive research literature review with any CDM dissertation proposal.

But with practitioner-initiated projects, instead of beginning with a literature review, I find that it is most helpful to begin looking at the literature *after* the central study questions have been initially framed and *before* final decisions have been made about the data-extraction instrument and the plan for analysis. Then, available research can be used on an *as-needed* basis to possibly sharpen or add to the questions so that they help locate the local study in a broader research context. Likewise, other studies may be used to modify instruments, scale construction, or plans for analysis so that the potential for *comparisons* of findings with prior studies is maximized. Clearly, however, every CDM researcher should, at some or several points in the process, consult prior research literature for

• alternative ways of framing the research question;
• alternative theoretical perspectives;
• key variables that may have been overlooked in the data-extraction instrument;
• descriptions of comparable clinical interventions;
• comparative client populations (both similar and different);
• findings (both content and presentation);
• clinical, programmatic, or policy implications.

Certainly, once practitioners are thinking about conference presentations and publication, we return to the literature in a more comprehensive, less selective, and more conventional manner to frame the presentation or paper with reference to previous research and research findings.

Now, a final few tips on literature review, publication, and conference presentations. I often find that the best place to start a literature review is not in the library or on the computer, but in a single, recent, empirical research article that appears in a journal that the agency or practitioners subscribe to. Together we can review that article, see how analyses are done and findings presented, use the bibliography for locating other relevant articles, and identify a possible outlet for future publication.

Once a potential publication site is identified, I encourage practitioners to find an article in that publication site that does something analogous to what they have done. I emphasize that it can be on a completely different topic but seeing how much attention is given to literature review and methodology, how tables are constructed, and how practice and program implications are discussed can be extraordinarily helpful in completing the paper. Likewise, by loosely mimicking the structure and style of the paper and sending it to the journal with small changes that make it appear "printer ready" enhances the likelihood of acceptance.

On the other hand, sending a CDM paper to a journal that does not value practitioner-research, that prides itself on how "scientific" it is, and/or that emphasizes RCTs is just asking for rejection. In a few cases, however, more hardy CDM-types have made good use of these rejections and of the more civil critiques that have accompanied their rejections. Then, after shedding a few tears, they've gone on to publish their work in other more practice-oriented journals whose readership was more likely to make use of the knowledge generated in the first place. Clearly, their papers benefited from the critiques they received, but only they can say whether it was worth the grief. In one instance that I know of, a reviewer resigned from an editorial board over the journal's publication of a CDM article. CDM can be enlightening and it can be fun, but the clinical data-mines are not the place for sissies.

As for conference presentations, I find that sending the abstract in before the study is completed is an excellent motivator. If the abstract is rejected, it's an opportunity to develop some CDM calluses and apply elsewhere. Naturally, it's better if the abstract is accepted. Better still, if the conference is in a terrific location and the agency will finance attending.

CONSULTING PRINCIPLES

CDM consultation with practitioners is the closest I come to witnessing social work practice and mentoring doctoral students through their dissertation research process, is the closest I come to doing a form of clinical practice myself. It's no surprise then that some of my PBR and CDM "principles" and "practices" appear remarkably similar to classic clinical social work principles and practices such as "starting where the client is," "establishing rapport and mutual trust," "setting a treatment contract based on nonjudgmental, active listening," and so forth.

Before I began doing CDM studies extensively, I listed the principles that informed my PBR consulting with practitioners who were collecting original data (Epstein, 1995). Subsequent to the original articulation of my PBR consultation principles, I discovered that they worked for me in practitioner-initiated CDM studies as well as CDM dissertations. Hence, whether the practitioner-researchers or doctoral students with whom I am working are conducting studies involving original data, available data, or both, I make a serious effort to

- establish positive, trusting relationships based on mutual respect and appreciation;
- let practitioners and/or doctoral students set the research agenda;

- accommodate research concepts and techniques to practice norms and requisites;
- recognize practitioners' and doctoral students' unique abilities to contextualize, interpret, and apply research findings;
- employ active listening for concerns, theories, metaphors, and contradictions that surface;
- validate practitioners' and doctoral students' desire to know and to reflect;
- maintain a firm belief that practice-based, research informed reflection will lead to more effective social work practice and knowledge about practice.

Although the foregoing consultation principles were developed in the context of previous PBR efforts, an additional principle emerged in the context of CDM studies; that one has to do with coauthoring and publication. In contrast with former PBR studies which rarely did, since CDM studies have frequently led to publication it was necessary for me to establish a principle for how I handle the issue of coauthorship. My "practice" in this regard is to let practitioners know that I will help them with consultation about publication but that I will expect coauthorship only if I do actual writing on the paper. Although I do not "need" further publications for my CV, if I do any writing, no matter how limited or extensive, I let them know that I will expect to be listed as the final author.

By offering my conceptual and editorial assistance, first-time authors feel reassured that they will have the support they need to complete the research and dissemination process. By making it clear that if I do any "hands-on" writing I will require listing as the final author, they are assured that I am not unduly advancing my academic career on their "data-mining" backs. The clear understanding about this at the *beginning* of the CDM process and the mutuality of expectations further contribute to building trust. And while it makes clear that publication is a distinct possibility and a desirable CDM outcome, it dispels fears and neutralizes commonly held practitioner stereotypes of academic exploiters. Consequently, I would add to the foregoing list of consultation principles:

- Establish early in the CDM consultation process mutual expectations regarding publication.

CONCLUSION

This chapter described basic steps in the CDM process. The following chapter presents a wide range of published, practitioner-initiated CDM studies. These are all *quantitative*, making use of very simple and straightforward, practitioner-friendly approaches to conceptualization, data-analysis, and presentation. The chapter that follows it describes CDM dissertation studies that are more methodologically sophisticated. Though primarily quantitative, they may include *original* as well as *available* data. Or, they may be *mixed-method* studies based on *quantitative available and qualitative original* data. A subsequent chapter explores *qualitative* CDM. Regardless of the different degrees of methodological sophistication and data combinations, these studies demonstrate how practitioner-researchers and doctoral students can contribute to practice knowledge through CDM studies.

4

Practitioner-Initiated CDM
Studies: Principles and
Exemplars

The previous chapter described basic steps in the clinical data-mining (CDM) process, the basic elements of CDM consultation, and the central importance of "strategic compromise" in both. Virtually all of my experience with CDM projects has been with individual social workers and social work teams, single or multidisciplinary health care or mental health teams, or with social work doctoral students. The health care teams sometimes were comprised exclusively of single allied health professional units, for example, physiotherapists, occupational therapists, podiatrists, and so forth. Other groups were multidisciplinary teams devoted to particular patient or client health or mental health problems, for example, liver transplant, renal dialysis, child abuse, and so forth.

As I indicated earlier, the CDM studies that have been most innovative from the point of view of scope and methodology have been those conducted by social work doctoral students with whom I have worked in the United States and abroad. These will be described in detail in Chapter 5, which is devoted specifically to the quantitative CDM doctoral dissertation, and in Chapter 6, which introduces qualitative CDM. Some of the dissertations make use of multivariate analyses of one kind or another. Others creatively meld qualitative and quantitative as well as available and original information. Two are entirely qualitative.

This chapter focuses on *practitioner-initiated* CDM studies—all of which happen to be quantitative. This is because available data are more likely to lend themselves to quantitative rather than qualitative analysis and require lesser methodological sophistication and/or epistemological flexibility. A lone practitioner-initiated, qualitative CDM study is described in the following chapter. To the neophyte-practitioner researcher or doctoral student who mistakenly thinks that qualitative research (aka no statistics) is easier to do than quantitative, this pattern may appear contradictory. More to the point is the fact that as narrative case recordings becomes less detailed and more truncated, their suitability for qualitative research diminishes.

Though generally less ambitious and methodologically variegated, CDM studies initiated by practitioners have been extremely useful from a program and practice point of view. And they cover an extraordinary range of substantive topics. Indeed, they are as varied as the data on which they are based and the applied research interests and decision-making needs of the practitioners involved. But from a data-analytic point of view, they are generally quite simple. No apologies for that. Often they are purely descriptive studies employing simple, univariate percentages and measures of central tendency or bivariate cross-tabulations with Chi-square analysis. Many begin with information that is already in quantitative form or involve the conversion of qualitative case record data into quantitative data-sets.

Despite their methodological straightforwardness (perhaps because of it), many CDM studies have generated presentations at conferences attended by practitioners and/or publications in peer-reviewed journals targeted at practitioners. For the majority of the practitioner-researchers who conducted these studies, they produced their first professional publications and for many, their first professional conference presentation. Some have gone on to pursue doctorates after having positive experiences with CDM, but here in life as in research we shouldn't confuse correlation and causation.

Still, it's a plausible hypothesis, and though I don't have the numbers nor the qualitative testimonials to support any of this claim, several of these first research publications and CDM doctoral dissertations will be cited in this and the next two chapters and used for illustrative purposes. However, before describing some practitioner-initiated, quantitative CDM studies, let me reiterate some of the most important CDM principles and practices mentioned in the previous chapter.

CDM PRINCIPLES

Whoever is conducting the study, what the study is about, or however sophisticated the data-analysis, the most fundamental questions facing any potential CDM researcher are as follows:

- What is the purpose of the study?
- What data are currently available that is relevant to the study purpose?
- Is the study based entirely of available data or does it combine available and original information?
- Is the CDM component of the study qualitative, quantitative, or a combination of the two?

Having presented the foregoing questions in their most epistemologically "correct" order, let me again "confess" that several CDM studies—particularly those conducted by practitioners—really began with a simple expressed desire to do some kind of practice-relevant research and my asking them to tell me what data they routinely collected. Then, in exploring the practice and program problems that confound them, questions that bedevil them, concepts that intrigue them, or practice innovations that inspire them, we frame a study purpose that somehow fits the data sources that are currently available.

To conventionally trained researchers this undoubtedly seems backward, at best, and to post-positivists even tautological. Certainly, it often engages the principle of *strategic compromise* discussed in the previous chapter because once a study purpose is articulated, the CDM researcher inevitably confronts the less-than-ideal aspects of available and unavailable data. However, let me remind the reader that this does not imply "cherry-picking" only data that support "practice-wisdom," practice-based theories, or any other theories for that matter. In fact, to the extent that it is even possible, many of these studies approach the atheoretical. Certainly, few involve formal hypothesis-testing but many involve validating or invalidating "hunches" or expectations based on practice-wisdom.

Nonetheless, in articulating a study purpose, locating relevant data, and planning the analysis, I hold myself and my practitioner colleagues firmly to the positivist principle of *conducting research in such a way that they can discover that they are wrong.* In so doing, I engage practitioners in a collaborative process of enquiry that might challenge their most cherished beliefs about who they serve, what they do, and what their work accomplishes? In addition, I make it clear that as a researcher, I am not there to debunk or to trash their practice-wisdom. Finally, I suggest (and strongly believe) that we learn the most from results that surprise us because they weren't what we expected. (Researchers may read this as findings that negate our hypotheses.)

In my well over a decade of CDM consulting experience, every study—even the most rudimentary—has produced surprises of one kind or another. Admittedly, not all have delighted the practitioners. I take that as a good sign. An even better sign, however, has been the willingness of practitioners to honestly and openly confront the possible meaning and explanations of those findings in a manner that was not self-serving. In my opinion, working through that process is as important a part of my work as coming up with a researchable question as a practice-based research (PBR) consultant. Clearly, however, the study gains traction when its purpose and the available data are connected. Which comes first is immaterial.

When the available data are already quantitative, the choice of quantitative versus qualitative is a "no-brainer." Until someone cracks the quantitative-to-qualitative conundrum, it's going to be a quantitative study. However, if the available data are in qualitative form, the decision about whether to use it as such or convert it to quantitative data is more complex. Here, the answer rests on recognizing whether both the study purpose and available data lend themselves best to qualitative or quantitative analysis. Simply stated, if the study is intended to describe a complex process and available data sources are sufficiently rich, a qualitative study is an option.

CDM that begins with available computerized client or program data, information derived from intake face-sheet data, or client-based self-administered questionnaires necessarily produce *quantitative* studies. Typically, in CDM studies, *qualitative* clinical data from case records are translated into *quantitative* data-sets that ultimately produce quantitative studies as well. In rare instances, available *qualitative* data are sufficiently rich to support *qualitative* analysis and interpretation. This possibility is discussed in greater depth in Chapter 6.

SOURCES OF QUANTITATIVE DATA FOR PRACTITIONER-INITIATED CDM

Having asked what data are currently available that can inform a practice or program-relevant set of questions, a comprehensive survey can yield various types of information. From a "gold-standard" research standpoint, the ideal would be information derived from standardized quantitative measures of psychosocial consumer attributes, practice interventions, and/or outcomes. Even better, one discovers that these data are available for all service recipients. From a quantitative research point of view, best of all is when these standardized quantitative measures on all clients or patients are already computerized.

In my CDM consultation, I feel that God is smiling on me on the days when I find that these conditions are met. For the clinical data-miner, it's the closest one gets to striking gold. Most frequently, it happens in agency settings that have extensive management, client, or patient information systems. However, the irony here is that in such settings practitioners rarely have any institutionalized means to access these rich, informational resources for their own practice-relevant research and reflection. More likely, these data are routinely available only to managers for program monitoring and/or to funding sources for accountability purposes. Or, there is a research division or a university-affiliated research center wherein academic researchers exploit these practitioner-generated riches. More commonly, mining available client data involves nonstandardized forms recorded on paper or in computer files. Likewise the information recorded in them may be quantitative, already, or qualitative, requiring conversion to quantitative data.

Whatever their data sources, the least complex and most straightforward quantitative CDM studies simply *describe* client characteristics, the services they receive and/or the psychosocial outcomes that follow these interventions. Often, they do only one of the above. Though such studies may seem prosaic and methodologically simplistic to academic researchers, they are most comprehensible to practitioners and inevitably produce findings of interest and utility to them. In addition, the studies may be an important first step toward the conduct of future, more complex studies, and/or further education. Hence, readers and potential CDM consultants are urged to not be too quick to dismiss the value of frequency distributions, percentages, and measures of central tendency in quest of more refined results or inferences. "Descriptive" is not a dirty word!

Ratcheting up the level of sophistication a bit, when these variable sets are *correlated* with each other in some type of *bivariate analysis*, they can tell us something about relationships (e.g., between client characteristics and interventions and between interventions and outcomes). When the number of cases is sufficiently large and the range of variables sufficiently broad to lend themselves to *multivariate analysis*, explanations can be tested or spurious relationships eliminated. Here CDM studies approach and approximate the experimental ideal of correlating intervention and outcome while controlling for client variations.

Whatever the type of data-analysis or degree of methodological sophistication, the reader is reminded that these practitioner-initiated CDM studies are, in Scriven's vocabulary, *formative* rather than *summative* (1995). In other words, the findings they generate only *approximate* causal relationships and are initially intended to provide local knowledge that informs clinical or programmatic decision-making. Accordingly, unlike with "gold-standard" randomized-controlled trial (RCT) studies, in CDM studies, referring to psychosocial "outcomes" by that term already *assumes* that they are the result of intervention rather than simply a co-occurrence. Turning again to Scriven's useful distinction, with sufficient available information, the right available data, knowledge of multivariate analysis, and experimental logic, these studies can inch their way closer toward the summative end of the continuum (Sainz & Epstein, 2001).

This possibility is dicussed more fully in the final chapter and is where the "dreaming of gold" portion of the "mining for silver" metaphor (Epstein, 2001), is worth keeping in mind—especially for the CDM consultant or doctoral student. *The point is to stretch the methodological and inferential possibilities as far as they can reasonably go.* On the "silver" side, despite their methodological limitations, simple descriptive CDM studies are excellent devices for engaging practitioners in research and informing practitioners about their own work in ways that their unsystematic observations and reflections never do. That's why there are always surprise discoveries in CDM.

Although critiques of the limitations of empirical analysis are daily fodder for researchers of all epistemological persuasions, they are best left to the academics. Consequently, in working with practitioner-researchers, I always point out some of the limitations of their studies—especially in the context of drawing practice implications—but I don't dwell on these. Emphasis on the shortcomings is the international pasttime for academics but in heavy loads is "undermining" to CDM practitioner-researchers. And, it is an unfortunate legacy of evidence-based practice (EBP) pedagogy that focuses on the evidentiary weaknesses in prior research. In my experience students and former students socialized in this approach to "critical thinking" internalize this message rendering them completely incapable of doing anything that is methodologically imperfect. The result is more research alienation and less practitioner-research.

Whatever their limitations, the contributions these practitioner-initiated CDM studies make are not restricted to descriptive findings concerning interventions and outcomes. So, for example, if the consulting is balanced properly—that is, supportively as well as critically—practitioner data-miners inevitably discover problems, inconsistencies in their own practice theories and data sources, as well as the limits of existing empirical research studies. In this crucible, practitioners are impelled to refine their practice theories, improve their data sources, and identify gaps in their own as well as professional knowledge. Good CDM consulting helps them do this.

What remains most remarkable to me, however, is that notwithstanding their study findings, practitioners who participate in the CDM process neither become despairing about their practice nor cynical about research. Instead, they come away enriched by the experience in multiple ways and embrace research as an integral part of their practice (Hutson & Lictiger, 2001; Ciro & Nembhard, 2005). In view of their prior educational experiences in research, perhaps, less surprising is that in many of these practitioner-initiated projects, I have had to spend time persuading practitioners that "descriptive" is not a pejorative and descriptive research is not something to apologize for. In response, I remind them that many scientific fields and significant discoveries are based on detailed observation, description, and careful categorization rather than controlled experimentation. Clearly, they acquired this bias somewhere—very likely from their research instructors in graduate school.

Here again, once they are disabused of these attitudinal "trained incapacities" and privileging of experimental studies, we can move on to doing useful and pragmatic practice-research. More refined yields that come from conducting CDM studies will be discussed more fully in the following two "descriptive" chapters and the potential for more in the more "exploratory" concluding chapter. This chapter focuses on the most basic practitioner-initiated, quantitative CDM studies for which their originators have every reason to be proud.

TYPES OF QUANTITATIVE CDM STUDIES

As stated earlier, the possible variety of quantitative CDM studies is as varied as the clinical data from which they are mined. In working with social work and other health care practitioners, however, I have always found it useful to place studies into the same broadly descriptive categories that Tripodi and I used to characterize different types of evaluation research in our book dealing with evaluative techniques for program administrators— that is, need studies, monitoring studies and outcome studies (Epstein & Tripodi, 1978).

> *Need studies* use available data to describe patient or client population profiles, diagnostic variations, perceived problems, stated needs, service requests, and so forth.
>
> *Monitoring studies* use available data to reflect on the extent to which the desired clientele is being reached or not, the services they are receiving, and the extent to which these services are consistent with the program's intervention model. Evaluation researchers sometimes refer to this as treatment or program *fidelity* (Bickman, 1987).
>
> *Outcome studies* focus on available information concerning short-term and/or long-term indicators of program-relevant service or treatment goals.

The most basic form of each is the descriptive study in which univariate and bivariate analyses are employed. Of course, studies need not be limited to one or another of these categories. In fact, most overlap to one degree or another. But having the categories, to begin with, helps practitioners to conceptualize the range of study possibilities available to them and helps them organize their data. And while each of the studies cited began with a programmatic purpose, all were published in peer-review journals indicating a contribution to knowledge beyond the local practice-research site.

Need Studies

Needs of Pediatric Diabetic "Frequent Flyers" and their Families

From a methodological standpoint, the least complex way to approach any of these three CDM study types involves simply aggregating and percentaging information about clients, services or outcomes. So, for example, in a study of adolescent "frequent flyers," that is, patients with poorly controlled, insulin dependent diabetes mellitus (IDDM), in a children's hospital in Melbourne, Australia, Nilsson (2001) describes the psychosocial attributes of patients and their families derived from the case records of a sample of 18 young persons that had more than four times the average rate of admissions as others with the same diagnosis (p. 60).

Even without comparison with patients with more typical hospital stays, Nilsson's findings revealed exceptionally high frequencies of parents and children with psychiatric disorders, parental overinvolvement, familial conflict, and so forth. And while practice-wisdom might predict these findings or practitioners might suggest that they are obvious, there is nothing as powerful as empirically documenting what we know as well as discovering what we don't know. In this CDM study, however, inferences were made about the service needs of families that weren't made before and certainly weren't translated into practice. Most impressive, conducting this study as an individual practitioner in a pediatric diabetes unit, Nilsson reports that "[t]he knowledge gained from this study has been subsequently incorporated both directly and indirectly into the practice of social workers employed within the diabetes unit…." (p. 67).

Needs of Family Care Providers for Elderly Patients

A more methodologically complex needs study by Dobrof et al. (2006) surveyed telephone requests for information, referral, and emotional support from a caregiver resource center. Consistent with the program's purpose, telephone requests came primarily from family members caring for terminally ill, elderly patients in New York City. Sponsored by a grant from the Soros Foundation Project on Death in America, the study involved a small group of social work staff-members collecting and coding existing but previously unresearched program records, categorizing service requests, and cross-tabulating them with demographic characteristics of care providers and patients. Findings were particularly useful in noting culturally driven differences in service requests, needs, and the likelihood of following through on referrals. While none of these findings relate directly to patient- or family-support provider outcomes, they made important contributions to program refinement. The study was based entirely on the contents of brief, semistructured records of telephone contacts between elderly patient family members and social workers (Dobrof et al., 2006). It did however support the value of having a Spanish-speaking social worker on staff.

Adolescent Mental Health Needs

From the standpoint of study scope and practitioner involvement, the most ambitious CDM need study to date evolved into a collection of 10 distinct explorations of the self-assessed mental health needs, risks, and resources of close to 800 adolescents requesting counseling at Mt. Sinai Hospital's Adolescent Health Center. This collection of published papers focused separately on the self-assessed desires for counseling with regard to health, safety and violence, sex, substance use, school and work, and racism by adolescent applicants to a mental health program, taking into account gender, age, and racial differences (Peake, Epstein & Medeiros, 2005). The data were all mined from a single, self-administered intake questionnaire originally constructed for clinical assessment of individual applicants for service but never before aggregated and analyzed for research purposes.

Working with 10 separate direct service social worker groups based on their particular substantive interests, bolstered by the active involvement of their social work administrator, a staff psychiatrist, and a staff psychologist, but each led by a line worker, the project produced 10 publishable, quantitative-descriptive planning studies. Each of the published studies began with a literature review and a prestructured format for univariate and bivariate analysis followed by an opportunity to empirically explore unanticipated findings, and a section devoted to practice and program implications of their findings.

Ultimately, the findings from all 10 studies were combined in a more complex quantitative analysis employing multivariate and factor analysis to consider multiple risk factors, what at-risk youth worry about, and how their worries cluster. In that final empirical paper, the lead author was a research-sophisticated psychologist on staff (Surko, Peake, Medeiros & Epstein, 2005). With the exception of that summary paper, all others were methodologically quite simple. Taken together, however, they made significant contributions to programmatic reflection, new program planning, future evaluation systems planning, and practitioner-research skill development. In addition, the book that the collected studies produced helped the agency in future funding efforts. For several line social workers, however, participation in the project promoted practice-research, group leadership, and writing-for-publication and presentation skills. One is currently entering a PhD program where she intends to focus on research on adolescent mental health and another already has her PhD and is in a full-time teaching position teaching courses and conducting workshops on clinical work with adolescents.

None of the foregoing CDM studies could consider services received or treatment outcomes. These data were not routinely available or collected at the time the studies were conducted. However, the intake instrument, the data-analytic format, and the findings introduce the possibility of practitioner-initiated CDM outcome studies based on re-administration of the "intake" instrument at later points in treatment. This possibility is currently under consideration by agency administration.

Social Relationship Needs of Young Adults in Early Psyhosis

Conducted in the context of an Australian group-work program for young adults (aged 16–30) showing signs of early psychosis, this study data-mined 126 self-administered, open-ended, initial assessment forms routinely given to prospective groupwork program participants over the course of four years of program implementation. Responses to very basic questions such as "Would you like to make more friends?" and "Do you have someone to confide in, and what is their particular relationship to you"? constituted the informational source of this CDM effort (Macdonald, Carroll, Albiston & Epstein, 2006, pp. 155–166).

This study conducted by social workers under the guidance of an experienced occupational therapy research-academic and with my assistance generated programmatically useful findings that empirically documented the relationship needs of this at-risk population. These young adults are often extremely marginalized and socially isolated. The excellent group-work program in which they participated attempted to provide for some of their social needs and to build skills for meeting those needs outside the program. However, until this study was conducted, there was no systematic effort to empirically assess and analyze their needs in the aggregate other than what practitioners might do informally and impressionistically. What makes the study all the more useful beyond the particular setting and target population is that it concisely and effectively retraces their steps in the "recursive" PBR and CDM evidence-based process (Macdonald, Carroll, Albiston & Epstein, 2006, p. 157).

Although their sequence of steps do not necessarily replicate those taken in other CDM studies, most of the basic elements are all there. My Australian co-authors of this study have presented on its findings and on CDM methodology at several practice conferences and practice-research workshops throughout Australia and in the United States.

Patients at Risk of Intimate Partner Violence

Another CDM need study made use of a practitioner-devised, self-administered patient questionnaire that included some previously published scales to assess whether patients were at risk of intimate partner violence (IPV). The questionnaire was originally and routinely administered as a clinical screening device to identify women at risk at two different outpatient settings within the same hospital—a hospital OBGYN clinic and a Neonatal clinic at Mt. Sinai Hospital.

Although the questionnaire was not initially thought of as a research tool, aggregating and analyzing the data it provided concerning 431 patients made it possible to compare the prevalence of IPV risk in the two clinics and to correlate relationships between patients' witnessing domestic violence as children, experiencing it as adults, and fearing that they themselves might physically abuse their own children. The findings of the study based on several hundred women in each of the two clinics reinforced the importance of such screening in both clinical settings and supported existing theories concerning intergenerational domestic violence and child abuse as well as providing locally based information for a domestic violence training program that the lead author provided for medical students in the hospital (Ross, Walther & Epstein, 2004). The practitioner who initiated the study is currently a doctoral student who does adjunct teaching in a master's level research course.

Psychosis and Drug Use

In a much smaller and less complex study of Australian adults referred to a Melbourne dual diagnosis service, Cole and Ryan (2006) data-mined a sample of 25 client files to determine whether there were any discernible patterns in the relationship between patient sex, psychiatric diagnosis, and illicit drug use. They refer to their study as only a "snapshot" but one that was used to "check the accuracy" of their "anecdotal observations" that a very high proportion of their clients self-medicated with marijuana. Despite the very small sample and minimal cross-tabulation of the available data, they found much more than their "practice wisdom" allowed them to perceive. In fact, the data revealed some surprisingly dramatic and differentiated patterns of drug use and attitudes toward drug use that had extremely important clinical implications.

So, for example, male schizophrenics were five times more likely to use marijuana than other male patients and 10 times more likely than female schizophrenics. What was most surprising to the experienced practitioners who did this study was the finding that 40% of the sample concurrently used cannabis and amphetamines, which has particularly detrimental effects for psychotic individuals.

Cole and Ryan (2006) conclude their brief CDM paper with the following:

> Finally, our data mining shows that formal assessments provide a rich source of information, which if systematically audited, assists our understanding of and response to clients with a dual diagnosis. (p. 21)

As illustrated in the foregoing exemplars, when the data are available, they can serve as a basis for *descriptive* (i.e., univariate) analysis of service applicants and/or consumers and their needs. More complex bivariate analysis might involve cross-tabulations between demographics and service requests or referral sources and problems presented. Multivariate analysis might consider the prevalence of different kinds of presenting problems controlling for demographic variables such as age, sex, and race. Ultimately, these descriptors of need may function as predictors, that is, independent variables, in subsequent analyses of interventions received and outcomes achieved.

When additional data sources *are* available, of course, practitioners need not limit themselves to studying needs, service, or outcomes separated from each other. If they have data that cut across these categories, they may study relations between and among them.

However simple or complex the analysis of need might become, the starting point is always the collection and categorization of information concerning the following potentially available information.

- Demographics
- Referral sources
- Service requests
- Diagnostic categories
- Problems and risk factors
- Strengths and resiliency factors
- Clinically relevant knowledge, attitudes, and behaviors

Monitoring Studies

Arguably, the most neglected type of published evaluation research and the most common unpublished evaluation activity concern program monitoring. Practice activities and program efforts are of great significance to funding sources and have profound consequences for service recipients but seem to hold little interest for academic researchers. This is why so few studies describing practice get published in peer-review journals. Likewise, it is why the annual reports of nonprofit agencies are filled with statistics concerning number of program contacts with clients or patients and units of service delivered.

Available quantitative data concerning these "program contacts" (Tripodi, Fellin & Epstein, 1978) are abundant in any organization that must account for what it does with its resources. That means every nonprofit agency. Similarly, practitioners who "process record" their activities generate and store extensive qualitative data regarding their activities with service recipients. In addition, the advent of electronic records will place even more potentially analyzable data in relatively easy access to practitioner-researchers who are interested in reflecting on what it is they do and with whom they do it. One hopes that there will be infrastructural opportunities, administrative vision, and academic support for practitioners to mine and make use of these data.

Prenatal Clinic Services

For now, however, most practitioner-initiated CDM studies draw their data from clinical case records and other noncomputerized, available data sources. So, for example, Mason et al. (2001) began their practice-research CDM project with an interest in describing social work services provided to patients in a prenatal clinic population at Mt Sinai Hospital. By extracting and quantitatively codifying information from primarily qualitative case records plus demographic intake forms, they were also able to describe the demographic and psychosocial characteristics of patients served and how these were associated with the receipt or nonreceipt of services. Next, they were able to quantitatively profile the psychosocial problems that patients brought to the clinic and the relationships between patient characteristics and treatment objectives. Racial differences in service requests were noted as well.

Unlike the previous exemplar studies where available data sources were limited to intake questionnaires or screening devices, however, Mason and her supervisees mined 435 full records of closed cases. Although they did not have standardized measures of treatment outcomes, they *did* have narrative accounts of objectives achieved and a brief patient satisfaction questionnaire that they had devised and routinely administered to patients upon case closure.

As a consequence, the final section of their published study could consider relationships between interventions and treatment outcomes as well as patient perceptions of the helpfulness of various kinds of intervention. Their empirical findings provided correlational support to the contribution that social workers made to ameliorating anxiety and ambivalence towards their pregnancy and reinforced the program's commitment to prenatal social work as a part of clinical preventive medicine (Mason et al., 2001, p. 34).

In addition to generating the foregoing findings and providing a first publication experience for the team members, the study had a valuable unintended program outcome. In the process of developing a data-extraction instrument for mining their process records, practitioners discovered that they emphasized different content areas in their intake interviews. One focused more on extended family as resources, another on the possibility of domestic violence and another on the role played or not played by the father of the expected child.

As a result of this discovery, practitioners and their supervisor together developed a more comprehensive and "standardized" approach to patient screening than any had employed in the past. Because it came from them, they endorsed this program change and never once raised question about its being bureaucratically imposed on them in or its being a threat to their professional autonomy and creativity. Nonetheless, it can be seen as a step in the direction of more uniform programmatic effort and bureaucratic rationality, if one is so inclined.

Services to End-Stage Renal Disease Patients

Another quantitative CDM monitoring study by Dobrof and her colleagues was intended to empirically describe and empirically document the complexity of social work practice with patients suffering from end-stage renal disease (ESRD) during their first year on dialysis (Dobrof, Dolinko, Lichtiger, Uribarri & Epstein, 2001). The unstated "political" impetus behind this study was a move in other hospitals to "de-professionalize" social work services to ESRD patients. Sponsored by a grant from National Kidney Foundation's Division of Social Work, the Mt. Sinai CDM study was conducted in a setting in which all the social workers on the Dialysis Unit had master's degree training and certification. Consequently, no "natural" comparisons could be made between patients receiving care from MSW *versus* BSW practitioners. Certainly, there was neither an opportunity nor an inclination to devise a "gold-standard" RCT to compare their effectiveness.

Beder (1999) comes close to this, however, in an RCT outcome study comparing the impact on standardized measures of patient depression and adjustment to illness based on whether they received the federally mandated minimal services required (i.e., one brief visit and an informational pamphlet) *versus* an "enriched" package of social work services (i.e., multiple visits and extensive counseling). As will be discussed in chapter 7, Sainz and I (Sainz & Epstein, 2001) critiqued the Beder study on ethical grounds in our attempt to find a more congenial and less intrusive approach to approximating her experiment. Ethical considerations aside, Beder was able to "prove" that although all patients who received services improved, those patients who received more extensive and more complex counseling did considerably better (1999, pp. 29–30).

In reviewing the available literature, this almost contemporaneous finding pleased but came as no surprise to the social workers in the Mt. Sinai team. However, they were appalled at the thought of those seriously at-risk patients who were randomly limited by the research design to one brief counseling session. Likewise, they were concerned about their social work colleagues in the Beder experiment who were constrained by study requirements from providing more than perfunctory services to patients who were seriously in need, all to make a research point.

Working with available data, within the constraints of practitioner norms and ethical priorities, in a setting that only employed MSW nephrology social workers precluded both prospective and retrospective comparisons of patient outcomes by social workers' level of professional training. However, what we *could* do with the data they did have was to describe in *relatively* complex ways how master's-level social workers served patients at different stages in their dialysis treatment process and to shed some light on the outcomes of their interventions. In several ways, however, this practitioner-initiated, CDM monitoring study was more methodologically complex than the Beder study or Mt. Sinai prenatal care study previously discussed.

First, it was multidisciplinary and involved social workers as well as medical and allied health staff in different stages of the study's implementation. Second, the study involved data extracted from patient medical records as well as from social workers' clinical case records. Third, the study included patient "resiliency factors" as well as risks. Fourth, the study was cross-sectional and looked at patients at different quartiles during their first year on dialysis.

Like Beder, however, Dobrof and her supervisee co-researchers demonstrated that patients who received more than the federally mandated minimum of social work services improved. Unlike Beder's prospective, "gold-standard" RCT, in the retrospective CDM study, all patients who wanted or needed more than minimal social work services received them. However, in describing social work practice with patients at different stages in their dialysis, the Mt. Sinai study was able to empirically demonstrate naturalistically the "complexity" of social work practice with dialysis patients and consider the extent to which clinical judgments (rather than standardized measures) of patient psychosocial depression and adjustment indicated improvement.

Although the findings of this primarily CDM monitoring study were informative to the practitioner-researchers as well as to me as a CDM methodologist, what surprised me most was the response of a group of nephrology social workers from other hospitals to a presentation Dobrof made early in the study process offering only descriptive findings regarding the complexity of practice. As she presented the quartile-based, cross-sectional tables, the audience appeared fascinated, validated, and "empowered" by the study findings, independent of the question of psychosocial outcomes.

While the presentation and the monitoring portion of the study emphasized the differential practices of masters-level dialysis social workers, it eventually linked these activities to psychosocial outcomes (from the case records) as well as to medically- and organizationally relevant outcomes such as adherence to medical recommendations, use of the emergency department, and rehospitalization (from medical records).

Presentation of the latter findings resulted in several "secondary benefits" that empirically demonstrated the value of social work in this service (Dobrof, Dolinko, Lichtiger, Uribarri & Epstein, 2001, pp. 124–125). Because of the grant sponsorship of the study, Dobrof presented all of the findings at a national conference sponsored by the National Kidney Foundation in whose journal a version of the study was published (Dobrof, Dolinko, Lichtiger, Uribarri & Epstein, 2000).

The study and its CDM methodology were later replicated by Auslander—a university-based social work research colleague and social work practitioners with 67 ESRD patients in Israeli health settings. A comparative analysis of the American and Israeli data revealed dramatic differences in patient characteristics and the structuring of dialysis service delivery in the two countries but numerous similarities in the role of social workers (Auslander, Dobrof & Epstein, 2001).

Doubling back in our story, with this very positive CDM experience under her belt, Dobrof went on to apply for and receive the Soros Foundation grant that sponsored the telephone advice and support to caregivers of elderly patients program and evaluation described earlier in this chapter. And while in that study, direct measures of patient "outcomes" remained beyond the reach of the data-miners, it meaningfully reported interventions received (e.g., emotional support, community resource referral, support group information, homecare, etc.) during the first telephone contact and over the course of all contacts (Dobrof, Ebenstein, Dodd & Epstein, 2006).

Returning to the present, at the time of this writing, Beder (2008) recently published another study on the effectiveness of social work intervention with ESRD patients. Citing Dobrof et al.'s (2001) findings but not Sainz and Epstein's (2001) ethical critique, Beder employs the same standardized outcome measures as in her previous study and random sampling of patients. However, rather than an RCT, she makes use of a more "naturalistic" research design whereby differential access to social work services is a function of existing staffing patterns rather than "classical" experimental requirements. Although the findings of her more "objective," external researcher-conducted study indicates that more naturally available access to services is significantly associated with positive patient outcomes, what is striking to me is both how her methodology has changed and how little her study has to say about practice itself. The former pleases me, but the latter remains of concern.

On this final point, I quote from Dobrof et al.'s original CDM paper.

> ...although there was sufficient information in medical records to make record review a highly feasible methodological strategy, some aspects of patients' experiences were not documented and the lack of documentation could affect the validity of our findings. Finally, although there is potential bias among practitioner-researchers studying their own patients, the secondary benefits to their practice and the efficiency brought to the project far outweighed the possible negative consequences. (Dorbof et al., 2001, p.125)

However simple or complex the CDM monitoring study might become and/or whether outcomes are ultimately considered, the starting point is the collection and categorization of the following potentially available data:

- Types of psychosocial services offered
- Types of psychosocial services received
- Frequency and intensity of interventions (i.e., "dosage")
- Quality of interventions and the extent to which they approximate an ideal treatment or service model (i.e., "fidelity")

Although the fidelity issue has not been systematically explored in the practitioner-initiated CDM studies described, it will be discussed in detail in relation to Hannsen's CDM doctoral dissertation in the following chapter.

Outcome Studies

Clearly, for social work academics and evaluators, "outcomes" represent the most desirable "pay-dirt" of evaluative research but "outcome-only" studies represent the "slag heap" of evaluative research. Thus, for EBP purists committed to the experimental "gold standard" proving or disproving social work effectiveness, the purely descriptive "after-only" or "posttest only" design is so methodologically flawed that some refuse to even consider it as a *bona fide* evaluative strategy, even worse if it's based on available data generated by practitioners. (Do I remind the reader of the archaeological study of "coprolites" referred to in the previous chapter?)

Obviously, there are major inferential weakness (i.e., "threats to validity") in the design that are understandably associated with (1) the absence of associated, highly specified intervention data; (2) the absence of a matched control group or counterfactual; (3) the absence of a design structure (i.e., environmental isolation) or extraneous control variables that would make it possible to eliminate other causes of outcome differences; and (4) the absence of variables that might be used to "explain" the possible successful links between interventions and outcomes. And yes, from the standpoint of high-minded "truth-seekers" who are looking for "proof" that the interventions "really worked" or antipractice martinets who would prefer to "demonstrate" the flaws in practice-wisdom, the absence of definitive proof is sufficient to raise rhetorical questions about practitioner incompetence, chicanery, gullibility, and ethical inferiority. (Sorry about that.)

CDM practitioner-researchers can only dream of demonstrating the causal connection between specific "evidence-based" practice interventions and standardized outcome measures that is intended to yield the "gold" that some social work research academics seek for themselves or require from practitioners. Stretching the metaphor a bit further, "platinum-standard" designs would allow us to definitely determine "why" the intervention works, that is, by controlling for and eliminating or not eliminating alternative explanations.

But, for CDM practitioners working in the trenches, these are luxuries that neither they nor their clients can afford. Despite their acknowledged epistemological limitations, to the practitioners, simple descriptive studies about practice and program outcomes are both highly valuable and often much more empirical evidence than they have ever had that their practice works or doesn't work. But simple is not simplistic. More valuable yet is knowledge about with whom and with what intervention objectives they are more or less successful. Hence, some CDM studies *do* produce empirical information concerning patient or client outcomes (sometimes even on standardized measures) and may even be able to correlate outcomes with data about worker interventions. "Silver" perhaps, but in the more pragmatic realm of the possible, highly valuable nonetheless. Here again, however, I frequently have to reassure practitioners (especially the ones that did well in their graduate research courses) that after-only evaluations are legitimate, worth doing, and knowledge-producing. Once I convince them that it's "O.K." we can get back to work.

Thus, when the data are available, a CDM study can begin modestly by describing patient and/or program outcomes. In quantitative form, these outcomes can be expressed in percentages, measures of central tendency, or where sample sizes are small even "lowly" whole numbers (Nillson, 2001). Sometimes, if we are lucky, the available data are already recorded on standardized instruments that provide greater assurance of validity and reliability and which also allows for comparisons with other comparable client or patient populations— providing norms for establishing "cutting points" that might distinguish among different values on frequently measured variables such as depression, anxiety, adjustment to illness, intimate partner violence, and so forth.

More likely, clinical case records will yield less numerically calibrated but not necessarily less refined clinical assessments of these variables based on practice-wisdom and behavioral observation. Thus, instead of a standardized depression or anxiety score, a case record might report that a postsurgical patient appeared "no longer depressed but still anxious about returning home." In crudest, but by no means inconsequential terms, such a patient would receive a coding of "no" for depression and a "yes" for anxiety. Even less refined, as in some studies, the distinction might be between depression or anxiety being mentioned or not. In other words, a mention of "anxiety" is coded as a "yes" but the absence is coded as a "don't know" or "no information."

Naturally, if standardized measures are not available, one would prefer assessments that are reliably articulated by more categories, for example, "slightly depressed," "moderately depressed," "severely depressed," and so forth. However, while dichotomous variables such as those described above may seem dreadfully simplistic, categorically inadequate, and unscientifically generated to some, they can be quite useful even in after-only studies. And they remind us that some standardized measures are highly correlated with the answers to one or two simple clinical questions.

I've learned through my own consultation experience with the liver transplant study that started me on this CDM journey and many subsequent CDM projects that simple and dichotomous indicators can have profound implications. Is there a more definitive and less subjective outcome than whether the patient survived the transplant and/or how long post-transplant the patient remained alive? In addition, it provided invaluable information about the comparability of outcomes for liver transplant patients with histories of substance abuse and those without; this study contributed by describing pre- and post-hospitalization service patterns delivered by the social work team (Zilberfein, Hutson, Snyder & Epstein, 2001).

In other CDM studies with more refined designs, one might compare such simple indicators of patient well-being at program-entry (Time-1) and program completion (Time-2). In the renal dialysis studies described in the previous section, dichotomous measures of more proximate outcomes such as patient no-shows, completion of dialysis sessions, use of the Emergency Room, re-hospitalization, and so forth were very meaningfully employed. Using a slightly more sophisticated cross-sectional design, looking at group percentages at 3, 6, 9 & 12 months in dialysis, it was possible to consider program and organizationally relevant outcomes over time and ultimately to correlate these with patient characteristics and intervention patterns.

In the ESRD study, the closest we were able to come to definitively documenting the impact of social work services on psychosocial variables was based on a cross-sectional decline in the percentage of cases in which the workers noted patient anxiety and depression over the four quartiles of dialysis reflected in the study. For example, by showing that references to patient anxiety in the charts dropped from 52% during the first three months of dialysis to 30% during the last three months and depression dropped from 43% to 10%, an inference was made about the positive impact of social work services as well as an acknowledgment that anxiety remained an issue for nearly one-third of the patients on dialysis for 10 months to a year (Dobrof, Dolinko, Lichtiger, Uribarri & Epstein, 2001, pp.114–115).

Whether these declines are attributable to social work intervention, to external factors, to getting used to dialysis, or all of the above (and in what degree) is in some sense irrelevant. From a practice point of view, what is most important is to know it *and* to identify what patient needs persist. Finally, because some of the outcome indicators used were so organizationally relevant (e.g., rehospitalization and ER use) and had such profound economic implications, clinical administrators and physicians who attended the groups' hospital presentations of their findings did not raise any of the "gold-standard" methodological objections. Here, real money as well as concern for patients was the driving force since hospitals lose lots of money on ER admissions. Providing data that showed that patients who received information from social workers about when to come in to the ER (another "yes"/"no" variables) were half as likely to do so was seen as extremely compelling.

Discovering this, it reinforced the practice among social workers, informed other allied health team members of something they didn't know social workers did, and led the chief of nephrology to suggest that medical units in the hospital should be doing this kind of research. Clearly, many decisions in this CDM study involved "strategic compromises" but they produced findings that were highly valuable, pragmatically and professionally useful.

However simple or complex the CDM outcome studies might be, the starting point is the collection and categorization of data concerning the following potentially available information:

- Attendance, participation, and "uptake" of social work services
- Adherence to treatment recommendations
- Clinically relevant client knowledge, attitudes and behaviors
- Client satisfaction and/or dissatisfaction
- Unintended outcomes

TRANSCENDING CONCEPTUAL AND DISCIPLINARY BOUNDARIES

Although for heuristic and consultation purposes, I have found it useful to divide quantitative CDM studies into three categories, that is, need studies, monitoring studies and outcome studies, available data may be found that pertains to each. Moreover, in discussing the foregoing studies, I have accentuated their "goodness of fit" and minimized the extent to which they overlapped each other. Accordingly, the data-miner rarely has the luxury of being able to forego one type of data for another. One mines and refines whatever "ore" is available.

Consequently, what is most practical is to collect all three types of data and make decisions about data-analysis *after* the data are collected. Accordingly, some quantitative CDM studies describe *both* interventions *and* outcomes. In fact, many studies provide information relevant to all three categories, that is, client need, services received, and outcomes achieved.

Hence, the study of telephone support services for caregivers reported a description of the demographics of the population that called the services they requested, the interventions they received, and to a minimal extent, the outcomes that were achieved (as reported by the social workers). Only one of these outcomes related directly to patient care (i.e., satisfactory discharge from hospital) while others referred to the caregiver (e.g., improved emotional coping, attendance at a support group, etc.). Some had implications for both patient caregiver (e.g., completed advanced directives; obtained assistance for financial, insurance, or legal issues, etc.) (Dobrof, Ebenstein, Dodd & Epstein, 2006).

In Australia, where my data-mining consultations and workshops extend much beyond the disciplinary boundaries of social work, outcome-oriented CDM studies have focused on social adjustment activities of young adults diagnosed with early signs of psychosis cited earlier in this chapter (Macdonald, Carroll, Albiston & Epstein, 2006), with the "impact" on length of stay of a "transdisciplinary" rapid response team in a suburban hospital (Freedman, Joubert & Russell, 2005), with the "impact" of a multidisciplinary "Integrated Care Program" on length of stay of patients who might otherwise return to that same hospital multiple times (Joubert & Power, 2005), and with the unmet biopsychosocial needs and outcomes of discharged patients relevant to all disciplines in an urban hospital setting (Posenelli, Joubert, Power, Vale, Lewis & Elliot, 2005).

TYPES OF QUANTITATIVE DATA-ANALYSIS IN PRACTITIONER-INITIATED CDM

Although more conventional, business-oriented forms of data-mining make use of highly sophisticated quantitative data-analytic techniques and data-mining software packages, practitioner-initiated CDM studies are perforce more rudimentary and less ambitious. In these studies, EXCEL, Statistical Package for the Social Sciences (SPSS), or Statistical Analysis System (SAS) generally provide a sufficient repertoire of analytic and statistical options. On rare occasions, however, doctoral students conducting their dissertation research projects based on CDM methodology have employed data-mining and/or qualitative data-analytic software (see Chapters 5, 6, and 7).

For the most part, quantitative CDM studies have made productive use of conventional univariate, bivariate, and multivariate analyses employing percentage tables, cross-tabulations, measures of central tendency, Chi-Squares, measures of correlation, t-tests, Analysis of Variance (ANOVAs), and so forth. Perhaps more relevant to the practitioner-researcher are the various uses of these different types of analysis.

So, for example, univariate analyses are useful for describing the following:

- Demographic profiles, diagnostics, risks, strengths, and so forth
- Service requests and presenting problems
- Contextual factors (i.e., family and community supports)
- Referral sources
- Adherence patterns
- Outreach efforts
- Social work and allied health interventions
- Social work and related outcomes

Bivariate analyses are useful for considering the following:

- Relationships among demographic characteristics for a more refined description of patient or client profile
- Relationships between demographics and diagnostics, service requests, and so forth
- Relationships between demographics and services received (e.g., to study possible institutional bias)

- Relationships between services received and externally derived standards of care (e.g., to study treatment or program fidelity)
- Relationships between interventions and outcomes (e.g., to study treatment or program effectiveness)
- Relative costs of interventions and outcomes (i.e., treatment or program efficiency)

When sample sizes are large enough to sustain them, multivariate analyses allow us to reconsider relationships between interventions and outcomes, controlling for the following:

- Demographic factors
- Diagnostics
- Risk and recovery factors (e.g., adherence, family supports, spiritual beliefs, etc.)
- Program and personnel factors (e.g., worker training, professionalization, etc.)

QUANTITATIVE CDM DESIGN VARIATIONS

Clearly, the multivariate analytic possibilities described above are informed most directly by experimental logic and has been used most explicitly in a paper by Sainz and Epstein (2001) that envisions the potential for the creation of experimental analogs in CDM. Such *ex- post- facto experiments* are arguably as close as we might get to the "gold standard" using available clinical information. The possibilities and special requisites of such designs are discussed in the final chapter. However, less ambitious and restrictive possibilities exist.

So, for example, clinically relevant intake data that lend themselves to a descriptive needs study may also serve as the basis for a *before/ after* (i.e., t1/t2) study if the same variables are assessed at the completion of intervention. In this instance, what began as an indicator of need is also an indicator of outcome.

If we are fortunate enough to have this information for the same service recipients at more than two time periods, a *longitudinal study* is possible; if not, but have sufficient information about service recipients at different stages in treatment, as in the renal dialysis study, a *cross-sectional study* is possible and quite desirable.

A remarkably concise cross-sectional CDM study of the psychosocial needs and services provided to 46 families of children who have received allogeneic stem cell transplants was conducted by Edberg-Posse and Forinder (2007) in the Karolinska University Hospital in Huddinge, Sweden. Having attended one of my CDM workshops, Edberg-Posse, a social worker at the hospital, joined with Forinder, a senior lecturer at the Department of Social Work at Stockholm University, in conducting this study. Drawing on available clinical data, the authors had sufficient data to develop a five-category scale combining parent/child need and therapeutic response for 39 of the 46 patients and their families. Then they presented a single table, cross-tabulating this information with the sex and age of the child and whether the consultation took place at the time of the transplant or at a follow-up visit.

From the data, Edberg-Posse and Forinder concluded that "it is important to offer all families and children/adolescents continued support of a generally psychosocial nature." In their paper they specify the types. From their CDM experience, however, my Swedish colleagues offered some final "methodological reflections":

> Despite the fact that the study was done retrospectively and with a method, which, to a certain degree, is descriptive in nature, we feel that it has led to valuable new insights. It is clear that the intervention identified a whole series of important problems encountered by both children and parents. The study supports the assertion that the health social worker has access to an extensive knowledge bank that can be used for purposes of both case evaluation and research (Epstein, 2001). Since the health social worker is already legally obligated to systematically enter notes in the patient's record, making use of the knowledge bank does not entail extra work. What is, in fact time-consuming is the systematic assembling of these data into compelling and useful information. The study is the result of the combined efforts of a clinician and a researcher, which we found very stimulating for both a clinical and analytical perspective. Working closely together like this also helps make the results more rapidly and efficiently transferable into clinical practice, which of course is the ultimate goal of this type of research. (Edberg-Posse & Forinder, 2007, p.2)

CONCLUSION

The selection of any of the foregoing combinations of analysis and design assumes that the practitioner-researcher and/or the CDM research consultant possess a sufficient conceptual and methodological repertoire to envision what is possible given the quantitative data that are potentially available. In many respects, doing this involves working in just the opposite direction from how academic researchers are trained to work. In fact, it is closer to the inductive way clinicians approach their practice. It begins by asking what is possible given the data that are available and when the data are routinely gathered. Still, maximization of the knowledge-generating potential of any quantitative CDM effort requires a solid grounding in experimental logic, quantitative methodology as well as openness to how they can be used to inform practice.

This chapter has discussed a number of practitioner-initiated CDM explorations that vary in purpose and are modest in methodology but have made important contributions to knowledge about practice. Their publication in peer-reviewed journals attests to the contribution they have made to the practitioners who did the data-mining as well as to those who might read these publications. For obvious reasons, methodologically uncomplicated quantitative CDM has been most typical of practitioner-initiated CDM studies and are most likely to be published in journals that target practitioner audiences.

The following two chapters prospect some less typical data-mining territory via quantitative and qualitative CDM doctoral dissertations and variations. Here, new ground is broken in several ways. More methodologically sophisticated their methodological procedures are employed. Mixed-method studies employing *available* and *original* data are described and initial exemplars of *qualitative* CDM are introduced.

However, before thinking about going on for a PhD, readers who are research-oriented practitioners are encouraged to do the following:

- Identify a practice-decision-making problem that would benefit from research.
- Consider what data are already available that might be helpful in informing your understanding of the problem.

- Identify others who might be interested in joining together in a CDM research effort.
- Think about what resources (i.e., technical, consultative, released time, etc.) will be necessary to pursue your interest.
- Secure administrative and IRB approval.
- Find a practitioner-friendly researcher (either in your agency or from a local university) who is willing to work alongside you.
- Start digging!

Who knows, what you discover may turn out to be your doctoral dissertation topic. Whether it does or doesn't, conducting the study will teach you much more about your practice for having done it. If you do it right, you'll also learn about where improvements need to be made and new programs need to be introduced. Doing it with other team members or social work colleagues with have additional personal and organizational development benefits such as team-building, communication, and possibly greater efficiency.

Finally, for readers who are academic or agency-based researchers but are willing to support practitioners in the CDM process, it might help to reiterate the slightly revised PBR consultation principles stated in the previous chapter:

- Establish positive, trusting relationships with practitioners on the basis of mutual respect and appreciation.
- Let practitioners set the research agenda.
- Establish early in the CDM consultation process mutual expectations regarding publication.
- Accommodate research concepts and techniques to practice norms and requisites.
- Recognize practitioners' unique ability to contextualize, interpret, and apply research findings.
- Employ active listening for concerns, theories, metaphors, and contradictions that surface.
- validate practitioners' desire to know and to reflect.
- maintain a firm belief that practice-based, research informed reflection will lead to more effective social work practice.

5

The Quantitative CDM Doctoral Dissertation

Not until William Reid (1979) suggested the "model development dissertation" (MDD) as an alternative paradigm for social work doctoral programs has anyone offered anything that departs from the conventional research dissertation. Although Reid argued forcefully that as a "practice profession" social work should use doctoral research in the development and testing of practice interventions, to my knowledge no doctoral programs have emphasized or adopted his MDD recommendation.

Since his innovative proposal appeared, the only discernible change in the dissertation-research paradigm has been the increase in qualitative dissertations (Brun, 1997). More recently, Sales et al. (2006) proposed that Secondary Analysis (SA) of large, easily accessible, quantitative databases offers future promise for social work master's and doctoral research education. Sales and her colleagues do not go so far as to advocate SA doctoral dissertations though several have been done in policy-oriented doctoral programs, such as Columbia University's.

Still, critics as well as proponents of conventional social work doctoral programs recognize the increasing need for research-trained social workers with doctorates who are qualified to teach practice courses in universities but who possess research and writing skills that will enable them to regularly contribute to the practice-knowledge base of the profession and survive in the academic marketplace.

This problem is not new. In the 1990s, Lindsey and Kirk (1992) described the shortage of such teacher-researchers as representing a "continuing crisis" in social work education and proposed the expansion of PhD programs in major research universities. Since then, social work doctoral programs have proliferated in schools known for their research as well as those with more modest research reputations (Khinduka, 2002). But these eminent research authors and former deans were talking about the need for "teacher-researchers." Anyone who has interviewed recent PhDs seeking entry-level academic positions soon recognizes that their knowledge of social work practice is extremely limited. Hence the shortage of "practice-teacher-researchers" is even greater and, some would say, more critical.

Earlier in this book, I employed Veblen's (1914) concept of "trained incapacity" to describe the ways in which social work practitioners are pedagogically alienated from the research that they are exhorted by evidence-based practice (EBP) proponents to embrace. Another and perhaps doubly ironic manifestation of Veblen's concept applies to the alienation from practice of recent PhDs.

Hence "trained incapacity" might be even more descriptive of the impact on PhD graduates of "tier-1" research universities who have conducted conventional PhD dissertations and even those who have done SA dissertations—the former because "practice-wisdom" tends to be disregarded or disparaged in their doctoral programs and the latter because the data-sets they work with are so far removed from practice. Since these data-sets are frequently originated by the academic-research-professors or by some external research organizations, students working with them are that much more removed from the experience of practice. In fact, they could conceivably complete a social work doctorate without ever entering a social work agency. SA dissertations are convenient and suggest a quick and easy route to a PhD. However, my impression is that more often than not, the faculty member who makes the data-set available has already gleaned the more interesting findings and the research questions that are potentially researchable are of greater interest to the mentor than to the student.

From an andrological point of view, I think it is always advisable for doctoral students to choose their own dissertation topics. As a veteran dissertation advisor, I know that *every* dissertation requires a certain amount of passion to overcome the inevitable obstacles along the way. With SA dissertations it's hard to be passionate about someone else's data. And once completed, they may not yield findings upon which to base a future research or teaching trajectory.

In the evolving academic marketplace so heavily influenced by the EBP perspective, the prospect of doctoral programs producing practitioner-researcher-teachers seems even more unlikely. So, despite doctoral program expansion, Robb (2005) describes a "deepening doctoral crisis" in which the "magnum opus" research dissertation remains a major obstacle to PhD program enrollment as well as to successful degree completion—especially for social workers who are identified with practice. In response, some social work educators are even advocating the return of the DSW degree and the abandonment of the research dissertation requirement entirely (Robb, 2005, p. 13).

Encouraged by the positive experience that I've had with practitioner-initiated clinical data-mining (CDM)studies for over a decade and that I've documented in the previous chapter, in the last few years, I've begun encouraging doctoral students to routinely consider CDM as a dissertation-research methodology. Fortunately, my doctoral program colleagues at Hunter College School of Social Work where I teach, the University of Hong Kong where I was for the last 3 years an external examiner, and the University of Melbourne and the University of Auckland where I have been a visiting professor have not discouraged me from doing so. Based upon my experiences as a dissertation advisor, external examiner, and visiting professor at these schools, this chapter and the next describe and illustrate an alternative paradigm for doctoral research, that is, the CDM dissertation. This chapter emphasizes the *quantitative CDM dissertation,* and the next, the *qualitative CDM dissertation.*

Not surprisingly, a CDM dissertation is especially appealing to mature students who (1) are grounded in practice; (2) have access to agency-based data; and (3) identify practice-based "evidence" as a *bona fide* potential source of knowledge generation. This, of course, requires that their Dissertation Committee chairs and members agree. With that in mind, I'm hoping that the excellent and creative CDM dissertation exemplars contained within this chapter and the next will be persuasive to both doctoral students and, at least, a few doctoral faculty members. Since opening myself and doctoral students to this possibility, I have supervised and served as a dissertation committee chair, committee member/or as an external examiner on a growing number of successfully completed CDM doctoral dissertations. More are on the way.

What makes them especially exciting is that the students who conduct them keep extending the boundaries of CDM both methodologically and substantively. In other words, they are mining new territory and doing it in increasingly sophisticated ways. For many, their studies have produced publications as well as serving as springboards to academic teaching careers that are grounded in both practice *and* research. Most of the authors of the studies cited in this chapter and the next are seasoned practitioners who now occupy teaching positions in several schools of social work in the United States and abroad. Others occupy senior administrative, clinical, and/or research positions in hospitals, schools, and other social agencies but also teach as adjuncts or conduct trainings in their area of interest. To me, they epitomize that splendid and elusive rarity—the practitioner-researcher-teacher. And, the CDM dissertation is the vehicle that got them there.

Though I am an unabashed advocate, this chapter reveals the strengths as well as the limitations of the quantitative CDM dissertation—especially in the current academic environment. In doing so, it begins with perhaps the first CDM dissertation that I have ever supervised. It certainly wasn't labeled as such and ironically was conducted in the 70s at a tier-1, research university—the University of Michigan—where I was teaching at the time. Since then, and in much more recent years, several doctoral students have successfully completed CDM dissertations at the Hunter College School of Social Work of the City University of New York where I teach, at the University of Hong Kong, and the University of Melbourne. This chapter describes some of these dissertations and their varied uses of quantitative CDM methodology.

Among other areas of social work practice, the dissertations discussed in the following two chapters concern neonatal care, child welfare, and foster care, adolescent and adult mental health, family preservation, individual adult and family homelessness, oncology, and palliative care, and so forth. Thus, they involve social work clients and patients quite literally from before the cradle to the grave and from Australia, Chile, Hong Kong, and the United States.

Some exemplar dissertations combine CDM with original data-collection and analysis. Others are entirely based on CDM but make use of advanced quantitative analytic techniques that social work practitioners are unlikely to embrace or fully comprehend. Still others rely on quantitative analysis of available data for making generalizations about *programs* or *organizations* rather than about clients, patients, or participants, *per se*. And, in the following chapter, two dissertations are described that represent a completely new CDM pairing, that is, the purely *qualitative CDM dissertation*.

Leaving aside their variations in topic and/or research design for the moment, CDM dissertations require a timeline, a degree of sustained intellectual investment, research sophistication, and individual persistence that one can appropriately expect from doctoral students but not from practitioners who experience so many competing pressures in the routine performance of their jobs. This is why group or team projects are more advisable for practitioner-initiated CDM studies.

For doctoral students contemplating doing a CDM dissertation, it is important to keep in mind that in many ways, carrying out a CDM dissertation is as challenging as a more conventional one; in some ways, even more so. However, despite their unique problems and acknowledged "gold-standard" limitations, such studies yield practice-relevant findings and produce practice-research reflective future academics. In my opinion, both are well-worth their weight in gold.

MY FIRST CDM DISSERTATION

Dissertation supervision is something that I have done and loved doing for many, many years. At the University of Michigan, where I began doing dissertation supervision and taught research for 13 years, it was one of my favorite academic activities. It still is at Hunter. Nonetheless, at the University of Michigan (U of M), those that I supervised generally followed conventional quantitative or qualitative dissertation guidelines.

Perhaps the only exception at U of M was one conducted by Edward Pawlak dealing with institutional racism and sexism in the court processing of juvenile offenders (1977). Long before I thought of CDM as a distinct dissertation-research strategy, I remember Pawlak courageously struggling with 96,000 (give or take) computer cards based on available data collected from 66 county juvenile courts in 1 state during a 3-year period. We called it a "secondary analysis" because the data used had been originally collected for planning purposes by the state court system from which he secured the data. However, Pawlak was passionately invested in documenting and undoing institutional racism and sexism in the processing of delinquents. Still, Pawlak anticipated that this would be a very speedy as well as meaningful dissertation project. Not so. This was before the advent of the PC when data entry involved IBM computer cards and keypunch machines, and analysis required hand-carrying the cards to a mainframe computer center and praying that the technicians would not scramble their order or destroy them in the processing.

As I recall, just "cleaning" the data cards, that is, eliminating contaminated variables, hanging "chads" and ambiguous "punches" and emotionally letting go of "key" variables for which there was no reliable data took well over a year and a half for him to accomplish. In the cleaning process, I think he went from about 79 anticipated variables to about 18 usable ones, so much for the "quick and dirty" dissertation.

Still, Pawlak doggedly persisted, and when he finished, his understanding of the ways in which institutional racism and sexism were manifested and interacted together was far more complex and differentiated than he had originally hypothesized. His findings also challenged simplistic rhetoric concerning the ways racism and sexism manifested themselves in the juvenile court system. Moreover, because Pawlak had unexpectedly unearthed some limited data about whether court social workers had consulted on cases and, if so, the diagnostic assessments that resulted, he got a glimpse of the way in which well-meaning and ideologically liberal practitioners were unwittingly implicated in this complex race and gender-influenced process.

Although based entirely on available data, simple data-analytic techniques, and experimental logic (i.e., cross-tabulations of race and sex with various court dispositions; controlling for offense categories), Pawlak was able to provide a much more refined, empirically based analysis of racism and sexism than he had anticipated. Indeed some findings were quite surprising and countered prevailing "expert" opinions concerning institutional racism and sexism. Perhaps his most surprising findings were that non-white females were least likely to be detained and white females, most likely. In a published paper based on his available-data dissertation, Pawlak concludes:

> While some findings point to discriminatory handling of non-white juveniles, other findings suggest that nonwhites are not always treated more harshly than whites. (Pawlak, 1977, p. 152)

Ironically, it was easier to get Pawlak to accept the complexity of these findings than his dissertation chair, who was so ideologically invested in the study that the findings were problematic to her "expert" opinion.

But that is precisely why we do research. And how we do good research is in a way that we can discover that our original premises were incorrect. Though we referred to it at the time as an SA dissertation, I now see that Pawlak's work planted an extremely long-germinating seed for the CDM dissertation. The much more recent exemplar studies that follow, however, are consciously defined as such. Pawlak went on to a successful academic career teaching and writing about social work administration. I am grateful to him for his inadvertent contribution to my late-blooming CDM career.

MIXED-METHOD CDM DISSERTATIONS COMBINING AVAILABLE AND ORIGINAL DATA

Instrument Construction for a Study of Bereavement among Hong Kong Chinese

Although the practitioner-initiated CDM studies discussed in the previous chapter and Pawlak's PhD dissertation relied entirely on CDM, some doctoral students have employed it productively in "mixed-method" dissertations that combine *available* and *original* data. So, for example, in her doctoral research on the bereavement experience of Hong Kong Chinese, Amy Chow (2005) mined available videotapes of 52 clients who had received bereavement counseling in a community mental health setting in advance of a larger survey that was based on original data. Chow's specific purpose in using CDM was to identify salient bereavement dimensions for the purpose of questionnaire construction and subsequent hypothesis testing.

In doing so, she felt that she was able to avoid placing what she felt might be an undue burden by interviewing bereaved individuals who were going through the grieving process solely for the purpose of original instrument construction. Because she had been a clinician in the agency setting, she knew about the existence of the tapes and, after Ethics Committee approval at both the agency and the university, was given access to them.

Starting with 60 available videotapes that had been recorded for training and supervisory purposes and following Ethics Committee requirements, she was able to contact 52 of the individuals who received counseling in order to secure consent for the use of the tapes for research purposes. All 52 consented.

She then transcribed 10 complete tapes—some involving several sessions—that were randomly chosen and engaged practitioners who provided the counseling in closely analyzing them in order to extract key psychosocial dimensions of the grieving experience. One-hundred-forty-eight dimensions were identified under general headings such as "responses," "coping," "functioning," and "transformation." To assure the reliability of the coding of these items, Chow used university-based researchers to review a single session from each of the 10 tapes and found only 5 code category disagreements. These were reconciled in meetings that included both researchers and practitioners. In so doing, Chow made use of *available qualitative* data to devise an *original quantitative*, self-administered survey questionnaire.

In her study, Chow was particularly interested in the elements of the coping process and the positive transformations in self, relationships, philosophical views, and sense of life's purpose that some bereaved individuals can experience. She went on to do an original survey of bereaved Hong Kong Chinese giving particular attention to the factors that predicted extreme and dysfunctional grief reactions versus more positive adjustment to loss.

A seasoned mental health practitioner, Chow is now an Assistant Professor in the Department of Social Work and Social Administration at the University of Hong Kong. Based on her dissertation research, she has presented at several international conferences. Most recently, she copresented at a workshop on the CDM dissertation that I conducted at the University of Hong Kong in June 2008.

Population Description and Typologizing of Homeless Women Female Shelter Residents

In her mixed-method dissertation concerning women and their families who are "long-term-stayers" in homeless shelters in New York City, Adina Goldstein (2007) used quantitative CDM to describe the demographic characteristics of her population and to typologize those with whom she wanted to conduct in-depth qualitative interviews.

Using de-identified 2003 intake data secured from the NYC Department of Homeless Services, she employed cross-tabulations, t-tests, bivariate correlations, Analysis of Variance (ANOVA), and linear regression analysis to identify predictors of shelter length of stay among female-headed families. Working with only 7 variables but with a study N of 1820, she determined that age, number of children, number of adults, and number of previous episodes of homelessness, each made a contribution to length of stay (Goldstein, 2007, pp. 71–84).

Based upon her *available quantitative CDM* effort, she chose a purposive sample of 30 women with whom to conduct *original qualitative interviews*—15 short-term and 15 long-term stayers. Interview questions and probes were informed by her knowledge of these predictors. Moreover, by demonstrating that her two sets of interviewees differed markedly on each of the quantitative predictors of length, she established the representativeness of the groups and, by inference, the external validity of her findings. These interviews were then supplemented, corroborated, and informed by interviews with seven key-informant practitioners and policy-makers, who were service providers in the shelter system, to further validate the findings and to explore their practice and policy implications.

In her dissertation, Goldstein remarks that her mixed-method study findings "shed light on both systemic and personal factors that contribute to the increased length of stay of families in the shelter system…and have implications for program development and for public policy making at municipal and federal levels" (Goldstein, 2007, p. v.). Although she approached her research from the standpoint of a program administrator, because she had been a clinician, her remarkable qualitative interviews provide a powerful voice for the homeless women in her sample and have clear implications for case advocacy and psychosocial casework with homeless women and their families. Only clinically sensitive, focused, qualitative interviews could do that.

An experienced clinician and administrator of services to the homeless, Adina Goldstein, DSW, is currently Deputy Commissioner in the Department of Social Services, Greenwich, Connecticut.

Clinical Evaluation of Treatment Termination

Long concerned with the often precipitous ending of mental health treatment of adolescents at Mt. Sinai's Adolescent Health Center where she was a clinician, Diane Mirabito (2001) conducted a mixed-method dissertation study of the termination process. In contrast with the previously mentioned studies, however, Mirabito began by conducting *original qualitative interviews* with her coworkers. The purpose of these interviews was to construct a "grounded theory" based on practitioners' views that described who and explained why some clients drop out of mental health treatment abruptly with neither warning nor therapeutically structured ending. In this regard, her intent was to capture the prevailing "practice-wisdom" that she and her colleagues had accumulated over the years.

Although the theoretical literature that she reviewed emphasized the importance of a clinical termination process, previous studies of adolescents in mental health treatment indicated high levels of unannounced dropout. Likewise, Mirabito's practitioner peers believed that this was the norm rather than the exception but that those with whom a clinical termination process was most likely to take place were adolescents who were most effectively engaged in the treatment process—in other words, those who benefited most from counseling.

Once the first phase of her study that relied on original qualitative data was completed, Mirabito conducted a *quantitative CDM* study of 100 closed patient records to determine the extent to which terminations were "acknowledged" or "unacknowledged" by the clinician prior to termination. As predicted, and consistent with practice-wisdom, CDM data demonstrated that most terminations went unacknowledged, and if they were, it was more likely to be via a follow-up telephone conversation rather than in a face-to-face treatment session. This came as no surprise.

What surprised Mirabito and what contradicted prevailing practice-wisdom was that the adolescents who abruptly dropped out of treatment were those who were *most successfully engaged* rather than those who appeared resistant to counseling or were there because they had to be. While these empirical findings contradicted conventional practice-wisdom, on reflection they made sense. It was because young persons who were missing appointments were obviously resistant and not meeting treatment objectives and directly or indirectly provoked discussion with their therapists about ending treatment.

At the same time, Mirabito remained most intrigued about the seemingly precipitous and unacknowledged endings of those who were highly engaged. To further understand how various young counselees perceived treatment termination, she developed a typology based on whether the ending was acknowledged or not and whether clients were successfully engaged or not in treatment. The purpose of the typology was to recruit different types of "terminators" for follow-up, *original qualitative interviews* with individuals who fell into each of the various combinations.

Among other uses, this final, qualitative phase of her dissertation was intended to explain why those who did well in treatment "dropped out" unexpectedly. Based on her interviews with various kinds of treatment terminators, Mirabito discovered that young people who benefited most from treatment but terminated precipitously felt that by not acknowledging the ending of treatment, they were, in fact, "keeping the door open" to future contacts if necessary. So, contrary to practitioner perception and official agency policy definitions, to these young persons treatment never ended.

A highly experienced clinician, Mirabito is currently a Clinical Associate Professor of Social Work at New York University School of Social Work. She has published from her dissertation research (Mirabito, 2001) and has presented it at national and international professional conferences.

CDM DISSERTATIONS USING ADVANCED QUANTITATIVE DATA-ANALYSIS

"Cultural Data-Mining" Depression and School Performance

In contrast with practitioner-initiated and implemented CDM studies, doctoral dissertations using available data may involve advanced statistical techniques and quasi-experimental designs that are beyond the ken of most practitioners. But, however rarified their statistics or designs, their focus necessarily remains on the "real world" problems and practice issues that social workers and other allied health professionals routinely confront and keep records about.

One such quantitative CDM dissertation was conducted by Vladmir Kochkine (2006). Trained as a psychologist in Russia before emigrating to the United States, Kochkine entered Hunter's doctoral program as a social worker providing individual as well as group therapy for Russian male adolescents who were performing poorly in school. His original dissertation interest concerned the relationship between depression and school performance among recently arrived Russian adolescent males and the impact of individual and group intervention within this population. Based on his prior training as a psychologist, his first dissertation plan involved designing a small randomized-controlled trial (RCT), using *original quantitative data* based on standardized measures of depression and *available quantitative data* regarding school performance such as grades, graduation, and so forth.

Serving as one of his doctoral program research instructors and eventually his dissertation advisor, I had many opportunities to discuss his study plans with him over a period of years while he was taking doctoral coursework. In those conversations, the ethical, programmatic, and practical issues associated with the use of a control group inevitably arose. He raised them, and we discussed and dismissed using a "cross-over" design on ethical grounds because putting depressed and poor-performing adolescents on a waiting list for research purposes was unacceptable to him as a practitioner. Another question I raised concerned the possible burden of using standardized instruments to measure depression at two points in time, prior to intervention as a "baseline" for young persons awaiting the treatment phase of the experiment.

In the course of these discussions about obstacles to his ideal "gold-standard" study design and long-held research fantasy, what very gradually became clear to me were a number of highly desirable sources of available data in the program records in the agency in which he worked. First, the program served hundreds of adolescent males and females from various cultural backgrounds including nonimmigrants. Second, the program routinely administered standardized instruments measuring students' psychological functioning for clinical assessment and evaluation purposes before and after treatment;

while also collecting routine data regarding grades and other aspects of school performance. Third, his agency program offered both individual and group therapy with some clients receiving both. Finally, Kochkine averred that it would be possible to match data concerning students and the services they received with information about their social workers' cultural background, languages spoken, level of training, and so forth.

For me, the picture that very gradually emerged was CDM heaven, while for Kochkine it began as RCT hell. The shift in focus to a shared vision of the remarkable possibilities took several months. Clearly, I was looking at things through a broad set of multinational CDM "lenses" whereas his was a narrow RCT and Russian *pince nez*. I was talking "silver," he was wanting "gold" (Epstein, 2001). But to me, this was as good as it could get.

Once we began speaking the same research language, his study went extremely efficiently. Using the experimental logic and statistical sophistication he had garnered in his Russian training as a research psychologist, he dug in to and totally uncovered a rich source of CDM possibilities. Easily gaining approval to access a vast amount of *available qualitative and quantitative data* that had never been used for research purposes by his agency, Kochkine received Institutional Review Board (IRB) or Ethics Committee approval without needing to "re-consent" clients whose data could easily be de-identified.

Then he specified eight distinct cultural groups, and using a computer program for randomly selecting recently closed cases, chose 50 males and 50 females in each cultural group. Employing multivariate analytic techniques, he was able to look at the relationship between depression and school performance controlling for client variables, for example, gender, cultural group; for intervention, for example, casework, group work, combined casework and groupwork; and for social worker variables, for example, cultural background and language spoken, level of training, and so forth.

As one might expect (and I had hoped), Kochkine's findings were quite complex and highly diverse: far too complex and diverse to summarize here. Suffice it to say, they revealed very different but statistically significant relationships between depression and school performance at the beginning and at the end of treatment for males and females as well as for different cultural groups. Likewise, they demonstrate differential responses to individual, group, and combined individual and group interventions, as well as variations in the significance of the match between the cultural background of workers and clients.

Though his findings are more complex but *less* causally definitive than what his idealized RCT with Russian male adolescents would have produced, one can argue that his findings are *more* valuable in that they reflect on multiple gender, cultural, and intervention patterns simultaneously. That comes much closer to the reality of his agency practice than his original RCT fantasy. Kochkine's enormously rich and complex study findings are yet to be further refined and "mined" for their publication possibilities. His dissertation title, however, refers to his research as a form of "cultural data-mining."

Kochkine now provides training to practitioners as well as clinical services for poor-performing students in the New York City school system. He has given several workshops based on his findings in his own agency in the United States and in Russia.

Mining "Good Death" in a Palliative Care Program

There are some practice contexts in which RCTs, let alone original data-collection with lengthy standardized instruments, are almost unthinkable from an ethical standpoint. End-of-life research is one. Nonetheless, social workers and other health professionals routinely work in palliative and hospice care with dying patients. To the extent possible, their purpose is to relieve physical and psychological distress for patients and to minimize the pain of loss for surviving loved ones. In other words, their practice is intended to maintain a reasonable and meaningful quality of life while patients are in care and, ultimately, to help patients achieve a "good death" when the former is no longer possible. The sensitivity of this topic does not preclude us from wanting to know more about how to help such patients and their families. While RCTs are hard to envision, the need for practice-relevant research is not.

Though there is a general consensus among practitioners of the value, if not the indicators, of "good death," for understandable reasons, empirical research on this existentially profound topic is rare. Patients and their loved ones could not be more vulnerable than at this time. Family members are understandably "resistant"—coping with intense emotions and often confronting very difficult, end-of-life decisions. Similarly, in helping patients and their families, practitioners are intensely occupied in ways and in matters that generally preclude research. So, it is the rare practitioner, doctoral student or indeed academic researcher who ventures into this sensitive but important research venue. I have been fortunate enough to know two such practitioner-researcher-doctoral students—one from Australia, the other from Hong Kong. One conducted her dissertation with original data; the other conducted his using CDM; her PhD was in nursing, and his was in social work. For our purposes, both are worth describing and comparing.

In her remarkable dissertation, Carrie Lethborg (2006), a very experienced social work clinician has pursued both a qualitative and quantitative enquiry into "meaning-making" among dying Australian cancer patients. Although her qualitative research is exquisitely rendered and her quantitative analysis extremely sophisticated, her study is limited by substantial interview refusal rate by patients, a small N, a relative lack of consideration of the impact of palliative care as an intervention and a "narrowness" of focus that gives limited attention to the psychosocial dimensions of dying. Despite the foregoing limitations, Lethborg's mixed-method study based entirely on original data and employing some standardized instruments provides considerable, empirically based insight into how cancer patients make their own death meaningful to themselves and their family members.

Sharing similar practice-research interests with Lethborg, but working as a clinical social worker in a hospital in Hong Kong rather than Melbourne, Wallace Chan also had extensive practice experience with dying cancer patients in a palliative care program. Sensitive to patient needs and struggling with the ethical problems of conducting original research in this context, he was aware of CDM through a workshop I had given at the University of Hong Kong where he was a doctoral student and chose to conduct a CDM dissertation on his great passion—palliative care. However, in exploring available clinical data collected by social workers in his hospital, he was discouraged by the limited amount and scope of psychosocial data that social workers in the palliative care program routinely recorded. While thoroughly devoted to their practice, Chan's social work colleagues had little interest in participating in research, involving a *prospective* practice-based research (PBR) dissertation employing either *original quantitative or qualitative data-collection.*

Disheartened by this set of circumstances, he e-mailed me for advice, and I suggested that he consider other available clinical information sources. This simple suggestion led to another incredibly rich "vein" of institutional data (Chan, 2007). Hence, it was the palliative care nurses rather than social workers whose task it was to conduct comprehensive assessment interviews with patients. As a result, nurses routinely recorded vast amounts of medical and psychosocial data about newly admitted patients. Further, they regularly checked on patients, monitored, and recorded all kinds of data about physical and psychological dimensions of well-being and routinely inquired about their relations with family members, anxiety about death, religious beliefs, and so forth. These data were routinely recorded in all patient charts from the time patients entered until they died.

Working in collaboration with the nurses, Chan was able to enlist their help in extracting data—some based on *available qualitative data* and others based on *available standardized quantitative* measures that were already used for clinical assessment but *not* as research tools. For many patients, whose palliative care journey took weeks or months rather than days, data were available from the time they entered the program to a few days before they died. At the very least, this made possible time 1/time 2 comparisons. Choosing a CDM "sampling window" that included only deceased patients precluded hospital Ethics Committee or University IRB objections. In Hong Kong, I was told that the dead no longer have legal rights over their own data. Nonetheless, Chan's CDM strategy offered no intrusion to patients or their families during this sensitive time and de-identified data-analysis and safeguarded their identities in the research.

By the time data were extracted by nurses and reliability was operationally and statistically assured, Chan's sample exceeded 900 patients who died between 2003 and 2005 and included data describing their demographics, medical conditions, pain levels, depression, grief, anxiety, and their interactions with family members. In comparison with Lethborg's study, Chan's wide range of data resources and large N is mitigated by the relative crudeness of the coding of critical dimensions of "good death" into dichotomous categories rather than in more refined scales that might have been built into a self-administered patient questionnaire (Chan, Epstein, Reese & Chen, 2009).

Thus a principle advantage of the quantitative portion of Lethborg's dissertation study was that on her narrower range of variables her interval measures were highly refined and standardized (Lethborg, C., Aranda, S. & Kissane, D., 2008). However, criticism of this shortcoming in Chan's study is countered by the fact that many of the patients he studied were illiterate, spoke no English, and couldn't respond to existing self-administered instruments even if they could be ethically employed. CDM was the only practical as well as ethical option available to Chan—albeit from a research standpoint another "strategic compromise."

Using descriptive statistics and hierarchical regression analysis, Chan was able to create two composite scales that represented physical and psychosocial indicators of "good death" that is, physically pain-free on the one hand and psychologically at peace and with positive feelings toward family on the other. In so doing, he was able to document the positive effect of palliative care based on time1/time 2 differences. Programmatically, that was quite valuable.

From a practice-knowledge development standpoint however, what was even more valuable was the discovery of what he identified as a "support paradox" whereby patients are most likely to achieve "good death" when they are supported by family members but when they don't think they are too much of a burden. Chan sees this "paradox" as unique to the Chinese who place great emphasis on intergenerational familial bonds and reciprocity. However, to some degree, one could argue that this finding is universal to all cultures that value family relations.

In this context, it is interesting to consider the differences between Kochkine's and Chan's original dissertation aspirations and ultimate CDM dissertation findings. Kochkine began with a universal assumption and theory about depression and school performance hypothesizing that patterns would be the same for both genders and all cultural groups. Instead, he found quite different patterns controlling for gender and culture and differential response to interventions and interveners. This set of findings was only possible in a comparative study and later raised significant, empirically based questions about what is universal and what is particular to different cultures?

Alternatively, Chan has argued that his findings are particular to Chinese culture. Because he has no comparative data on palliative care in other cultural contexts, there is no way to know whether this is true or not. However, anyone who has ever cared for a dying patient, relative, or friend can recognize the salience and "truth value" of providing support while allowing the patient to maintain a sense of not being a burden. Based on his findings, Chan, Epstein, Reese & Chen (2009) posit two distinct "pathways of intervention" with dying patients—one focused on the patient and the other on family members. CDM studies in palliative programs in other countries and cultures could determine how unique these pathways are.

In a recent workshop that I did on the CDM Dissertation at the University of Hong Kong at which he was one of the presenters, Chan, who was at this writing in a training and research position at the Centre for Behavioral Health, University of Hong Kong and will be an Assistant Professor of Social Work at the Chinese University of Hong Kong by the time this book is published, closed by saying that while his data-mining involved the records of deceased patients, he did it "dreaming" of enhancing quality of life and meaning of death for future palliative care patients and their families. Though they employed different dissertation-research methods, I'm sure that in doing so, both Chan and Lethborg shared the same dream. Who is to say which version of the dream is better?

Mining Breast Cancer Patient Narratives

Another presenter at my 2008 CDM dissertation workshop in Hong Kong was Fu Wai. From a quantitative methodology standpoint, his is the most sophisticated CDM dissertation completed to date. His clinical database is drawn from the narratives of 202 Hong Kong Chinese breast cancer patients who participated in clinical trial RCTs of various psychosocial interventions with breast cancer outpatients. As a therapeutic coping device, all of these women were encouraged to keep personal journals over the course of their breast cancer treatment. Until he recognized their research potential, the available qualitative data were considered a clinical residue of an RCT.

But Wai gathered and "mined" these narratives—converting them from *qualitative patient narratives* into *quantitative CDM data*. In addition, he could link these data to standardized psychosocial, self-administered questionnaires administered to the women over the course of their involvement in the clinical trials. As a result, he had the best of both methodological worlds. He not only had their qualitative narratives describing their cancer experiences in their own words and metaphors but linked quantitative data with numerous *standardized quantitative measures* of psychosocial adjustment that were employed in the RCT intervention studies.

Having attended a prior workshop that I did at the University of Hong Kong, Wai decided to do a CDM dissertation focused on the content of the narratives and how the themes contained within them were associated with standardized psychosocial markers from available self-administered, quantitative data over the course of cancer treatment.

In some sense then, his study may be seen as a *mixed-method* study that involved secondary analysis of quantitative data collected for other research purposes combined with CDM conversion of qualitative to quantitative data from information that was a byproduct of a routine clinical intervention. Less important than how it is categorized, what makes Wai's study stand out from other CDM dissertations is his highly sophisticated and inventive use of various data-mining software programs, for example, ITALASSI, QDA Miner version 2.0.6, SIMSTAT version 2.5.5 as well as SPSS 11.5 (Wai, 2007, p. 34).

Inspired by prior content analytic studies of suicide notes, personal accounts of recovery from trauma and cancer narratives, Wai "mined" the narratives for themes concerning cancer causality, death, relationships with doctors as well as family members, body image, sexuality, helplessness, anger, hope, gratefulness, letting go, and so forth. Creatively employing the foregoing data-mining software, he was able to represent complex multivariate relationships with striking three-dimensional graphics. At the same time, he does not allow the impressive graphics to obscure his awareness of the limitations of the study in which patient behaviors are not charted and important psychological constructs may be absent from the narratives.

It would do his many rich and complex findings an injustice to try to summarize them here. Simply stated, Wai's study sheds light on how women preserve their spiritual integrity and quality of life during breast cancer treatment and how their fears and concerns about death are associated with standardized psychosocial markers. Unlike other CDM studies that are more exploratory in their style of presentation, Wai tests specific hypotheses about "self-integration" of the cancer experience. Ultimately, he presents an empirically based typology of patient adjustment to their condition derived from the narrative content of their journals in which a subset of women labeled as the "metaphysical group" experiences more social support and displays more "fighting spirit" than either the "psychosocial group," which is highest on perceived stress, or the "environmental group," which emphasizes environmental explanations of their cancer. He concludes with recommendations for interventions based on these very different patient orientations.

Although they employed a wide array of research methodologies, designs, and data-analytic techniques, Chan, Lethborg, and Wai share common humanistic and practice-research purposes. Who is to say which of their contributions to knowledge ranks higher than the other? And each considered important, practice-relevant questions that were not answerable via an RCT.

In contrast with Chan and Lethborg, who were both seasoned clinical practitioners, Fu Wai was trained as a psychologist as well as a social work researcher. He is currently teaching in the Department of Counseling and Psychology at Hong Kong Shue Yan University. A gifted data-miner as well as an inveterate boundary-spanner and paradigm-stretcher, he is currently translating the writings of the noted French psychoanalyst Jacques Lacan into Chinese.

Mining for Predictors of Length of Stay of Male Homeless Shelter Residents

Another soon-to-be completed CDM dissertation that employs data-mining software and advanced statistical techniques is by Louis Rodriguez (2009) within the Hunter College School of Social Work doctoral program. In many ways, his dissertation can be viewed as a counterpoint to and replication of Goldstein's dissertation cited earlier in this chapter. They each focused on the homeless—she on homeless women, he, on homeless men. Each employ quantitative CDM secured from the same agency database. Their mutual interest in the plight of New York City's homeless population emerged from their many years of administrative practice in settings serving the homeless. In fact, they both worked together for years as administrators in the St. John's Family Center in Brooklyn, New York, where Rodriguez is Executive Director.

From my first dissertation seminar meetings with each of them, it was clear that both were passionately concerned with why individuals and families often languish in homeless shelters rather than moving into housing rentals long beyond the shelter program's intended length of stay (LOS)? In their "clinical" work with the homeless families, both recognized that even with difficulties associated with changes in the economy and availability of low-cost housing in New York City, with proper support, some homeless found housing relatively quickly while others, referred to as "long-term stayers" seemed to make "temporary" shelters their permanent homes.

As described above, Goldstein conducted a *mixed-method* CDM dissertation that made very limited use of available quantitative data-analysis and extensive use of original qualitative interview data. In her study, CDM only set the quantitative stage for an in-depth qualitative comparison of homeless women—some who left the shelters success-fully and expeditiously and others who far exceeded their intended length of stay.

Rodriguez took another route. His *entirely quantitative* CDM dis-sertation relies exclusively on data-mining. Hoping to mine many more variables than Goldstein did from State records, using business-oriented, data-mining software (Shmueli et al., 2006) and advanced statistical techniques, Rodriguez set about to identify multiple predic-tors of LOS and their relative weights for homeless shelter men and their families. Once a predictive model was generated with half of his sample, he would test its "goodness of fit" with the other half of his sample. In effect, the second portion of his study served as a replication of the first.

More specifically, using a systematic sampling of every 8th home-less male head of household who entered the shelter system in 2003 and 2004, Rodriguez arrived at his sample of 811. Because he drew his de-identified data from a Client Tracking System rather than from Intake data as did Goldstein, Rodriguez had access to both demographic variables as well as data concerning the reason for shelter placement, marital relationship, medical conditions, prior shelter eligibility and exit disposition, as well as LOS, making his quantitative database potentially richer than Goldstein's. Nonetheless, other more process-oriented variables that he had hoped to include in his study were not made available to him directly (on ethical grounds) or in coded form (on grounds of efficiency and cost).

Working with the 12 variables remaining, Rodriguez used SAS soft-ware, Kaplan-Meier Survival Analysis, and Cox Proportional Hazards

Modeling to test the goodness of fit of these predictor variables with LOS in various predictive models. Consistent with Goldstein's findings for homeless women, Rodriguez found that age and family size were significant predictors of LOS. In addition, and because he had a wider set of variables to mine than Goldstein, he found that reason for placement and destination upon discharge, that is, "disposition" were predictive of LOS as well. In fact, the latter was the strongest predictor indicating that those men who were successfully housed in desirable apartments also spent the least time in shelters. This implies that certain client profiles (be they male or female) are easier to place in their own apartments and these profiles can be empirically described.

What is striking about these Goldstein's and Rodriguez's dissertations is that though they used somewhat different methodological approaches with populations that differed by gender their major findings were quite similar. They differ significantly, however, in that Goldstein's qualitative portion of the study gives "voice" to the women she interviewed and makes possible an empathic understanding of the range of experience of women who live in homeless shelters whether for short or long periods. Moreover, she provides deep insight into the perceived incentives and obstacles to leaving the shelter that homeless women perceive. This provides a profound sense of the internal validity of her findings.

Rodriguez acknowledges that because he has not done qualitative interviews with the men, he did not know how they experienced shelter life and shelter services. That is the strength of Goldstein's study. On the other hand, the more refined quantitative CDM methodology that Rodriguez employs allows him to empirically describe in quantitative terms various "paths to independence" and the risk ratios associated with different characteristics. Thus, he substitutes predictive power for interpretive richness and empathic understanding. Her findings have more obvious micro-level practice implications, and his, macro-level policy implications. Here again, who is to say which methodology or set of findings is superior? And, could social work practitioners comfortably contemplate an RCT with homeless adults and children?

Louis Rodriguez is Executive Director of St. John's Family Center, which provides housing and social services for homeless families in New York City. Upon completion of his PhD, he plans to provide CDM consultation to homeless administrators and policy-makers.

CDM DISSERTATIONS FOCUSING ON THE ORGANIZATIONAL AND SOCIETAL LEVELS

While practitioner-initiated CDM was initially conceived as a PBR strategy to provide clinically relevant knowledge to practitioners working directly with individual clients and their families, doctoral dissertation students like Rodriguez have "mined" available quantitative data to make empirically based statements and to test theory at higher levels of abstraction—that is, the organizational and/or policy levels. In so doing, they extended the scope of CDM methodology beyond what some might comfortably label "clinical." Their inclusion in this chapter is based on the fact that all of these dissertation studies were

- conducted by social work doctoral students;
- concerning issues of direct interest to social workers and social work agencies;
- based on available quantitative data that were not originally collected for research purposes.

The following quantitative CDM dissertations focus respectively on a single agency's program, multiple programs within a single agency, multiple agencies, and an entire society. The first looks at an agency that is dedicated to a single intervention model—that is, Intensive Family Preservation. It uses available case record data to test how faithfully the agency implements the intervention model and to identify the client characteristics with whom the model is most effective.

The second dissertation uses available quantitative program data gathered from multiple programs within a single community mental health agency. In that dissertation, the author tests a broader, widely held theory of the conservative effects of privatization on social agencies. Here, the author employs available quantitative clinical data from several agency programs to test a political theory in what is ultimately a case-study of a single organization.

The third exemplar employs available quantitative accreditation data study to evaluate the impact of an accreditation process on applicant organizations. In this dissertation, the accreditation process is viewed as an organizational intervention, and various aspects of organizational change are viewed as potential study outcomes.

The fourth study is in many respects broadest in scope. Though the unit of analysis is individual service recipients, it uses publically available quantitative data to evaluate the antipoverty program of an entire nation. This study both assesses the implementation of a broad social policy and tests a political theory concerning social capital formation and social networking on national poverty reduction.

More important than the label attached to their methodological strategies, these exemplars are intended to demonstrate the potential usefulness of available quantitative data in social work data-mining dissertations *beyond* the most restrictive definition of "clinical." In addition, they demonstrate the creative contributions to knowledge that some doctoral students can make when they are freed to consider an alternative dissertation-research paradigm.

Mining for Program Fidelity and the Differential Effectiveness in a Family Preservation Agency

For several years prior to her entry into Hunter's doctoral program, Daria Hanssen was a caseworker, supervisor, and subsequently a clinical consultant to an agency in New England that was viewed within the Intensive Family Preservation (IFP) community as exemplary in its commitment to the goals of the movement, that is, the prevention of foster care placement. In contrast with other intervention models, IFP and its intended outcome had been rigorously specified by its funders who promoted its evaluation in an unusually large number of RCTs testing its effectiveness. These programs and evaluations were conducted in the United States and several other countries throughout the world.

Conversant with the many RCTs conducted on IFP, Hanssen's practice-research interest originated in her desire to find out how closely her own agency adhered empirically to IFP program theory and practice. Using Bickman's terms (1987), she was interested in doing a "black box" study of "program fidelity." Moreover, as a former caseworker, supervisor, and consultant, she was well aware that no matter how effective IFP was shown to be in prior experimental studies, it did not work with many troubled families. Consequently, her second study objective was to assess the differential impact of IFP with different kinds of client presenting problems and types of families.

Hanssen's inductively derived, practice-based interests suggested a more refined and differentiated set of questions than EBP proponents generally ask (Fraser, Pecora, & Haapala, 1991) and conventional RCTs can answer (Macias, Jones, Hargreaves, Wang, Rodican, Barreira & Gold, 2008).

Because her study was initially driven by her own program and practice interests, a PBR research strategy was attractive to her. Rejecting a "gold-standard" RCT for "ethical" reasons, she envisioned conducting a *prospective quasi-experimental study employing original data-collection.* However, she was still concerned about the potential intrusiveness to clients as well as former coworkers of original data-collection. Although her agency did relatively little in the way of evaluation research, it did an exemplary job of process record keeping and took pride in the way case-records were used "the old-fashioned way" to train and supervise workers. Moreover, Hanssen's standing in the agency was so positive that a *retrospective* CDM dissertation based primarily on *quantitative data* extracted from available, closed case-records was then considered and easily approved (Hanssen, 2003).

As her dissertation advisor and just beginning my exploration of CDM as a dissertation-research strategy, hers was of particular interest to me as a test of the "feasibility" of CDM methodology for testing program fidelity and for specifying the conditions under which interventions were effective. In addition, I wondered whether CDM could add to the knowledge already generated by RCTs. In this early CDM dissertation study, Hanssen's and my research dreams happily coincided.

In addition to the quality of the case-records available to her, two features of the IFP movement facilitated a CDM study of intervention and outcomes. First was the fact that IFP intervention involved highly prescriptive practices, for example, a 24-hour availability, the provision of specific kinds of concrete services as well as psychosocial interventions, emphasis on teaching parents cognitive-behavioral child-management as well as homemaking skills, and so forth. In other words, the intervention principles of IFP were easily converted into a "yes" versus "no information available" checklist, which was taken from previous prospective IFP studies and modified for CDM purposes. Second, for better or worse, the universally agreed-upon measure of IFP effectiveness was remarkably specific. Hence, the intended outcome or measure of success was nonplacement 30 days after intervention was withdrawn.

With her former agency's permission and IRB approval, Hanssen used systematic sampling to select 116 de-identified closed cases dating from January 2000 through December 2001. From these, she extracted and converted largely qualitative case narratives concerning interventions into coded quantitative data. Drawing on previously published studies of IFP, she was able to efficiently arrive at code categories for services provided, with another colleague to establish the reliability of her coding, and to demonstrate empirically that IFP practices in her agency compared favorably to studies of other IFP agencies. With these data comparisons, she was able to demonstrate that her program was "faithful" to the principles of IFP in its actual practice.

The second portion of her dissertation focused on the overall and differential effectiveness of IFP. Consistent with her practice experience and better than many prior RCT research studies, Hanssen found that 88% of the cases studied prevented placement for at least 30 days after they were was closed. By IFP standards, her program was highly successful and as exemplary as everyone thought. For the first time, however, they had evaluation findings to demonstrate that.

Hanssen's next steps, however, were not routinely taken in "gold-standard" RCT studies. In the latter, through random assignment, study participant differences are assumed to be equivalent. In other RCTs, equivalence is sought through matching strategies. Only recently, have Macias et al. (2008) argued that "[p]ractitioners need to know for whom evidence-based services are most or least effective, but few services research studies provide this information" (p. 283). However, the statistically sophisticated solution they propose is intended for RCTs.

In Hanssen's retrospective study, random assignment to intervention or nonintervention was impossible, and matching was rejected because of the relatively small sample size and lack of variation in outcomes. At the time, I knew nothing about Propensity Score Matching (PSM), a technique for analyzing available data that might have been useful with a larger quantitative data-set. (The potential uses of PSM in CDM will be discussed in the final chapter.)

Instead, employing a much less sophisticated statistical approach, Hanssen followed with a series of bivariate and multivariate cross-tabulations that revealed specific child and adolescent problems and family configurations that were differentially accessible to successful

IFP intervention, for example, whether the young person at risk was from a single-parent family or not, was male or female, whether the parent was mentally ill, and so forth. In research terms, she *specified* the relationship between IFP intervention and outcome in ways that RCTs make an effort to *universalize*. But in working with clients and families that vary in their outcome-relevant characteristics, practitioners require more refined knowledge than universal EBP generalizations and RCT studies provide.

Although several of Hanssen's findings were strong enough to achieve statistical significance, they should be treated as *hypotheses* for future studies rather than as generalizations for all IFP programs. Limited by a relatively small sample size from a single IFP agency and very modest Chi-square statistical analyses, Hanssen's study was informed by her own practice sophistication and explanatory feedback that she received from agency staff with whom she shared her findings before completing her data analysis. And while RCTs using advanced statistical techniques make claims to generic "proof" of effectiveness, their design and frequent intention is to "strip" away contextual variations in the quest for generalization.

In that respect, they mimic drug studies. From a social work program and practice point of view, however, one can argue that the more important and useful findings involve statements about the conditions under which intervention is effective or not. From an "evidence-based medicine" point of view, a similar critique could be directed toward drug studies. But that is taking us too far afield.

Closer to home, one might suggest that some social work research journals that place RCTs at the top of the EBP hierarchy might reconsider their priorities. So, it comes as no surprise that initial efforts to publish articles based on Hanssen's research in a prominent social work research journal were rejected on the grounds of their methodological weaknesses relative to the number of previously published RCTs and meta-analyses of RCTs already available concerning the effectiveness of IFP. One of the more kindly rejections asked why one would even think of doing such a study when there are all the RCTs around. Leaving aside the methodological merits of the more brutal and dismissive rejections, it is noteworthy that two articles based on Hanssen's dissertation were quickly and enthusiastically accepted by the *Journal of Family Preservation* (Hannssen & Epstein, 2006, 2007).

Daria Hanssen is currently an Assistant Professor of Social Work at Marist College. In addition to her publications, she has presented on the basis of this study in conferences in the United States and the United Kingdom.

Mining for the Programmatic Effects of Privatization in a Community Mental Health Agency

Upon entering the doctoral program at Hunter College School of Social Work, Edye Schwartz was already Executive Director of a community mental health agency in upstate New York. An experienced manager and administrator, both she and her agency were confronted by a major environmental change. The county in which her agency was situated was privatizing all local mental health services. If her agency was to survive, she would have to change it from a public to a nonprofit private agency with all the attendant fiscal, legal, structural, and staff requirements associated with privatization.

For her and her staff, this was not only an organizational challenge but an ideological confrontation. Virtually, all of the social work literature on privatization, mostly written by academics, and much of the thinking among rank and file social workers emphasized its *conservatizing* effects. Indeed, there was a general consensus that privatization and managed care necessarily meant cost-reduction at the expense of quality of care, efficiency at the expense of effectiveness, disengagement of the poor, "creaming" of those clients who had private insurance, and the greater possibility of positive treatment outcomes, decreased length of stay, and so on.

Schwartz believed this as well but was determined to avoid these negative organizational outcomes if she possibly could. Her administrative strategy for avoiding these negative programmatic outcomes was heavily influenced by the Psychiatric Rehabilitation (PR) model of change developed by Anthony (2000). Employing an organizational analogue of PR, Schwartz assessed her agency's readiness for change and carefully guided it through the change process. Once having done so, both she and her staff as well their service recipients and community seemed satisfied. Naturally, Schwartz was pleased that the agency had weathered some stormy years and had achieved a new equilibrium. However, while a doctoral student, she became aware that despite the newfound program stabilization, she had never empirically evaluated the organizational impacts of privatization in her own agency. Nor could she offer any "evidence" that a PR model of organizational change "worked." Finally, other than her own subjective impressions, she had nothing to say in the privatization debate to which she felt she had something important to contribute.

Although her original intention for her dissertation research was to do a qualitative case-study based on organizational documents and interviews with clients as well as staff, her position as Executive Director raised Hunter-IRB concerns about ethical conflicts and the possibility that clients as well as social work staff might feel compelled to report positively about the organizational change process that she promulgated. In addition, they objected to a qualitative case study as insufficiently scholarly. Consequently, our IRB rejected her original proposal on ethical as well as methodological grounds.

Instead, she decided to use available documents and her own personal diaries to describe the PR-guided change process and CDM to evaluate it. The latter would make use of available quantitative data drawn from agency reports to funders and from de-identified client records to which she could easily gain access. Her final, IRB-approved quantitative CDM study design involved looking at various privatization theory-relevant outcome indicators extracted from organizational records over the course of two years prior to privatization, six months during the period of change, and two years after privatization had been achieved (Schwartz, 2007).

Early in her study, Schwartz provided a brief summary of some of the key outcome indicators that she used. Quoting her, they included but were not limited to

- length of stay, to see if privatization caused staff to discharge clients prematurely;
- diagnosis and functionality to see if 'creaming' occurred after privatization;
- payor source, to see if clients who could not pay were denied services;
- number and diversity of staff interventions, to see if the array of services available to clients changed;
- client and clinician perception of treatment, to see if outcomes changed. (Schwartz, 2007, p. 54)

The last set of indicators was drawn from client and staff satisfaction instruments that were routinely administered in the agency rather than from interviews as originally planned. In addition to the foregoing data, Schwartz used fiscal reports to assess in various ways agency productivity, cost-effectiveness, and efficiency.

Ultimately, Schwartz demonstrated that in virtually all of the measures she employed, her agency performed either better or the same as it had done prior to privatization. She reports that only one variable, payor source, changed in a manner consistent with privatization theory. Thus, after privatization, she discovered that "the number of self-pay only clients decreased and the number of clients with commercial insurance increased" (Schwartz, 2008, p.154). However, she concludes that this finding is somewhat ambiguous. Hence, she suggests that to properly interpret this finding:

> Further study would have to be done…to assure that those who were self-pay only were not denied access to treatment and to see if some of those clients who were self-pay before privatization actually had insurance but just didn't use it because the agency was not enrolled in their insurance panels. (Schwartz, 2008, p. 154)

These are the kinds of refined and, at the same time, practical questions that a "reflective" administrator should be asking, but it was her CDM study findings that provoked her to ask them. She concludes the CDM portion of her study saying that it "evidences a community mental health agency that experienced a disruptive organizational change and yet emerged a more efficient and cost effective organization without experiencing the dire consequences to the quality of service provision that has been reported or predicted in the literature" (Schwartz, 2008, p. 154).

Shortly after completion of her dissertation, Edye Schwartz was contacted by a publisher who was interested in publishing her dissertation as a book. She has since published it and continues in her capacity as Executive Director of the community mental health agency in which she conducted her study. In addition, she has presented on the use of the PR model in promoting organizational change at local, state, national, and international conferences.

Mining the Organizational Impact of an Accreditation Process

During her years as a social work doctoral student at Hunter College School of Social Work, Brenda Williams-Gray was a child welfare administrator. Subsequent to that, she became a program officer at the Council of Accreditation (COA), an organization that accredits social work and other human service agencies in the United States and Canada. Like Schwartz, Williams-Gray had a long-standing interest in organizational development and capacity-building, but prior to moving to COA, her expectation was that her dissertation would focus on foster care and child placement—a field in which she had worked successfully for many years as a direct-service practitioner, supervisor, manager, and administrator.

After a considerable hiatus resulting from her career change, the inescapable subject of dissertation possibilities surfaced in our discussion of her new job responsibilities. As an accreditation program officer, Williams-Gray provided information and consultation to agencies that were seeking accreditation—before, during, and upon completion of the accreditation process. When asked what kinds of data COA routinely collected about the organizations seeking accreditation, Williams-Gray indicated that they employed standardized organizational self-assessments before and on completion of the process in the form of questionnaires with sets of forced-choice items concerning eight dimensions of organizational capacity. These included mission and goal clarity, governance and leadership, fiscal resource management, human resource management, information resource management, cultural competence, community linkages, and performance improvement (Williams-Gray, 2008).

In our discussion, what was remarkable to me was the fact that COA collected and computerized all these data and established the statistical reliability of the measures of these dimensions computing *alpha* scores but never aggregated and analyzed these data for self-evaluative purposes. Instead, they used the "intake" data in much the same way that the Adolescent Health Center (AHC) at Mt. Sinai Hospital (see Chapter 4) had used their self-administered intake forms to assess individual clients and set treatment goals on a case-by-case basis. Just as prior to our CDM effort, AHC had not exploited the knowledge-generating potential of what they referred to as their "database," so too had COA not seen the potential in aggregating and analyzing the data collected from the many agencies that participated in the accrediting process. Of course, the participating agencies and COA were most interested in the individual decision concerning whether or not they received accreditation, but it occurred to me that it would be extremely useful for COA to know whether and where the accreditation process promoted organizational capacity.

In conducting her literature review and writing her dissertation proposal, Williams-Gray discovered a literature on accreditation as an organizational process and linked it with developmental theory. Ultimately, within the one-year, prospective "window" that she chose, she studied 256 agencies participating in the process in which accreditation consultation is considered an "intervention" and before/after differences in organizational capacity and type of accreditation received are treated as "outcomes." In that sense, the study might be seen as analogous to a "clinical" evaluation.

Without detailing her findings, both Williams-Gray and COA learned as much from where change took place (e.g., fiscal management, information resource management, performance improvement, etc.) as where it didn't (e.g., governance and leadership, community linkages, cultural competence, etc.). An analysis of the agency profiles at "intake" suggested that the latter were already up to standard via a process of "anticipatory accreditation" whereby participating agencies meet accreditation requirements in advance of application. Separate from the implications for COA, Williams-Gray's her dissertation raises more general questions about the impact of the accreditation process on human service organizations, schools, and so forth.

Brenda Williams-Gary is currently an Assistant Professor of Social Work in the MSW program at Lehman College of the City University of New York.

Mining for the Societal Effects of Social Capital Formation and Social Networking on Poverty in Chile

By far, the CDM doctoral dissertation that "mined" the largest data-set and client population was recently completed by Mahia Saracostti (2008). Conducted in Chile, her study combined two available national data-sets that were never before linked and made possible an evaluation of the early impact of the Chile Solidario System (CSS), a program intended to relieve poverty in the entire country. In contrast with the relatively small sample sizes in other CDM dissertations that required the labor-intensive location, extraction, and conversion of qualitative case information into quantitative data-sets, Saracostti was working with and linking two already available and computerized quantitative national data-sets. From a data-extraction and coding point of view, it was a "piece of cake." But it was an enormously big cake to study.

Based in part on census data and in part on data collected by the Chilean Department of Social Planning, in principle, her study enumerated the entire population of Chilean heads of households who lived below the poverty line. Consequently, hers was an N = 66,073 study. Moreover, it involved no sampling. Accordingly, there was no question of representativeness or external validity. Everyone about whom she wanted to make inferences was included. From a numerical and statistically inferential standpoint though not from an RCT-causal standpoint, she had indeed struck "gold."

Broadly speaking, the intervention theory behind CSS was that by creating opportunities for social capital formation and social networking, extreme poverty would be ameliorated. Unlike various prior program-policy experiments to eliminate poverty in the United States, however, the Chilean government made no effort to randomize CSS implementation. Nor were there any evaluation efforts reported.

Nonetheless, because the evaluative window that Saracostti chose looked at CSS implementation in its second year, only about half of its intended program beneficiaries had been engaged in the program. However, employing experimental logic in her data-mining, once the comparability of those who were enrolled in CSS and those who were not at T1 was established, she could assess whether the program made a difference by looking at T1/T2 differences for those who were enrolled and T2 differences between those who were and those who weren't.

From the standpoint of program engagement and outcome indicators, she also struck "gold." More specifically, her database routinely included items concerning access and use of health services, dental services, employment services, social subsidies, housing loan programs, savings programs, health insurance, and so forth, which she used as independent variables. Likewise, at T1 and T2, she had measures of family income, government-indexed poverty level, home ownership, occupation and workforce participation, and total family income, which she used as dependant variables. Finally, she had information about CSS participants' perceptions of the program as well as reasons given for nonparticipation by those to whom the program had offered services but who had declined.

Saracossti states that her general objective was to "evaluate the early impact of the CSS on social networking and economic well-being indicators of Chilean families living in extreme poverty" (Saracostti, 2008, p. 2). Using cross-tabulations, Chi-squares and relatively unsophisticated multivariate analytic techniques, she concludes that at this relatively early stage of program implementation, CSS showed

> a limited impact on the social and economic well-being of the participating indigent households. More specifically, the CSS had a moderate but statistically significant positive impact on the social participation level of the household heads, the level of family registration in medical centers or in public primary health establishments, and on the application to government housing programs. Second, CSS had a moderate but statistically significant positive impact on the employment activities of the household heads and on the level of autonomous family income. Third, CSS had no significant impact on the dental care and healthcare received by the household heads. Fourth, CSS had a small but statistically significant impact on the level of participation of the household heads in employment specialization courses, and on the level of the total family income. Finally, indigent families participating in the CSS made less use of homeownership government subsidies than those indigent families that did not participate in the program. (Saracostti, 2008, p. iv)

Naturally, with a sample size so large, if sampling were employed, would be statistical significance easily achieved. Moreover, the strength of her positive correlations is not especially impressive. However, what is perhaps her greatest contribution is not in her findings but in her establishing a baseline and creating a format and a methodology for a national evaluation of this ongoing antipoverty program for her country.

Mahia Saracossti is currently Director of the Andres Bello School of Social in Santiago, Chile. She was also the first Hunter College School of Social Work doctoral student to defend her CDM dissertation via satellite tele-conference.

CONCLUSION

This chapter amply illustrates various dissertation possibilities inherent in quantitative CDM. More important than the label attached to their methodological variations, these exemplars are intended to further illustrate the potential usefulness of available quantitative data in the conduct of social work doctoral dissertations within and beyond the most restrictive definition of "clinical" data-mining. In addition, they demonstrate the creative contributions to knowledge that practice-research oriented doctoral students can make when they are freed to consider the more practice-friendly dissertation-research paradigm that CDM provides.

The following brief chapter presents an even rarer "find"—that is, the qualitative CDM study. In Chapter 6 are presented only three exemplar CDM studies: two doctoral dissertations and one practitioner-initiated study. All, in my opinion, are worthy of consideration for their practice as well as their research and methodological implications.

6

Breaking New Ground: Qualitative CDM

Although *quantitative* data-mining appears to be the norm in the business world, in practitioner-initiated practice-based research (PBR) studies and in clinical data-mining (CDM) dissertations, in this chapter, three rare examples of *qualitative* data-mining are presented. I begin with the first and only entirely qualitative CDM dissertation-research project that I've supervised. That study opened my eyes to the possibility. For me, it serves as the "touchstone" for other qualitative CDM practice-research dissertations that I hope will follow. Consequently, I describe its evolution in some detail.

The second, also a PhD dissertation, is one that I had little to do with but was fortunate enough to learn about from a brilliantly inventive Australian practitioner-researcher who attended one of my CDM workshops in Melbourne. Because I was not involved in the development of her study, I can't describe that in detail. However, together with my University of Melbourne colleague and coeditor Lynette Joubert, I was able to publish a paper based on that dissertation in our Australian CDM collection (Joubert & Epstein, 2005).

Though not a direct product of my work as a dissertation advisor; this study is an exemplar in many ways. First is its highly sophisticated epistemological sensibility; second, its extensive use of qualitative research software; and third, its evocative presentation of findings. This qualitative CDM dissertation is so impressive that I wish I could take more credit for its development.

The third exemplar, rarer still, is a qualitative CDM study initiated by research-minded Australian practitioner-researcher. It is not a doctoral dissertation. Moreover, it is informed by a psychoanalytic theoretical base. Although the author is a friend and colleague of many years who is well aware of my CDM workshops, the idea for her qualitative data-mining venture originated in a Melbourne café. Once open to CDM, one never knows where and with whom data-mining fever will strike.

At this point in the development of qualitative CDM, however, such exemplars remain isolated and unique. Nonetheless, the character of the practice-knowledge they produce and the power with which they can communicate complex clinical processes and client experiences render them worthy of consideration as a practitioner-initiated and/or dissertation-research strategy. What makes them possible, of course, is the availability of a rich vein of qualitative clinical data.

WHY SO FEW QUALITATIVE CDM STUDIES?

I suspect that qualitative CDM studies are rare for two reasons, one practical, the other paradigmatic. Practically, qualitative CDM requires unusually rich deposits of available data—for example, highly detailed case records, diaries, logs, or qualitative interviews that are consistently, copiously, and meticulously recorded. If one is fortunate enough, the latter are already transcribed. If not, as in original qualitative research, transcription is tedious and costly.

Analogous to the field notes of a *prospective* conventional qualitative researcher with *original data*, clinical data of this richness are rarely available for *retrospective* analysis. In this age of managed care, detailed "process-recording" is a luxury most agencies can't afford. Social workers and other health professionals under enormous pressure to work efficiently have neither the time nor the inclination to keep extensive records. With the move toward electronic records in many health and mental health settings, the likelihood of quantitative

CDM will clearly increase, very possibly at the expense of its qualitative alternative. As a result, those seeking qualitative CDM opportunities will have to be all the more observant, resourceful, and sensitive to the possibility.

Arguably, a second reason for the rarity of qualitative CDM is that we simply haven't thought about it. The standard data-mining paradigm and the popular association with the "data-mining" concept is quantitative data-analysis with large available numerical data-sets. Virtually all of the energy for technological innovation in data-mining is in the direction of more and more sophisticated statistical analysis and graphic displays. Indeed, the dedicated data-mining software employed and graphics presented in Fu Wai's (2007) quantitative CDM dissertation discussed in the previous chapter made it all the more memorable. Data-miners in the business world, government, and medical profession; social researchers who conduct secondary analyses; and even practitioners who conduct small-scale case-record reviews routinely think in quantitative terms.

Likewise in a book intended for the general public, Ayers (2007) exalts the emerging cadres of data-miners in everything from medicine to government, business, to baseball and wine-making (but alas not in social work) as the "Super-Crunchers." He subtitles his popular market, data-mining book "Why Thinking-By-Numbers is the New Way to Be Smart."

In contrast, in his book entitled "How Doctors Think," Groopman (2007)—a doctor and a frequent popular press contributor—is less enthusiastic about the positive effects of physicians' thinking-by-numbers—especially when he is the patient. Writing critically about "evidence-based medicine," Groopman and a senior colleague share their concerns about "young physicians who relinquish their own thinking and instead look to classification schemes and algorithms to think for them" (p. 238).

In fairness to each, both Ayres and Groopman, value randomized-controlled trials (RCTs) highly, the former in combination with data-mining and the latter wherever ethically possible and medically feasible. However, whereas Ayres downplays the future importance of "intuition" in decision-making versus large-scale, quantitative studies, Groopman champions case-by-case reflection and the ongoing accumulation and refinement of individual clinical skill and judgment.

A position somewhere between the two is exemplified by a recent medical data-mining study of 2,702 postlaparascopic surgery, prostate cancer patients reported in the *New York Times* (Bakalar, 2008). As anticipated, the study—published in *The Journal of Clinical Oncology*—reported a lower risk of short-term postoperative complications and shorter hospital stays when compared with radical prostatectomy with more conventional, nonlaparoscopic surgical procedures. However, what was not anticipated was that over the long term, men who had the laparoscopies had a

> 40 percent greater risk of scarring that interferes with organ function, a complication that requires additional surgery. And, within six months of their operations, more than one-quarter needed additional hormonal or drug therapy compared with one in 10 of those who had conventional surgery. (Bakalar, 2008, F-7)

One possible explanation offered by a urological surgeon not involved in the study was that while laparascopic procedures are minimally invasive, surgeons "can't feel the cancer" with their hands in a robotic procedure. Though, as with all data-mining studies, questions are raised concerning variables not available for analysis, such as the equivalency of the severity of cancer in the two groups, the chairman of the surgery department at Memorial Sloan-Kettering Cancer Study praised the paper as "the first that has come out in the field using a national database to examine outcomes."

This is a medical context in which the range of treatment procedures available and the known equivalency of survival and mortality rates preclude the possibility of RCTs. A prostate cancer survivor myself, I know that much is made to the recently diagnosed of the many treatment choices available as well as nontreatment and the "opportunity" to choose from among them. And while in choosing, even the most research-sophisticated, "evidence-based" patient may feel like he is flipping a multisided coin. One would have to be terminally ill to consider entering a randomized clinical trial.

So, despite its "gold-standard" shortcomings, the "expert" surgeon interviewed by the journalist concluded by saying that the results 'fit everything we know' (p. F–7). Though only a social work data-miner and a former prostate cancer patient who had to make the difficult choice of a procedure, I would suggest that it did quite a bit more. In fact, it revealed things we didn't already know, and while it didn't answer them, it raised important questions about why. Questions, I might add, that are answerable with future data-mining studies and newly available statistical techniques that allow us to approximate RCTs using available clinical information (see Chapter 7).

Closer to the position taken in this book is one advocated by Douglas B. Kamerow, former Director of the Center for Practice and Technology Assessment, of the Agency for Healthcare Research and Quality a decade ago in a Grand Rounds presentation at Mt Sinai Hospital on "experience-based" versus "evidence-based" medicine. When asked what he anticipated the latter would be like 10 years hence (that's now), Dr. Kamerow imagined that "really good" doctors would not be choosing one or the other. Instead, they would be routinely accessing *external* evidence in the form of published studies but researching their own *internal* patient databases with handheld computers as well, making their decisions on the "best available evidence" from both together with their *clinical experience.* (I can't cite the title or date of that talk, but I saved my notes because I found his talk and his vision so validating on several counts.)

Despite its enormous and unrecognized potential for social workers and other health professionals, those who are aware of conventional data-miners are likely to think of them as either bureaucratic "bean-counters" or intrusive violators of personal privacy. To those trained in the positivist tradition of quantitative research like me, data-mining is scorned for its atheoretical approach to knowledge-generation. For neo-positivists, it lacks the articulation of theory and the testing of specific hypotheses. Finally, to traditionally trained qualitative researchers, data-miners are likely to be pejoratively cast as mindless "number crunchers." In this epistemological fog, the possibility of qualitative CDM is rarely seen. It exists outside several paradigmatic boundaries.

To the reader, I confess that I too thought only of CDM in quantitative terms at first. All of my experience with practitioner-initiated studies had been quantitative. However, it was only while working collaboratively with a practitioner-researcher-doctoral student that I began to think outside the quantitative CDM box long enough to consider the possibility of the *qualitative CDM dissertation.* This option and its successful implementation first emerged in a series of dissertation-planning conversations with a doctoral student who was grounded in practice but relatively new to research. The rest is hopefully qualitative CDM "prehistory."

In this chapter, three rare examples of qualitative CDM are described. Then some unique aspects of the qualitative CDM method are discussed. Finally, whether qualitative or quantitative or both, next steps are offered for doctoral students considering conducting a CDM dissertation.

Qualitative Data-Mining Family Reunification

A broadly experienced clinician and trainer, Antonia "Toni" Cordero had for years served as a staff trainer and consultant to a private foster care agency through which the New York City Administration for Children's Services (ACS) placed children in unrelated or kinship foster care for reasons of abuse, neglect, domestic violence, substance abuse, and so forth. On any one day in New York, ACS oversees thousands of such children in foster homes, working with families, if at all possible, to reunite them with their children. Sadly, the possibility of successful family reunification is more an ideal than a reality.

In this context, Cordero aspired to conducting a dissertation-research study comparing successful and unsuccessful reunification cases in a foster care agency in which she provided training and supervision to foster care social workers. In turn, these workers provided services to children in placement, to their foster parents, and to biological parents and extended family with the objective of successful reunification at some future point.

Like Hanssen's Intensive Family Preservation (IFP) agency discussed in the previous chapter, Cordero's foster care setting prided itself on the process-recording that its social work practitioners did for accountability, training, and supervisory purposes. As a trusted and valued consultant to the agency, she had access to these case records. And because many of the children in their care never returned to their natural parents but "aged-out" of the program, some of these foster care cases spanned many years.

This was precisely what Hanssen's agency and the IFP movement were trying to prevent. The latter was seen as a short-term intensive intervention strategy to obviate the pain and destructiveness associated with separating children from their families. Although most would agree with this objective and IFP has been subjected to numerous "gold-standard" evaluations, many practitioners have criticized it as a questionable "quick fix." Indeed, in a scathingly critical review of IFP studies, the highly respected evaluation researcher Peter Rossi remarked that, among several other methodological limitations, the success of IFP is vastly overstated by an outcome measure (i.e., nonplacement 30 days after termination of intervention) that is much too short to demonstrate the achievement of family stability (Rossi, 1992). As a result, "successful" cases that were reopened after 31 days were classified as "new" cases rather than an as intervention "failures" in these highly prized RCTs.

Cordero's setting, however, dealt with clients for whom ACSs child-protective workers felt placement could not be prevented. These children were assessed as being at too great a risk to remain in their homes. Once they were placed, however, even under the best of circumstances, it could take several months or years before reunification was possible. Rather than a "quick fix," reunification involved careful and painstaking work on the part of the foster care caseworker with the children, foster parents, and biological family members to assure that in the end the child returned to a healthy and stable home environment.

Although her original intent (and what I originally had in mind) was a quantitative CDM dissertation, the formidable labor-intensive task of *converting* all the available qualitative case-record data to a quantitative data-set seemed terribly onerous. Cases could be open for years. Process records were voluminous. Moreover, as a former practitioner, Cordero's research priorities were more about gaining insight into the subtleties of successful practice than in enumerating its quantitative correlates. Her dissertation proposal literature review revealed that several studies in the past had done that.

What's more, like Hanssen, she was interested in how successful practice might differ depending on the different multiproblem constellations that troubled families routinely presented. It's one thing to follow "best practice" guidelines with clients that have a single problem or can easily prioritize the problems they do have; it's quite another to work with children and families in crisis that present multiple pressing problems simultaneously. That's the norm rather than the extreme in child-protective work.

As Cordero and I discussed, her central interests and the vast amount of clinical data available to her, it occurred to me that a *qualitative* data-mining study was not only possible but more suitable to the question that was driving her inquiry.

In conceptualizing and designing her qualitative CDM dissertation (Cordero, 2000) over a number of weeks, because the time span of the cases were so long and there was so much case material to go through, we agreed to purposively sample only successful cases that were closed by the agency in the previous year. This yielded over 90 cases, but still too many for her to study as closely as a qualitative study of practice would require.

Rather than attempting to study all of these cases, a systematic sampling of every fifth successfully closed case was selected (N = 18) and *typologized* by the official reason for placement assigned by the court (i.e., neglect, domestic abuse, substance abuse) and type of placement arranged by the agency, (i.e., non-kinship or kinship foster care), (see Table 6.1). In taking this analytic decision, we were hoping that the reason for placement in combination with the type of placement would reveal "clinically" significant practice differences.

Next, Cordero made use of a meta-theoretical stage-model of practice drawn from the child-welfare literature that conceptualized the work in terms of Exploration, Assessment, Intervention and Termination that roughly corresponded with the beginning period of assessment and placement, the middle period (i.e., child in foster placement prior to any consideration of return home), and the ending period (i.e., discharge planning and follow-up). Ultimately, we agreed that her study objective would be to describe and analyze successful practice at each stage with each of three different stakeholders or targets of intervention (i.e., the child, parents, and kinship or non-kinship foster parents). Her study proposal was welcomed by her former agency and approved by Hunter's IRB with the proviso that the names of clients and their families not be used and that other "identifiers" not be revealed.

Table 6.1 Sampling typology

Families	Placement Precipitants		
	Neglect	*Domestic Abuse*	*Substance Abuse*
Foster Care	2	3	4
Kinship Care	2	2	5

Using the foregoing typology and stage-model to broadly organize her "observations," Cordero developed an open-coding data-extraction system based on a "grounded-theory" approach to the data (Strauss & Corbin, 1990). Though the study itself was *retrospective* in its data-source, it was *prospective* in its data-analysis. In other words, cases were studied as though they were evolving over time. Though not in conventional research jargon a "longitudinal study," it was an analog to one.

After confirming the inter-rater reliability of her open-coding with a social work colleague on 10 de-identified cases, Cordero went on to describe, analyze, and interpret the emerging elements of successful practice as well as typical problems that seem to arise with different stakeholders at different points in the placement process for each type of case presentation. Clearly, with such a small sample, with qualitative data and lacking the counterfactual of unsuccessful cases, Cordero's dissertation did not *prove* anything. Nor did it test any specific, predictive hypotheses regarding successful practice. It couldn't.

Despite its acknowledged limitations, her study provided a rare, complex, and in-depth understanding of what successful practice looks like with different types of cases and how skilled practitioners handle the inevitable problems that arise in working with multiproblem families. More importantly, though her findings could not be assessed in terms of statistical significance, they persuasively demonstrated contextual differences in treatment issues that arise in different kinds of cases with different types of foster families. Thus, our typological hunches (aka "hypotheses") paid off in much the same way that Hanssen's did using a quantitative CDM methodology.

In contrast with Hanssen's quantitative CDM study, however, Cordero's described clinical practice is a subtle, rich, and dynamic manner—a manner that is much more suitable for training and educational purposes. Such a rendering of practice experience is only possible with qualitative research. It's "truth value" is confirmed by the fact that it conforms to the experience of other practice professionals—or if it doesn't, provokes reflection.

From a practice point of view, however, what is most remarkable and arguably most useful about Cordero's findings is that they support *general* practice principles and how they apply in working with different client groups and also identify distinctive problems that arise with *particular* kinds of cases. Here, her qualitative descriptions and interpretations illustrate the inventive solutions that skilled social workers use to manage more or less predictable crises of one sort or another. In so doing, Cordero reaffirms both the "science" and "art" of effective social work practice. Less important to practitioners but germane to the purpose of this chapter is that Cordero's dissertation demonstrates that with the right available data resources, sound conceptualization, and hard, practice-informed effort, it is possible to do *qualitative CDM* following the sound research principles contained within that research paradigm.

After a long career in agency-based practice, "Toni" Cordero is currently an Associate Professor at University of Connecticut School of Social Work. Based upon her dissertation research, she has presented at national child-welfare conferences, authored and coauthored articles (Cordero, 2004; Cordero & Epstein, 2005) and provided training in multiple foster care agency settings.

Qualitative Data-Mining Music Therapy

Working an even more remote "claim" in Australia, Claire O'Callaghan came to CDM with professional training as a social worker and as a music therapist. Her clinical work was in a cancer hospital in Melbourne, where she conducted adjunctive music therapy with patients, the majority of whom had advanced metastatic or end-stage disease. Her qualitative CDM data-source was her own highly detailed personal reflective journals covering a three-month period during which she saw 207 patients and conducted 356 individual and group sessions (O'Callaghan, 2005, p. 221).

Unlike Cordero, whose approach to qualitative research was more descriptive than interpretive and who employed no qualitative software, O'Callaghan brought to her University of Melbourne PhD dissertation a highly refined epistemological sensibility. Moreover, she made extensive use of ATLAS/ti software (Muhr, 1997) for her data-analysis. Still, hers was not a "number-crunching" study in which the software did the analysis for her. Thus, she described her highly personal and intensely introspective research process:

> Writing a clinical reflexive journal for prospective thematic analysis unleashed a "self-dialogic" process, inspiring new questions and awarenesses, uncovering and extending [my] "practice wisdom." (O'Callaghan, 2005, p. 217)

Ultimately, O'Callaghan distills the effects of music therapy to demonstrate the cognitive, emotional, spiritual, intellectual, physical, and social benefits of music therapy to her patients *as well as the contexts in which music therapy is potentially damaging.* Both are important to her. Textual analysis makes possible illustration of all of these, but specialized software gives her a tool for efficient graphic representation of these themes (O'Callaghan, 2005, p. 223).

Claire O'Callaghan is currently a music therapist and social work practitioner-researcher at the Peter MacCallum Cancer Centre in Melbourne, Australia. In that capacity, she continues qualitative data-mining of her own reflexive journals and perceptive observations, publishing the results of her uniquely innovative practice-research efforts (O'Callaghan, 2008). In addition, she is now training other practitioner-researchers to conduct qualitative CDM studies.

Qualitative Data-Mining Maternal Loss

Although it falls outside the category of doctoral dissertation and might be considered by some a secondary analysis, I would ask the indulgence of the more conceptually vigilant readers to include a brief consideration of another rare example of qualitative CDM. This study was initiated by Sarah Jones, an Australian social work practitioner and psychotherapist who attended my first PBR workshop in Melbourne—years before I presented the "mining for silver" paper. In fact, she was assigned to video-tape my incredibly jet-lagged, day-long presentation.

Full disclosure requires that I tell you that she and I became good friends. Sarah is an experienced social work clinician, trainer, and consultant. Psychoanalytically trained, she is someone who loves to write and to do research, but not of the quantitative persuasion.

Over a terrific cup of coffee in a Melbourne café, I told her about the plans that Joubert and I had to publish a collection of Australian CDM studies. She said she'd love to write something for our collection but wasn't currently doing any CDM-type research. It all sounded like "number-crunching" to her. Then she recalled having assisted, a few years earlier, medical researchers in the United Kingdom who had a grant to study parental response to fetal abnormality (Statham, 2001).

While on a leave in England, Jones had done some interviewing and provided some clinical consultation on that research project. That study was a prospective, longitudinal study of 247 pregnant women who received a prenatal diagnosis of fetal abnormality; 72 of whom chose to continue their pregnancy. Original data were gathered on multiple occasions during and after their pregnancies between 1997 and 1999.

In discussing her role in that study of pre- and postnatal parental response, Jones recalled that she had interviewed a small subset of women who were so-informed but decided to carry their pregnancy to term. She remembered these interviews (which were tape-recorded and already transcribed) to be quite compelling from the standpoint of how these mothers coped with the sad news and subsequent medical and psychosocial consequences. Jones decided that she wanted to retrospectively "mine" their stories and their intervention implications; years after the original quantitative study had been completed.

Together we agreed that this subset of women could constitute the basis of a qualitative CDM study using the available interview data that was never subjected to *qualitative* analysis. Prior studies using this data-set were entirely quantitative and prospective. Although all of the study participants had been "consented" by the researchers and approved by an ethics committee years ago, doing this naturally involved securing permission and, ideally, collaboration from Jones' Cambridge University medical research colleagues.

"Consenting" her research colleagues, however, required some paradigmatic persuasion on both qualitative and data-mining grounds. The prior published studies emanating from this project had relied on quantitative findings gathered from parental responses to standardized, self-administered questionnaires administered at regular intervals during the study. Although collected in the course of a research study, because of the sensitive issues involved, the qualitative interviews were conducted largely for clinical purposes—that is, to identify parents who were psychologically at-risk and in need of counseling. In this respect, Jones' potential database resembled Wai's breast cancer narratives cited in the previous chapter. Both were linked to quantitative research studies but were created for clinical *rather* than research purposes—a distinction I am trying to obscure.

Not only was Jones' proposed methodology unconventional but the design was what qualitative sociological researchers might refer to as a "deviant case analysis." In other words, it gives its primary attention to *atypical* cases assuming that one can learn more from the *deviations* from the norm rather than from those who conform to the norm. What made Jones' proposal even more "outside the box" was that she wanted to employ a *psychoanalytic lens* in assessing and interpreting the qualitative data.

Although the principal investigators of this study had already published extensively about those mothers who made the decision to terminate pregnancy (Statham, 2002; Statham, Solomou & Green, 2003), about the parents' experiences (Statham, Solomou & Green, 2001), and about the health professionals' experiences (Statham, Solomou & Green, 2002), Jones was interested in qualitatively rendering the "crisis of motherhood" from a psychoanalytic point of view for women who knew that the child they were going to deliver would be abnormal. This was something that her potential coauthors and the original study's principal investigators had not done and had not previously considered. Nevertheless, the possibility remained inchoate in the clinical data that were available. Once persuaded that this research paradigm was acceptable, Jones' medical research colleagues agreed to provide access to the data and to be coauthors.

Since Jones already knew about the quality and depth of the interview data that had been collected since she had done some of the interviews, she persuaded her British colleagues to join in a qualitative CDM study of a very small (N = 7), purposive sample of women whose prenatal exams indicated would have a wide range of abnormality from treatable conditions with relatively positive outcomes to untreatable conditions where there was a high likelihood that the child would not survive the pregnancy. Consistent with principles of purposive sampling, cases were hand-selected based upon highly specified criteria.

To this point, the authors comment:

> Selection was on the basis of ensuring variation across a number of criteria, including type of malformation, maternal age, reproductive history, maternal mood, but with survival of the baby until the end of the study period. The range of abnormalities diagnosed had a range of likely outcomes, from cleft lip and palate, a treatable condition with a mostly good outcome to hypoplastic left heart, where there was a high likelihood that the baby would not survive the neonatal period. (Jones, Statham & Solomou, 2006, p. 198)

Informed by psychoanalytic theory that emphasized the "crisis" that motherhood presents under the best of circumstances, Jones, Statham & Solomou identify and illustrate three central themes that emerged in the interviews with these women—that is, ambivalence, uncertainty, and loss. For some, these themes are heightened and compounded as their pregnancies progressed. Using qualitative quotes from retrospectively "mined" interviews, Jones and her colleagues dramatically document the experiences of these women (Jones, Statham & Solomou, 2006, pp. 202–203).

The authors conclude with a discussion of the implications for psychotherapeutic practice with women in this tragically challenging circumstance (Jones, Statham & Solomou, 2006, p. 204). Although they do not consider it in this paper, these themes are potentially relevant for fathers facing similar challenges and disappointments. Nonetheless, Jones and her colleagues offer additional "evidence" of practice knowledge-generating potential of qualitative CDM.

Sarah Jones works as a social worker and psychotherapist in Melbourne where she is currently coauthoring a book about individual and group intervention with abused women who are parenting infants and young children. The intention behind her current clinical research is to make a contribution to ending the cycle of abuse that Ross, Walther & Epstein (2004) "mined" in their practitioner-initiated, quantitative CDM study (see Chapter 4).

UNIQUE METHODOLOGICAL ASPECTS OF QUALITATIVE CDM STUDIES

As indicated above, whether a doctoral dissertation or a practitioner-initiated study, qualitative CDM requires a special kind of available data. This form of data-mining requires rich and comprehensive narratives. When in the form of client records and/or diary accounts of practice, it also helps if the language and metaphors that clients and patients use in describing their own experience are directly recorded. Of course, if they are audio- or video-recorded, as in Chow's study (see Chapter 5), the major problem is transcription to an analyzable database.

Once such rich informational resources are unearthed, it is generally helpful to employ "theoretical" or "purposeful" sampling to organize the data-extraction and refinement. Rather than seeking representativeness or external validity as with quantitative research studies, the sampling in qualitative CDM studies is guided by the unique question that is driving the study. In many respects, this is no different from qualitative research studies based on original data-collection. In the qualitative CDM studies cited above, both Jones and Cordero employ purposive sampling. Cordero, in fact, uses both systematic and purposive sampling in the conduct of her research.

Although there are disagreements within the ranks of qualitative researchers about whether theory should be inductively derived from data or used to test deductively derived theory (Huberman & Miles, 1994; Strauss & Corbin, 1990), in the three studies described above, none involved hypothesis testing. However, both Cordero and Jones made use of a theoretical or meta-theoretical "lens" in analyzing their data.

In contrast, O'Callaghan, employs no sampling whatsoever. Instead, her qualitative database reflects all of the experiences she reflexively recorded, working 16 hours per week over the course of 3 months, in 365 music therapy sessions with 207 patients (O'Callaghan, 2005, pp. 220–221). Then, unlike Cordero or Jones, she made extensive use of sophisticated qualitative software. As a result, she allowed the software to help her construct an empirically based theoretical model of the mostly positive and rarely negative impacts of music therapy on patients (O'Callaghan, 2005, p. 223). In that respect, though by no means devoid of interpretive reflection, her qualitative CDM dissertation study was most like conventional quantitative data-mining approaches.

Returning to Wai's quantitative CDM dissertation on breast cancer survivors discussed in the previous chapter, had he chosen to do so, he could have conducted a qualitative study of patient narratives. Thus, instead of converting *qualitative* journal entries into a *quantitative* database, he could have used equally sophisticated *qualitative* software to analyze his available data as such. Or, now that there is software such as Nudist allows one to move easily from qualitative to quantitative analysis, he could have done both kinds of analysis using the same database as a mixed-method study. (Still, software developers note, no quantitative to qualitative software available as yet.)

I appreciate both Wai's and O'Callaghan's different choices. Finishing is important. And, the option that he chose was by no means an easy one—that is, based upon mindless number-crunching. In fact, he made remarkable and clinically insightful use of the option that he took. In doing so, he was also able to correlate patient scores on standardized quantitative measures with themes in their narratives. Moreover, wherever he could, he used brief illustrative quotes to enrich his quantitative analysis. However, in primarily mining the quantitative potential of his data, Wai did not make maximum use of the opportunity to tell patients' stories in their own words and metaphors—a form of communication that practitioners find especially compelling (Osmond & O'Connor, 2004).

At this point in its development, it is probably premature to try to formulate distinct principles of qualitative CDM. In most respects, other than those suggested above, the steps in the process are quite similar to quantitative CDM. Alternatively, other than the fact that qualitative CDM makes use of available rather than original material, and is generated for clinical rather than research purposes, the conduct of qualitative CDM appears to be quite similar to conventional qualitative research. In qualitative CDM, missing data is as problematic as in quantitative CDM. However, it is not as subversive to study completion as refusal to participate and subject attrition is in qualitative or quantitative studies based on original data-collection.

Though there are distinct practical advantages to working with available data of any kind, when one is fortunate enough to strike a rich vein of qualitative data, it should not suggest that such studies are "quick and dirty". Dirty they may be, but certainly not quick. Even with the assistance of qualitative software, they require as much diligence, rigor and mindfulness as any other form of research. On this point, I offer a final quote from O'Callaghan:

> The coding of the journal yielded almost 1400 codes. Table 1 illustrates a coded journal fragment. The codes were grouped into 52 categories. Thirty-two categories were discarded because they contained components beyond the research question, for example, professional and logistical considerations, rather than descriptions about what music therapy did and thoughts about whether or not it helped. Approximately 700 codes remained, which informed 20 categories and clarifying category statements. (O'Callaghan, 2005, p. 222)

Qualitative CDM is a methodological option, but certainly no shortcut to a pot of gold or silver, or a PhD, for that matter.

CONCLUSION

Notwithstanding the qualitative CDM study conducted by Jones et al. (2006), the last two chapters have provided a full range of exemplars of CDM doctoral dissertations that have been successfully conducted, completed and defended in doctoral programs in places around the globe. Notwithstanding local variations in dissertation requirements, they follow universal standards of scholarship and research. Several of these studies have already made important contributions to social work knowledge at different levels of intervention. Others, will undoubtedly do so once their findings are published and disseminated. All have made valuable contributions to the careers of their authors with several moving on to teaching and research positions in universities in multiple locations.

Additional CDM doctoral dissertations are currently underway. These are briefly described in the following chapter but are only the ones I know about because I am either chairing the students' dissertation committees or if at another school, serving as an external examiner. Perhaps there are others that I don't know about that make use of available data but aren't called CDM. That would be "OK" too. My hope however, is that practitioners who have read the previous two chapters might consider entering a doctoral program where they also might carry out a CDM dissertation on a subject that impassions them with data that are currently available.

Similarly, I would hope that doctoral students reading these chapters might consider either mixed-method dissertations that make some use of CDM or dissertations that are entirely based on quantitative or qualitative CDM, or both. Finally, I would hope that based on the foregoing "evidence" of scholarly contribution and practice-knowledge discovery, readers who are teaching in master's and doctoral programs would consider CDM as a viable and legitimate research methodology for the students in their charge.

For doctoral students currently contemplating a CDM dissertation research, your next steps are a follows:

• Identify a social work practice issue that you would like to explore in your PhD dissertation.
• Determine what data sources are already available that are relevant to that issue.

- What are the practical and ethical issues involved in gaining access to and using these data?
- In what form are the available data, that is, qualitative, quantitative, computerized, and so forth.?
- How does prior research inform your possible use of these data?
- Do the data lend themselves to qualitative or quantitative analysis?
- Do they require sampling?
- Will conversion from qualitative to quantitative data be required?
- Will qualitative or quantitative data-analytic software be required?
- What form of data-analysis should be employed?
- What resources (financial) and educational (dissertation supervisor & committee) are required to conduct the study?
- Secure the resources, faculty support and Do It!

For practitioners considering a qualitative CDM study return to the list of "next steps" for practitioners in the concluding section of Chapter 4 and entertain the possibilities of either a qualitative or a quantitative CDM study. Whichever you decide is more suitable to the practice questions that you have in mind and feasible given the information that you have available to you, get the right consultative support and Do It!

The next and concluding chapter considers future possibilities for CDM research methodology and offers a final "evidence-informed" rather than "evidence-based" exhortation to practitioners, doctoral students and research academics alike.

7

The Possible Futures of CDM
and Evidence-Based Practice

In the Introduction to this book, I defined CDM as a form of "clinical" research conducted by practitioner-researchers and based on available data. Later, I differentiated it from business forms of data-mining and from secondary analysis in the social sciences. I also situated CDM as a practice-based research (PBR) strategy that was especially suited to engaging practitioners in research, contrasting it with more epistemologically restrictive and/or disempowering paradigms of practice-research integration, which I referred to as research-based practice (RBP). CDM, I claimed, could serve the dual function of (1) helping practitioners integrate research and research ways of thinking as well as their own practice wisdom into their practice decision-making; and (2) give them the opportunity to contribute to knowledge about practice to the field. The latter function is tacitly but effectively denied by prevailing evidence-based practice (EBP) models.

Extending McNeill's (2006) critique but borrowing his paradigmatic label, I proposed that social work's epistemological paradigm be the more inclusive evidence-informed practice (EIP) rather than the academically popular but professionally contentious EBP. Next, inspired by Shyne's (1960) seminal article on use of available data, I chronicled my own personal "discovery" of CDM, and why I thought practitioners found it so useful. This was followed by a chapter on the scientific principles that underpin CDM and the "art" involved in doing it both as a research consultant and as a practitioner-researcher.

Then I presented two sets of CDM exemplars as "evidence" to support my claim for CDM's viability, flexibility, legitimacy, and current contribution to knowledge. One set involved almost exclusively quantitative CDM studies conducted by groups of practicing social workers and/or multidisciplinary health professionals. Though they produced knowledge that was clinically and programmatically valuable, from a methodological point of view, they were relatively modest; many were simply descriptive studies of need, services, and/or service outcomes. Consistent with our understanding of the limits of CDM, none made claims to empirically demonstrating causality. All, however, were found worthy of publication in the broader professional literature— most in peer-reviewed journals. There they could be shared with other practitioners and researchers.

A second set of exemplar CDM studies I presented was almost exclusively composed of doctoral dissertations. Predictably, perhaps, most were quantitative. A few were mixed-method dissertations that combined quantitative CDM along with original data-based qualitative research. Next, I introduced the possibility of qualitative CDM by offering three exemplar studies. Two were qualitative CDM dissertations and one was a qualitative CDM study initiated by a practitioner though coauthored with academic researchers.

Almost all of the authors of CDM doctoral dissertations are current or former practitioners. Understandably, their CDM/PhD research studies are more methodologically sophisticated and epistemologically ambitious than the practitioner-initiated set. One would expect that of doctoral students. Several of the dissertations cited have contributed to knowledge via publication and conference presentation as well as served as springboards from practice to academic careers. Other clinical dataminers have remained in practice settings but continue as practitioner-researchers who contribute to knowledge for the profession. All have advanced and refined my own thinking about CDM methodology and in so doing have made major contributions to this book.

This concluding chapter offers some personal thoughts about future possibilities for CDM based upon my current involvement as a research consultant and as a social work doctoral faculty member.

These adumbrations are all rooted in work that is already under way. In addition, they are based on relatively unsophisticated past efforts to extend the causal inferential possibilities of CDM research through experimental analogs and on more sophisticated new statistical approaches.

A final set of prognostications is chancier and less "evidence-based." These have to do with the future of EBP and EIP and result from my own possibly selective reading of trends in the most recent research literature. Here the metaphor of "fool's gold" may come to mind. Thus, my weighing and assessment of the small nuggets of "truth" embedded in the current writings of EBP advocates may be more about what I'd like to see than what is actually there. Only time will tell. I end where I began and occasionally returned throughout this book with one final reflection about the "gold standard."

THE FUTURE OF CDM

In Chapters 4, 5, and 6 respectively, I described a wide array of previously published practitioner-initiated CDM studies and CDM doctoral dissertations. Based on my most recent CDM workshops, consultation activities, and dissertation advising, the future of CDM studies, both in the United States and abroad, looks positive to me. After a brief but not especially influential exploration of the use of experimental analogs in CDM (Sainz & Epstein, 2001), the introduction of Propensity Score Matching (Barth, Guo & McCrae, 2008) seems especially propitious for extending the predictive power and causal inferences that can be drawn from large, available quantitative service data.

Practitioner-Initiated CDM Studies Currently Under Way

Although I am involved in CDM consultation on individual studies in several social work agencies, perhaps the most impressive listing of practitioner-initiated studies currently under way in one place is a collection of quantitative, health-related CDM efforts at the Hunter Valley Area Allied Health Services in Newcastle, Australia. This set of studies emanates from a series of annual, one-day, multidisciplinary CDM workshops that I began with my University of Melbourne colleague Lynette Joubert three years ago, continued with the assistance of my University of Sydney colleague Ros Giles with ongoing administrative support from the Area Director David Rhodes and Anne Vertigan, the Chief of Allied Health Services.

In this collective CDM effort by social workers, dieticians, physical therapists, occupational therapists, podiatrists, speech pathologists, play therapists, nurses, and physicians are actively engaged in quantitative CDM studies of patient needs, services, and outcomes. In addition to conference presentations that have already been given, plans are under way to coedit these studies in a second collection of Australian CDM studies in social work and allied health practice. The working titles of some of their studies are:

"An Analysis of Vocal Features in Patients Who Undergo Thyroid Surgery"
"Analysis of Aphasia Assessment Results in Acute Stroke"
"Dietary Needs of Elderly Stroke Patients"
"Improving the Nutritional Management in Hospitalized Stroke Patients"
"Rates, Types, and Possible Contributing Factors for Percutaneous Endoscopic Gastronomy Tube Complications at a Rural Referral Hospital over a Five Year Period"
"Supporting Child-Abusing Parents after Removal of Baby"
"Improving Service Provision to Farming Families through Geographic Mapping"

The majority of the foregoing projects are being conducted within disciplinary "silos" but others are multidisciplinary and transcend professional practice boundaries to where the patients and their families more fully reside. Still, all have the potential to make valuable use of relatively simple quantitative CDM methodology applied to routinely available clinical data. Indeed, my most recent Hunter Valley CDM workshop and subsequent practitioner presentations were attended by two radiation oncologists who were interested in applying the methodology to studying their own work with cancer patients receiving radiation treatment.

CDM Doctoral Dissertations Currently Under Way

Several CDM doctoral dissertations are currently under way. At Hunter College School of Social Work where I teach and universities where I serve as an external examiner, the following have received IRB approval and are at various stages of completion:

- A mixed-method (quantitative CDM/qualitative original interview) evaluation of a multidisciplinary consultation program in child-protective services in New York city
- A mixed-method (qualitative CDM & quantitative CDM) of Philippine domestic workers' return migration from the United States based on advocacy group data
- A mixed-method ("conceptual" CDM study of the theoretical research literature and a quantitative CDM) test of a theory of bullying behavior among school children in a New York city public school
- A quantitative CDM study of the effectiveness of group interventions by a national employee assistance agency with staff in organizational settings that have experienced collective traumatic events such as mass shootings, robberies, natural disasters, and so forth, in the United States
- A mixed-method CDM study of the organizational benefits and costs of "social entrepreneurship" in nonprofit agencies in the United States
- A quantitative CDM study of the effects of cognitive-behavioral therapy (CBT) on depression and anxiety with adults in a community mental health program in Hong Kong

The last study listed began as an M. Phil. thesis proposal and is now an approved PhD thesis being conducted at the University of Hong Kong School of Social Work by Herman Lo. Lo is a clinician-researcher in an adult mental health program in Hong Kong. Though not yet completed, his PhD dissertation research deserves further comment.

Lo's agency has been offering CBT to clients and routinely assessing individual levels of anxiety and depression on standardized quantitative measures before and after treatment for 8 years. It wasn't until Lo was introduced to CDM in one of my workshops that the possibility of aggregating the available data on hundreds of closed cases had ever been considered.

In a presentation given at my most recent University of Hong Kong CDM Dissertation workshop, Lo briefly summarized his findings to date. Working with a population exceeding 800 and consistent with prior research, CBT is shown to be quite effective at a high level of statistical significance. However, despite the demonstrated effectiveness of this treatment technique that has come to be seen statistically as "best practice," many clients remain anxious or depressed post treatment. Others return to the agency with anxiety and depression after a few weeks or months. Because Lo has access to available clinical data about client background factors as well as CBT outcomes, multivariate analysis has enabled him to profile which background factors are significantly associated with CBT effectiveness and which are not.

I'll leave the specifics of his findings for him to report after he completes his dissertation in future presentations and publications. Suffice it to say, prospective randomized-controlled trials (RCTs) that use the device of randomization to "strip" away client differences in the quest for a generalization about the universal effectiveness of CBT would not have produced such clinically useful findings. In addition, simplistic statements about "best practice" obscure the reality that many clients do not find CBT helpful.

Here, the data-analytic innovations proposed by Macias et al. (2008) cited earlier again invite comment. Their statistical techniques for analyzing RCT data do offer promise of determining the "differential service effectiveness" of interventions and can help provide more practitioner-friendly knowledge about who benefits most and least from experimentally implemented interventions. However, their approach does not "strip away" the ethical objections that many practitioners and clients might have to participating in RCT studies in the first place.

Lo's CDM dissertation is poised to answer such questions (albeit with lesser statistical certainty) but without the necessity of random assignment of clients or the use of control groups. With the guidance of his statistically astute and paradigmatically flexible academic advisor, Dr. Siu-man Ng, Lo's CDM dissertation promises to contribute important "empirically based" knowledge about the differential effectiveness of CBT without the "classical" experimental requirements of randomization and control groups. We await the contributions that his and the other above listed CDM dissertations will make to our knowledge of practice.

Experimental Analogs

Throughout this book, I have been careful to acknowledge CDM's limited capacity to make definitive causal inferences. As irreverent as it sounds, Lo's study and other previously cited CDM dissertations suggest that from a practice decision-making standpoint, a CDM study might even be considered superior to an RCT. But I prefer to avoid the ranking of research contributions by methodological choice.

Within the terms of the more conventional discourse about clinical or program evaluation, however, I accept the claim that CDM studies can never definitively "prove" anything about the effectiveness of specific treatment techniques or programmatic interventions. Of course, this shortcoming is hardly unique to CDM. It applies to all qualitative research, to descriptive quantitative outcome studies, and to a lesser extent to all quasi-experimental studies. From that standpoint, however, inventive or statistically sophisticated they might be, none of the foregoing doctoral dissertations can match a "gold-standard" RCT. This is precisely why the RCT stands at the peak of the EBP pyramid. For those who accept its hegemony, all else is considered "less-than" (Petr & Walther, 2008).

Cognizant of this limitation, and before my doctoral students began charting new data-mining methods, sites, and units of analysis, my Hunter colleague Anthony Sainz and I conducted a comparative case study (Sainz & Epstein, 2001). The purposes of our effort were to further test and possibly extend the knowledge-generating potential of CDM to approximate an RCT.

The idea for the "case-comparison" came from a coincidental publication of a published RCT (Beder, 1999) that in many ways remarkably paralleled the CDM study that Dobrof et al. (2001) had conducted with my consultation and Sainz's statistical support (see Chapter 4). Although their designs were fundamentally different, both studies shared the common objective of assessing the impact of master's degree level social work services on depression with end-stage renal disease (ESRD) patients newly on dialysis. In our subsequent study, Sainz and I reanalyzed and compared the results of the CDM study and the RCT. Although they shared a common purpose, the RCT made use of a standardized outcome measure of depression whereas the CDM study relied on clinical judgments extracted and quantitatively coded from available qualitative case records.

Another important difference was that unlike Beder's RCT, patients in the CDM study were not randomized, and interventions were not randomly rationed for research purposes. Nonetheless, some patients in the CDM sample did not avail themselves of social work services beyond the requisite initial interview that was mandated by law for all ESRD patients. This minimal legal requirement applied as well to patients in Beder's RCT.

Consequently, neither study had a "true" control group of patients that were randomly assigned to no intervention at all. That would have been illegal as well as unethical. Although the CDM study had no randomized approximation to a control group as in Beder's study, it did have a "naturalistic" approximation to one based on patients who for one reason or another saw a social worker only once. Admittedly, in some sense, it was an approximation to an approximation. But Sainz and I agreed that the comparison was still worth trying.

Both studies were relatively small (CDM N = 78) (RCT N = 46). In discussing her findings, Beder offers the standard caveats about small sample size, absence of information about prior psychological differences, and variations in physical conditions, but assumes that "random assignment to groups would address both of these possibilities and threats to internal validity" (Beder, 1999, p. 27). From the standpoint of external validity, however, her "gold-standard" design emboldened Beder to conclude "[t]he outcome of this evaluation study suggests the effectiveness of an MSW intervention on the lives of first-time dialysis patients" (Beder, 1999, p. 27).

Less concerned with making global statements about social work effectiveness and more with the comparability of our findings, Sainz and I applied experimental logic to Dobrof et al.'s available clinical data. In other words, we paralleled Beder's analysis with our available quantitative data performing a kind of *post-hoc experiment*. However, in addition to comparing the results of our experimental analog with Beder's prospective RCT, we critiqued her study from an ethical point of view raising trenchant questions about the implications for ESRD patients as well as the practitioners who were obliged by the randomization protocol to provide "minimal" services to those patients who might require much more than that while providing time and resource-consuming "enriched" services to some who might need much less.

Despite the differences in ethical concerns, research designs, implementation issues, and claims to causality, our CDM findings were strikingly similar to Beder's. Moreover, here again the CDM study was able to describe endogenous variations in service delivery and outcomes that could not be studied in Beder's carefully controlled experiment. In our conclusion, Sainz and I commented:

> ...there is neither research nor credible theory that suggests that making social work services available to patients in need is harmful. Assuming it is not, our exploration of a single experimental analog based on retrospectively 'mined' data was torturous at best. Nonetheless, it generated comparable intervention outcomes and surfaced naturalistic service patterns thus allowing for serendipitous findings impossible in prospectively structured studies. (Sainz & Epstein, 2001, p. 181)

Perhaps prematurely, and with evidence drawn from a single comparative case study with an N of only 2, our enthusiasm led us to make our own exorbitant claim that one-day experimental analogs based on available clinical data might become an ethically preferable "credible alternative to randomly controlled experiments" (Sainz & Epstein, 163). That was almost a decade ago.

Ruefully, I report no bibliometric evidence of anyone else agreeing with or replicating our valiant effort. On occasions, CDM doctoral dissertations such as Wai's (2007) have referenced the Sainz and Epstein paper but more for the use of experimental logic in CDM rather than in replicating our post-hoc, experimental methodology. However, it is not hyperbolic for me to claim that the use of experimental logic remains an extremely valuable tool in every practitioner-initiated CDM study on which I consult or CDM doctoral dissertation that I supervise.

And while I have continued to doggedly work the data-mines, Sainz has ascended to conducting workshops for clinicians and writing books on mindfulness, breathing and other less grubby and more ethereal pursuits (Sainz, 2008). There may or may not be a lesson in that. Clearly, however, our joint quest at the time was to push causal-knowledge generating limits of CDM studies as far as they could go. Despite the rather dismal response to our labors, a recent methodological innovation has given me new hope for extending the causal inferences of CDM studies and for avoiding the ethically objectionable aspects of RCTs.

The Promise of Propensity Score Matching

Based on logic similar to ours but far more statistically sophisticated, Barth, Guo, and McCrae (2008) have recently introduced Propensity Score Matching (PSM) to the repertoire of social work researchers. Briefly stated, PSM is a statistical method that approximates "randomized conditions to analyze service effects using nonexperimental data" (Barth, Guo & McCrae, 2008, p. 212). Drawing upon methods developed in econometrics, the logic of experimentation, and using logistic regression and/or probit models, these authors demonstrate how PSM has been effectively used in the evaluation of child and family services, the impact of substance abuse services on child maltreatment reports and kinship foster care.

This is not the place, nor am I the person to detail the statistical intricacies of PSM. More to the point, in a recent study of risk factors associated with foster youth transition to adulthood, Berzin (2008) applies multiple PSM and other matching schemes to available quantitative data samples exceeding 8,000. By my definition, the Berzin study is an SA rather than a CDM study because it was conducted by a researcher with data that were originally generated for research purposes. For my present purpose however, it doesn't matter what you call it and I don't know how many practitioners are likely to incorporate PSM into their practice-research repertoires, but certainly doctoral students can. Once mastered, with adequate sample sizes, the same statistical techniques can be applied to available clinical data.

Closer to CDM (although they don't call it that either) is a recent PSM study by John, Wright, Duku and Willms (2008) comparing the psychosocial effects of a community arts program on 183 Canadian children with a matched sample of 183 taken from a national sample. Although the authors give very little attention to the practice implications of their findings, they conclude that PSM "offers an alternative to true randomization that is cost-effective and convenient, particularly important for social work research in community-based organizations with a limited budget" (p. 20). Borrowing from another PSM researcher, they liken their study to a "quasi-randomized experiment" (p. 21).

Using a similar method but a much larger sample, Koh and Testa (2008) compare kinship and nonkinship foster care permanency outcomes. Starting with a longitudinal sample of linked state service records for over 30,000 foster children, these authors randomly selected matched samples of 1,500 kinship and nonkinship foster care clients. Employing experimental logic and retrospectively applying PSM to available service data, they were able to show that

> [p]rior to matching, differences in reunification rates, combined adoption and guardianship rates, and placement stability are all significant. After matching, the differences in permanency rates disappear. Children in nonkinship foster homes still show a higher risk for initial placement disruption after matching but there is no difference in rates of instability within a year compared with children in kinship foster homes. (Koh & Testa, 2008, p. 105)

From the various standpoints of administrative decision-making, ethics, programmatic intrusiveness, and causal knowledge generation, Koh and Testa's study makes a significant contribution to current knowledge about gross predictors of foster care outcomes. In this context, however, it is important to remind the reader that for all it tells us, their study has little to say about actual practice with children, family members, and foster parents to problems that arise in successfully achieving permanency. Here, a valuable complement in the form of practice knowledge can be drawn from the very modest (N = 18) but richly insightful qualitative CDM dissertation conducted by Cordero and described in the previous chapter.

My main point here, however, is that applied to quantitative CDM, PSM has the potential to move us closer to the causal knowledge that RCTs attempt to provide without the accompanying ethical problems or the professionally self-negating assumption that if we can't "prove" that it works, it means it doesn't.

In the more research-based words of Barth, Guo, and McCrae:

> Knowledge of the principle behind PSM and the use of these methods can prevent misunderstandings about the meaning of program evaluations that lack randomization. Indeed, even when clients are randomized to treatment and control groups, PSM can be used to check that randomization was successful in eliminating preexisting

group differences. If randomization is not successful and PSM is not employed, then the bias in human services research is toward a null finding and the possibly erroneous conclusion that services were not helpful. (2008, pp. 221–222)

This human services research "bias" has been the basis of much practice-bashing by EBP proponents and RCT advocates who assume that the absence of causal proof of efficacy implies that "unproven" social work interventions are at best ineffective or at worst harmful (Soydan, 2008). This serves as the rhetorical mortar that holds in place the building blocks of the EBP pyramid.

Alternatively, for those quantitative CDM dissertation researchers as well as academic and agency-based researchers who have access to large quantitative service databases, PSM offers promise. For practitioners and researchers alike, it suggests that the "humanistic bias" to provide more services to those with greatest need does not preclude the possibilities of rigorous evaluation and further specification of client populations with whom interventions work best.

THE POSSIBLE FUTURE OF EBP AND EIP

Although this book is intended as a CDM text, in some sense its subtext has been a dialogue with EBP. In previous chapters, I have advocated directly and indirectly for a broader and more inclusive practice-research integration paradigm than what EBP offers. Borrowing a term from McNeill (2006) but expanding his definition, I have tried to make a case for a more harmonious and inclusive EIP that embraces CDM and other forms of PBR (for a fuller discussion, see Epstein, 2009).

A new book by Petr (2008) also extends the EBP paradigm by including "consumer wisdom," professional experience, and qualitative research along with RCTs in identifying social work "best practices." Petr calls his approach "multidimensional evidence-based practice" (MEBP). Like McNeill's and my versions of EIP, Petr's MEBP seeks a more methodologically pluralistic and is less wed to the familiar EBP "hierarchy of evidence" (Epstein, 2009, p. 225).

However, neither McNeill's EIP nor Petr's MEBP envision practitioners as potential *producers* of social work knowledge. Both emphasize practitioners as research *consumers*.

Whether carried out quantitatively or qualitatively, in the hands of practitioner-researchers, CDM is both epistemologically and politically pluralist. In this book, I favor neither quantitative nor qualitative CDM recognizing the strengths and limitations of each. If pushed to do so, I might express a preference for mixed-method studies that provide multiple perspectives on a given practice problem. Most importantly, CDM does not treat practitioners as "second-class citizens" in the knowledge-production project of the profession. In other words, rather than stratifying the profession into knowledge producers (academics) and consumers (practitioners), this book welcomes and encourages practitioner-researchers and provides a more "practice-friendly" research approach than does EBP.

In this context, CDM is offered as an especially effective bridge between practice and research and as one of several PBR strategies for promoting research development and utilization in social work. The underlying thesis of this book is that the best way to do that is to empower practitioners with skills to actively participate in research-based reflection and ways of thinking as well as knowledge production. CDM is one way to do that.

Whatever PBR techniques are used or labels applied, my hope is that through my own work, the work of practice-oriented research scholars like Joubert, McNeill and Petr and, more broadly, through the palpable resistance to EBP that I experience at every practitioner conference I attend and every CDM workshop I conduct, there will emerge a "course correction" in the current practice-research integration trajectory. Ideally, out of this change, multiple research paradigms will be equally valued and academic researchers as well as practitioner-researchers will become equal partners in the social work knowledge production enterprise.

THE SEARCH FOR A MORE PRAGMATIC PRACTICE-RESEARCH INTEGRATION PARADIGM

There are already subtle indications in the writings of prominent EBP advocates that such a shift is taking place. Hence, a recent special issue of *Research on Social Work Practice,* a primary publication outlet for EBP champions, was dedicated to papers presented at an international conference entitled "What Works? Modernizing the Knowledge-base of Social Work: Evidence-based Knowledge as Capability and Promise of Efficiency for a Better Practice."

That issue begins with an article by two German authors acknowledging the conflict between interpretive approaches to social work knowledge production (*verstehen*) and approaches that place emphasis on causal analysis (*erklären*) (Otto & Zeigler, 2008). Much like the Canadian McNeill (2006), Otto and Zeigler suggest that there is room for both and that "social work is an applied, empirically grounded social and cultural science aiming at both causal explanation and interpretive understanding" (Otto & Zeigler, 2008, p. 273). Unfortunately, however, after offering an astute critique of the limitations of RCTs, Otto and Zeigler conclude that the dissemination of cookbook-like, evidence-based guidelines based on RCTs might be more effective and efficient than the

> quest to disseminate empirically grounded understandings, interpretation, and theories to empirically and theoretically well-educated professionals in social work. If this proves to be true, then it might actually be reasonable to renounce the idea of reflexive professionalism in social work and to join the evidence-based practice movement. (p. 276)

Working at a purely conceptual level, Gredig and Sommerfeld (2008), two Swiss academic researchers, posit a "model of cooperative knowledge production" that rejects the notion that "knowledge transfer" only occurs from science to practice and from academics to practitioners. Instead, they propose a "hybridized" approach to practice-research integration built around problem-solving in which scientists and practitioners alike are considered "repositories" of different forms of legitimate knowledge and all enjoy equal rights in the knowledge-production process (p. 298).

Similarly, two American academics (Cnaan and Dichter, 2008) argue that while enhancing EBP, we must not abandon the "improvisational" and artistic aspects of social work practice (pp. 280–281). Focusing on the limits of the RCT, these researchers comment:

> Typically, the experimental design is not able to control for the effects of worker-client dynamics and client characteristics that are not clearly defined, understood or measurable. (Cnaan & Dichter, p. 281)

Ultimately, under a more "modest version" of EBP, they call for an "on-going feedback of outcome evaluation" from individual social work practitioners that "will serve as a base of generating overarching knowledge" (p. 284).

In the same issue, two other American EBP advocates (McCracken & Marsh, 2008) focus at the micro-level and offer a hypothetical case example describing various ways in which practitioner expertise is viewed as "essential to implementing EBP in real-world clinical practice" (p. 301). They propose that "practitioner skill-sets" come into play at five critical decision-making points in the EBP process (p. 302).

McCracken and Marsh don't go so far as to anoint their hypothetical practitioner with "practice wisdom" or to suggest that she might contribute to research knowledge more generally by disseminating the results of her practice evaluation efforts. Nonetheless, the authors squarely argue that EBP should *not be* implemented as a "mechanistic process" in which practitioners are passive consumers and implementers of knowledge (p. 301). I couldn't agree more.

Focusing at the macro-level, Proctor and Rosen (2008), two venerable American and Israeli contributors to the EBP knowledge base, express concern about the "real-world" obstacles (read: practitioner resistance) to implementation of evidence-based interventions. As a possible solution, they propose "implementation of evaluation feedback loops" in which "questions about the goodness of fit between the needs of practice" and the effectiveness of intervention are actually studied. They go on to say:

> Unfortunately, social work practice and research are too often conducted 'in silo' form. The EBP processes are followed up, evaluated, and connected too rarely. (p. 289)

In a concluding paper presented at the same conference, Thyer (2008), one of America's most ardent and prolific advocates of EBP, opens his arms and softens his rhetoric by suggesting that despite our differences "We are all positivists!"

> By seeking to justify a social work program in terms of the effects it produces or the measurable results obtained from it, as opposed to the intentions of the providers of the service or the needs of recipients of care, in some way we are returning to a more positivist orientation to our field. (Thyer, 2008, p. 339)

I appreciate his caution against jumping on the "practice-guidelines bandwagon" or our limiting our research attention to social work as a discipline (Thyer, 2008, p. 344). However, I don't think provider intentions or recipients needs are irrelevant—even to positivists.

Writing in the United Kingdom, Morgan (2007) takes a position similar to Thyer's in his aptly titled article "Paradigms Lost and Pragmatism Regained." Appearing in the first issue of the newly minted *Journal of Mixed Methods Research*, Morgan advocates a more "pragmatic approach" combining qualitative and quantitative methods as a "guiding paradigm" in social science research (p. 48). Similarly, but outside the social work silo, Berman, Ford-Gilboe, and Campbell (1998) advocate "combining stories and numbers" as a "methodologic approach" for a "critical nursing science paradigm" (p. 1).

In discussing the practical limits of conventional social policy-research strategies for "evidence-based policy", Pawson (2002) seeks a 'realist synthesis' as a "third way" between the "two poles" of "ruthless arithmetic extraction of 'net success' and the intuitive extraction of 'exemplars' as guides to best practice...."(p. 356).

Is EBP moving closer to EIP, or is it just me? Whatever initials or label we apply to the newly emerging practice-research paradigm, for it to take root and thrive in applied fields like social work and allied health, we must make equal partners of practitioners and researchers, interpretavists and experimentalists, retrospective and prospective researchers, and everyone in between. All have knowledge contributions to make.

Writing over a decade ago, in a study of practitioner-initiated research in health care, Rehr et al. (1998), raise the same pragmatic question that Otto and Zeigler's special edition addressed and the recent international conference was devoted to. "What works?"

In response however, Rehr and her colleagues provide a fundamentally different answer than do EBP advocates:

> What is needed is the evidence of 'what works' in clinical, organizational and administrative terms. Practice wisdom and judgments can be found in practitioners' writings, it is also found in the writings of academics when findings are translated into application for service delivery. How to capture this knowledge base for the field-at-large still remains a conundrum. (Rehr et al., 1998, p. 76)

Rather than relegate practitioners to mere research consumers or cookbook followers, Rehr et al. call for a practice that is informed by practitioner as well as by academic research.

Drilling down to the central purpose of this book, I once again quote my methodological inspiration with Shyne's conclusion to her seminal article on the "Use of Available Material" written a half-century ago:

> Although no one would gainsay the desirability of the projected experimental study with the researcher in full control of data collection, the difficulty of attaining this ideal should not be underestimated, nor should the social work researcher underestimate the results to be derived from, nor the wisdom and skills required, in analysis of the wealth of material already available to him. (Shyne, 1960, p. 123)

A CONCLUDING METAPHOR AND A FINAL ALLUSION TO THE "GOLD STANDARD"

Having early in this book acknowledged my debt to my first academic mentor and coauthor Richard Cloward and more recently referenced my respective practitioner-research and methodological muses—Rehr and Shyne—let me conclude the book with an appreciative reference to my father Joseph Epstein who was a craftsman of fine jewelry.

In addition to teaching me other important life lessons, he quite literally taught me the benefits and limits of working with silver as well as gold. I recall a conversation that I had with my father, whose particular specialty involved "setting" diamonds into fine jewelry—rings, necklaces, bracelets, and so forth.

Talk about "trench-bench partnerships" (Proctor & Rosen, 2008, p. 288), I worked my way through college "Florentine-engraving" jewelry cheek by jowl with him in an 7′×12′, two-bench workshop in lower Manhattan. There were no textbooks for what he did. You became a fine diamond-setter by apprenticing to another diamond-setter. It took years before the apprenticeship was cost-effective enough to justify a living wage. Today, computerized robots set cheap stones in cheap jewelry, but fine diamond-setting is still done by expert hands—most likely in other countries where skilled labor is much cheaper than here.

Similar to Schön's (1983) accounts of how reflective practitioners learn their trades, my father taught me the logic of cause-effect "thought experiments" in a context where a slip of a sharp steel tool could chip a precious stone or severely slice a precious finger. The latter was an accepted occupational hazard, but if you chipped a customer's diamond or cracked an emerald, you had to replace it out of pocket. Insurance did not cover it, so if it happened, there was also hell to pay.

Like many immigrant fathers, mine wanted me to be a doctor or, if not, to follow his path. He loved his work, and he thought I had "golden hands." He never wanted me to become a social worker or a sociologist. My mother Rachel had more to do with that. Still, his ultimate career advice was to choose something that I loved doing as much as he loved diamond-setting. I took his advice on that.

Noting in our work together that even the finest gold jewelry was made of 14 Karat or, or at most 18 Karat gold—mixtures of pure gold and other "baser" metals—I asked why pure gold is never used since it is more highly valued and easier to work with? His response was that 24 Karat gold is impractical and could never stand up to "real-world" pressures of daily customer use.

Perhaps, in my gratitude for all I learned from him, I think that in their methodological purity and imagined perfection, "gold-standard" RCTs are impractical in social work and not especially robust, but that quantitative and qualitative CDM studies better serve "real-world" client needs and inform the daily decisions of "real-world" practitioners.

For the reader who is sufficiently persuaded by the logic of my argument, the many CDM study exemplars presented in "evidence" for my argument and my metaphorical allusions, I encourage you to think about doing a bit of CDM prospecting within your agency as a practitioner-researcher and/or as master's degree or doctoral student.

Use CDM by yourself or with social work colleagues or with professionals outside your "silo." Use it quantitatively and/or qualitatively. Use it to (1) replicate existing CDM studies cited in this book; (2) apply it to entirely new practice issues and contexts; (3) conduct CDM studies where there have been none and compare your findings with studies conducted with other methodologies—especially RCTs; and (4) if you choose to do a CDM/PhD dissertation "play" with the methodology and invent new uses for it.

Whichever you do, I hope you'll present your findings to practitioner colleagues *within* the agency in which the study was conducted and that you'll publish and present your findings *beyond* the agency in professional journals and at relevant conferences, policy hearings, and so forth. And, needless to say, if you do, I'd love to hear from you about *your* CDM experiences and discoveries <iepstein@hunter.cuny.edu>. You've heard a good deal about mine.

Thank you for accompanying me on this long and circuitous journey. And now, it's time for my nap.

"That will be the gold standard by which all other naps are judged."

Source: The New Yorker,
July 10th & 17th, 2006

Glossary

Before/after studies Studies that compare service or treatment-relevant psychosocial characteristics prior to and after intervention has taken place. Also referred to as Time1/Time 2 studies.

Bivariate analysis Cross-tabulation of pairs of variables.

"Black-box" evaluations Studies that focus attention on describing interventions or services in great detail.

Clinical data-mining Practitioners' use of available agency data for practice-based research purposes. These data were not originally collected or recorded for research purposes.

Clinical information systems Routinely computerized client data for agency reporting and programmatic decision-making.

Comparison group A subset of subjects in an evaluation study that receives some form of intervention other than the ideal in order to determine the relative effectiveness of the ideal intervention that another group receives.

Connectivity The extent to which different available data-sets are analytically compatible.

Control group A subset of subjects in an evaluation study that receives no intervention in order to determine the effectiveness of the intervention that another group receives.

Control variables Characteristics that must be taken into account statistically in order to demonstrate causality between interventions and outcomes.

Counterfactual What might have happened in the absence of an intervention.

Cross-sectional design A type of evaluation study that approximates a time series by comparing different subsets or aggregates of individuals at different stages in a treatment process.

Data-cleaning The process by which ambiguous and missing data are minimized.

Data-mining Any use of available data for research purpose.

Deductive Beginning with theory or prior research.

De-identified data Client data that has been stripped of any identifying information.

Dependent variables Psychosocial characteristics that are assumed to be consequences of intervention.

Descriptive studies Evaluations that make no attempt to consider relationships between variables but rather focus on describing client populations, intervention provided, or outcomes achieved (see also univariate analysis).

Dichotomous outcomes Dependent variables that can be characterized in two categories, for example, depressed/not depressed.

Differential clinical evaluation An approach to evaluation of individual treatment that involves matching the treatment stage to the type of data-gathering.

Differential social program evaluation An approach to program evaluation that involves matching the program stage of development to the type of data-gathering.

Empirical Based on observation or experience.

Evaluation research A form of applied research that seeks to determine the usefulness of an intervention of some kind.

Evidence-based practice (EBP) A research-based approach to intervention selection that privileges knowledge derived from randomized, controlled experiments.

Evidence-informed practice (EIP) A research-based approach to intervention selection that gives equal value to all forms of research, recognizing the unique strengths and weaknesses of each (see also Methodological pluralism).

Experimental analog An effort to approximate a randomized, controlled study by applying experimental logic to the analysis of available data. (see also Ex post facto experiment).

Experimental logic The application of cause-effect thinking.

Ex-post facto experimental studies (see Experimental analog).

External validity The extent to which one can generalize from study results to other populations, programs, and so forth. beyond the context in which a study was conducted.

Face validity The extent to which a variable measures what it is supposed to measure based entirely on logic and our understanding of what the variable means.

Formative evaluation Studies primarily intended to inform treatment or programmatic decision-making with little regard to generalization beyond the context in which the study was conducted.

"Gold-standard" research Studies based on randomized, controlled experiments.

Grounded theory An inductive, atheoretical approach to theory generation often based on qualitative data.

Heuristic A guide to understanding that often involves simplification of complex phenomena, for example, conceptualizing treatment in terms of "beginnings", "middles" and "ends."

Hierarchy of evidence A rank ordering of "levels" of evidence by proponents of Evidence-based practice that places randomized, controlled experiments at the top and qualitative research at the bottom.

Independent variables Presumed causes of a phenomenon, for example, in clinical evaluations the treatment intervention.

Inductive Beginning with the available data or the phenomenon under study itself, without regard to theory or prior research studies.

Inter-rater reliability The degree to which multiple, available data-gatherers code the same variables consistently.

Intervening variables Client, worker or other characteristics that might mediate or enhance the success of an intervention.

Intrarater reliability The degree to which multiple, available data-gathereres code the same variables consistently.

Longitudinal design A type of evaluation study in which the same individuals or groups are followed over time.

Methodological pluralism An approach to assessment of research that gives equal value to all forms of research, recognizing the unique strengths and weaknesses of each.

Missing data Variables for which not all clients have data recorded.

Mixed-method CDM Studies that employ both available and original data, qualitative and quantitative data or retrospective and prospective data.

Monitoring studies Evaluation studies that focus on who is receiving services and what services they are receiving.

Multidimensional evidence-based practice A research-based approach to intervention selection that incorporates consumer and practitioner values as well as qualitative research to a greater degree than Evidence-based practice routinely does.

Multivariate analysis Forms of statistical analysis that take into account the interactions of more than two variables.

Naturalistic studies Research designs that minimize their impact on the phenomenon they are studying.

Need studies Research that attempts to describe consumer wants and practitioner assessments of their service needs.

Nominal definition A way of describing a variable by using other words (as in a dictionary definition).

Nonreactive data-gathering Ways of gathering data that do not influence the responses one receives.

Operational definition A way of describing a variable via specific instructions for its measurement.

Original data collection Gathering data for the first time for research purposes.

Outcome studies Evaluations that focus on the consequences of interventions but look at relationships between interventions (presumed causes) and outcomes (presumed consequences).

Outcome-only studies Evaluations that focus entirely on presumed outcomes without regard to empirically demonstrating cause-effect relations.

Plan for analysis An advanced guide to how variable relationships will be analyzed and which will be treated as independent, intervening and dependent.

Practice-based research (PBR) An approach to research that begins with practitioner questions, is informed by practice wisdom and conducted by practitioners.

Pretest/posttest studies (see Before/After studies).

Program effectiveness The degree to which programs produce desired outcomes.

Program efficiency The programmatic costs (in staff time, money or other resources) that are required to produce desired outcomes.

Program efforts What the interventions the program actually provides.

Program fidelity The extent to which program efforts match "best practice" for that type of program.

Propensity score matching A statistical technique used with available data to approximate random assignment to different intervention groups.

Prospective CDM A future-oriented form of "data-mining" that involves the collection of original data based on retrospective analysis of available data.

Purposive sampling Selecting cases for analysis that are based upon a preconceived classification scheme. (see also "typology").

Qualitative CDM Data mining that makes use of qualitative available data without first converting it into quantitative form.

Quantitative CDM Data-mining that either converts qualitative data into quantitative data prior to analysis, or statistically analyzes already available quantitative data.

Random sampling A form of sample selection in which each client has an equal probability of being included in the study. Not to be confused with systematic sampling.

Randomized clinical trials (RCTs) A type of applied research that relies on randomized controlled experiments as in drug studies.

Reflective practice An approach to practice knowledge development that relies heavily on trial and error and self-reflection under the guidance of an experienced mentor.

Reliability The degree to which variables are measured and coded consistently.

Research-based practice (RBP) An approach to practice knowledge development that incorporates prior research and research designs into practice implementation, for example, single–system designs (see below).

Retrospective CDM An approach to data-mining that involves collecting data from the past and treating them as though they were prospective.

Sampling window The time span within which data will be mined.

Secondary analysis A study conducted with available data that were originally collected for research purposes. (Not to be confused with Clinical Data-Mining in which the data were not collected or recorded with research in mind.)

Single-system designs A research-based practice approach to quantitative evaluation of the impact of clinical intervention with individual clients.

Standardized instruments Data-gathering instruments, for example, questionnaires, assessment tools, and so forth. that have been tested and validated through prior studies for which there are statistical norms available, for example, an I.Q. test or the Beck Depression Scale.

Strategic compromise The process by which methodological ideals are balanced against ethical or practical constraints in order to successfully conduct an applied research study in a naturalistic environment.

Summative evaluation Studies intended to generate cause-effect inferences about intervention treatment or programmatic decision-making with little regard to generalization beyond the context in which the study was conducted.

Systematic sampling A sampling technique in which every Nth case is selected after a random starting point between 1 and N. If the population of cases sampled is large enough and the sampling interval is small enough it produces results that approximate a random sample in a much more efficient manner.

The "Mining Metaphor" The many ways in which Clinical Data-Mining is likened to actual mining.

Typology A multidimension classification scheme often used in purposive sampling for qualitative research or derived from qualitative analysis.

Unintrusive A manner of conducting research that does not interfere with on-going treatment programs as they naturally occur (see also "naturalistic studies").

Unit of analysis The primary analytic unit of any study, for example, individual, group, family, program, and so forth. It is the unit about which generalizations and inferences are intended to be made.

Univariate analysis Quantitative data analysis that treats single variables one at a time often using measures of central tendency (i.e., mean, median and mode) to describe them. (see also "descriptive studies").

Validity The extent to which a variable measures or reflects what it is intended to measure.

References

Aisenberg, E. (2008). Evidence-based practice in mental health care to ethnic minority communities: Has its practice fallen short of its evidence? *Social Work, 53*(4), 297–306.

Alexander, L., & Solomon, P. (Eds.). (2006). *The research process in the human services: Behind the scenes.* Brooks, MN: Cole.

Anthony, W. (2000). A recovery oriented service system: Setting some system level standards. *Psychiatric Rehabilitation Journal, 24*(2), 17–24.

Auslander, G., Dobrof, J., & Epstein, I. (2001). Comparing social work's role in renal dialysis in Israel and the United States: The practice-based research potential of available clinical information. *Social Work in Health Care, 33*(3–4), 129–152.

Ayers, I. (2007). *Super crunchers.* New York: Bantam Dell.

Barth, R. P., Guo, S., & McCrae, J. (2008). Propensity score matching strategies for evaluating the success of child and family service programs. *Research on Social Work Practice, 18*(3), 212–222.

Beder, J. (1999). Evaluation research on the effectiveness of social work intervention on dialysis patients: The first three months. *Social Work in Health Care, 30*(1), 15–30.

Beder, J. (2008). Evaluation research on social work interventions: A study on the impact of social work staffing. *Social Work in Health Care, 47*(1), 1–13.

Berman, H., Ford-Gilboe, M., & Campbell, J. C. (1998). Combining stories and numbers: A methodologic approach for a critical nursing science. *Advances in Nursing Science, 21*(1), 1–15.

Berzin, S. C. (2008). Difficulties in the transition to adulthood: Using propensity scoring to understand what makes foster youth vulnerable. *Social Service Review, 82*(2), 171–196.

Bickman, L. (1987). The functions of program theory. In L. Bickman (Ed.), *Using program theory in evaluation.* San Francisco: Jossey-Bass.

Bielawski, B., & Epstein, I. (1984). Assessing program stabilization: An extension of the differential evaluation model. *Administration in Social Work, 8,* 13–23.

Blumenfield, S., & Epstein, I. (2001). Introduction: Promoting and maintaining a reflective professional staff in a hospital-based social work department. *Social Work in Health Care, 33*(3–4), 1–14.

Briar, S. (1979). Incorporating research into education for clinical practice in social work: Toward a clinical science in social work. In A. Rubin & A. Rosenblatt (Eds.), *Sourcebook on research uilization* (pp. 1132–1140). New York: Council on Social Work Education.

Brun, C. (1997). The process and implications of doing qualitative research: An analysis of 54 doctoral dissertations. *Journal of Sociology and Social Welfare, 27*(4), 95–112.

Chan, W. (2007). *A clinical data-mining study of the psycho-social status of Chinese cancer patients in palliative care.* Unpublished doctoral dissertation. University of Hong Kong.

Chan, W. C. H., Epstein, I., Reese, D., & Chan, C. L. W. (2009). Family predictors of psychosocial outcomes among Hong Kong Chinese cancer patients in palliative care: Living and dying with the support paradox. *Social Work in Health Care, 5*(48).

Chow, A. (2005). *The bereavement experience of Chinese persons in Hong Kong.* Unpublished doctoral dissertation. University of Hong Kong.

Ciro, D., & Nembhard, M. (2005). Collaborative data-mining in an adolescent mental health service: Clinicians speak of their experience. In K. Peake, I. Epstein, & D. Medeiros (Eds.), *Clinical and research uses of an adolescent intake questionnaire: What kids need to talk about.* (pp. 305–318). Binghampton, NY: Haworth Press.

Cloward, R., & Epstein, I. (1965). Private social welfare's disengagement from the poor: The case of family adjustment agencies. *Proceedings of the annual social work day conference.* University of Buffalo. Reprinted in G. Brager & P. Purcell (Eds.), (1967). *Community action against poverty* (pp. 40–63). New Haven, CT: College & University Press.

Cnaan, R. A., & Dichter, M. E. (2008). Thoughts on the use of knowledge in social work practice. *Research on Social Work Practice, 18*(4), 278–284.

Cole, M., & Ryan, K. (2006). Agency snapshot: Psychosis and drug use. *Journal of Substance, 4*(2), 20–21.

Collins, M., Schwartz, I., & Epstein, I. (2001). Risk factors for adult imprisonment in a sample of youth released from residential child care. *Children and Youth Services Review, 23,* 203–226.

Corcoran, K. (1997). Use of rapid assessment instruments as outcome measures. In E. J. Mullen & J. L. Magnabosco (Eds.), *Outcomes measurement in the human services: Cross-cutting issues and methods.* Washington, DC: NASW Press.

Cordero, A. (2000). *When reunification works: A family strengths perspective.* Unpublished doctoral dissertation. Graduate Faculty in Social Welfare. The City University of New York.

Cordero, A. (2004). When family reunification works: Data-mining foster care records. *Families in Society, 85*(4), 571–580.

Cordero, A., & Epstein, I. (2005). Refining the practice of reunification: "Mining" successful foster care case records of substance abusing families. In G. P. Mallon & P. M. Hess (Eds.), *Child welfare for the twenty-first century: A handbook of practices, policies and programs.* New York: Columbia University Press.

Danto, E. (2008). *Historical research.* (Pocket Guides to Social Work Research Series). New York: Oxford University Press.

Dobrof, J., Dolinko, A., Lichtiger, E., Uribarri, J., & Epstein, I. (2000). The complexity of social work practice with dialysis patients: Risk and resiliency factors, interventions and health-related outcomes. *Journal of Nephrology Social Work, 20,* 21–36.

Dobrof, J., Dolinko, A., Lichtiger, E., Uribarri, J., & Epstein, I. (2001). Dialysis patient characteristics and outcomes: The complexity of social work practice with end stage renal disease. *Social Work in Health Care, 33*(3–4), 105–128.

Dobrof, J., Ebenstein, H., Dodd, S., & Epstein, I. (2006). Caregivers and professional partnership caregiver resource center: Assessing a hospital support program for family caregivers. *Journal of Palliative Medicine, 9*(1), 196–205.

Edberg-Posse, E., & Florinder, U. (2007). Long-term support for families of children who have undergone allogeneic SCT. Presentation given at the Karolinska Institute, Huddinge, Sweden.

Eisenberg, J. M. (2002). Globalize the evidence, localize the decision: Evidence-based medicine and international diversity. *Health Affairs, 21*(3), 166–168.

Epstein, I. (1987). Pedagogy of the perturbed: Teaching research to the reluctants. *Journal of Teaching in Social Work, 1,* 71–89.

Epstein, I. (1995). Promoting reflective social work practice: Research strategies and consulting principles. In P. Hess & E. Mullens (Eds.), *Practitioner-researcher partnerships: Building knowledge from, in, and for practice* (pp. 83–102). Washington, DC: NASW Press.

Epstein, I. (1996). In quest of a research-based model for clinical practice: Or, why can't a social worker be more like a researcher? *Social Work Research, 20*, 97–100.

Epstein, I. (2001). Using available clinical information in practice-based research: Mining for silver while dreaming of gold. In I. Epstein & S. Blumenfield (Eds.), *Clinical data-mining in practice-based research: Social work in hospital settings* (pp. 15–32). Binghamton, NY: Haworth Press. Reprinted in Hebrew in (2006) *Haifa Forum for Social Work, 3*(3), pp. 90–106 and in Japanese in (2006) *Social Work Research [Sosharuwaku Kenkyu], 32*(1), pp. 38–43.

Epstein, I. (2005). Following in the footnotes of giants: Citation analysis and its discontents. *Social Work in Healthcare, 41*(3–4), 93–101.

Epstein, I. (2007). From evaluation methodologist to clinical data-miner: Finding treasure through practice-based research. In H. Rehr & G. Rosenberg (Eds.), *The Social Work–Medicine Relationship: 100 Years at Mount Sinai* (pp. 107–111). Binghamton, NY: Haworth Press.

Epstein, I. (2009). Promoting harmony where there is commonly conflict: Evidence-informed practice as an integrative strategy. *Social Work in Health Care, 48*(3), pp. 216–231.

Epstein, I., & Grasso, A. J. (1990). Using agency-based available information to further practice innovation. In H. Weissman (Ed.), *Serious play: Creativity and innovation in social work*. New York: NASW Press.

Epstein, I., & Tripodi, T. (1978). *Research techniques for program planning, monitoring and evaluation*. New York: Columbia University Press.

Epstein, I., Zilberfein, F., & Snyder, S. (1997). Using available information in practice-based outcomes research: A case study of psycho-social risk factors and liver transplant outcomes. In E. J. Mullen & J. L. Magnabosco (Eds.), *Outcomes measurement in the human services: Cross-cutting issues and methods* (pp. 224–233).Washington DC: NASW Press.

Fraser, M., Pecora, P., & Haapala, D. (Eds.). (1991). *Families in crisis: The impact of intensive family preservation services*. New York: Aldine de Gruyter.

Freedman, C., Joubert, L., & Russell, N. (2005). Practitioner evaluation of a brief intervention approach in emergency services: The Sunshine Hospital Quick Response Team. *Social Work Research and Evaluation, 6*(2), 207–216.

Gambrill, E. (2003). Editorial: Evidence-based practice: Sea change or emperor's new clothes? *Journal of Social Work Education, 39*(1), 1–18.

Gambrill, E. (2006). Evidence-based practice and policy: Choices ahead. *Research on Social Work Practice, 16* (3), 338–357.

Glaser, B. G., & Strauss, A. L. (1967). *The discovery of grounded theory: Strategies for qualitative research*. Chicago: Aldine.

Goldstein, A. (2007). *"A place of my own" Homeless families in the New York City shelter system: The long-term stayers.* Unpublished doctoral dissertation. Graduate Faculty in Social Welfare. The City University of New York.

Grasso, A. J., & Epstein, I. (Eds.). (1992). *Research utilization in the social services: Innovations for practice and administration.* Binghampton, NY: Haworth Press.

Grasso, A. J., & Epstein, I. (Eds.). (1993). *Information systems in child, youth and family agencies: Planning, implementation and service enhancement.* Binghampton, NY: Haworth Press.

Gredig, D., & Sommerfeld, P. (2008). New proposals for generating and exploiting solution-oriented knowledge. *Research on Social Work Practice, 18*(4), 292–300.

Groopman, J. (2007). *How doctors think.* Boston: Houghton Mifflin.

Hanssen, D. (2003). *Looking inside the black box of intensive family preservation services.* Unpublished doctoral dissertation. Graduate faculty in Social Welfare. The City University of New York.

Hanssen, D., & Epstein, I. (2006). A "black box" study of intensive family preservation services: Utilization of clinical data-mining. *Family Preservation, 9*, 7–22.

Hanssen, D., & Epstein, I. (2007). Learning what works: Demonstrating practice effectiveness with children and families through retrospective investigation. *Family Preservation, 10*, 24–41.

Hartman, A. (1992). In search of subjugated knowledge. *Social Work, 37*, 483–484.

Hudson, W. (1997). Assessment tools as outcome measures in social work. In E. J. Mullen & J. L. Magnabosco (Eds.), *Outcomes measurement in the human services:Cross-cutting issues and methods.* Washington, DC: NASW Press.

Huberman, A. M., & Miles, M. B. (1994). *Qualitative data analysis.* Thousand Oaks, CA: Sage Publications.

Hughes, D., Elkin, C., & Epstein, I. (2004). Long-term Counseling: A feasibility study of extended follow-up services with high-risk EAP clients. *Journal of Workplace Behavioral Health, 22*(2–3), 27–41.

Hughes, D. C., Leung, P., & Naus, M. J. (2008). Using a single-system analysis to assess the effectiveness of an exercise intervention on quality of life for Hispanic breast cancer survivors: A pilot study. *Social Work in Health Care, 47*(1), 73–91.

Hutson, C., & Lichtiger, E. (2001). Mining clinical information in the utilization of social services: Practitioners inform themselves. *Social Work in Health Care, 33*(3–4), 153–162.

Imre, R. (1985). Tacit knowledge in social work research and practice, *Smith-. College Studies in Social Work, 55*(2), 137–149.

John, L., Wright, R., Duku, E., & Willms, J. D. (2008). The use of propensity scores as a matching strategy. *Research on Social Work Practice, 18*(1), 20–26.

Jones, S., Statham, H., & Solomou, W. (2006). When expectant mothers know their baby has a fetal abnormality: Exploring a crisis of motherhood through qualitative data-mining. *Journal of Scial Work Research and Evaluation, 6*(2), 195–206.

Joubert, L. (2006). Academic-practice partnerships in practice research: A cultural shift for health social workers. *Social Work in Health Care, 43*(2–3), 151–161.

Joubert, L., & Epstein, I. (Eds.). (2005). Special issue. multi-disciplinary data-mining in allied health practice: Another perspective on Australian research and evaluation, Special Issue. *Journal of Social Work Research and Evaluation, 6*(2), 139–141.

Joubert, L., & Power, R. (2005). Using data-mining to explore the outcomes of an integrated care program: Looking for meaning behing key outcome indicators. *Social Work Research and Evaluation, 6*(2), 185–194.

Kagle. J. D. (1996). *Social work records* (2nd ed.). Prospect Heights, IL: Waveland Press.

Kapp, S., Schwartz, I., & Epstein, I. (1994). Adult imprisonment of males released from residential childcare: A longitudinal study. *Residential Treatment for Children and Youth, 12*, 19–36.

Khinduka, S. (2002). Musings on doctoral education in social work. *Research on Social Work Practice, 12*(5), 684–694.

Kirk, S. A., & Reid, W. (2002). *Science and social work.* New York: Columbia University Press.

Klein, W., & Bloom, M. (1995). Practice wisdom. *Social Work, 40* (2), 799–807.

Kochkine, V. (2006). Depressive symptoms and academic achievement in immigrant and American-born adolescents of diverse ethno-cultural backgrounds: A cultural data-mining exploration. Unpublished doctoral dissertation. Graduate faculty in Social Welfare. The City University of New York.

Koh. E., & Testa, M. F. (2008). Propensity score matching of children in foster care and nonkinship foster care: Do permanency outcomes differ? *Social Work Research, 32* (1), 105–118.

Krysik, J. L., & Finn, J. (2007). *Research for Effective Social Work Practice.* New York, McGraw Hill.

Lethborg, C. (2006). *The Role of Meaning in Adjustment to Cancer.* Unpublished PhD Thesis, University of Melbourne.

Lethborg, C., Aranda, S., & Kissane, D. (2007). To what extent does meaning mediate adaptation to cancer?—the relationship between physical suffering, meaning in life and connection to others in adjustment to cancer. *Palliative and Supportive Care, 5*(4), 377–388.

Lethborg, C., Aranda, S., & Kissane, D. (2008). Meaning in adjustment to cancer: A model of care. *Palliative and Supportive Care, 6*(1), 61–70.

Lethborg, C., Aranda, S., & Kissane, D. (2008). Understanding the role of physical suffering, meaning in life and connection to others in coping with cancer—predictors of distress and meaning. Unpublished paper.

Lindsey, D., & Kirk, S. (1992). The continuing crisis in social work research: Conundrum or solvable problem? *Journal of Social Work Education, 28*, 370–382.

Liptak, A. (2007). Does death penalty save lives? A new debate. *New York Times*, November 18, p. 32.

Lo, H. (in process). A clinical data-mining study of symptom presentation of depression, anxiety and Cognitive Behavioral Therapy outcomes in a community-based mental health program. Unpublished doctoral dissertation. University of Hong Kong.

Lunt, N., Fouche, C., & Yates, D. (2008). Growing research in practice (GRIP). *Report Published by New Zealan Families Commission Innvoation Practice Fund (2)*, January.Wellington, NZ, www.nzfamilies.org.

Macdonald, E. M., Carroll, A., Albiston, D., & Epstein, I. (2006). Social relationships in early psychosis: Clinical data-mining for practice-based evidence. *Journal of Social Work Research and Evaluation, 6*(2), 155–166.

Macias, C., Jones, D. R., Hargreaves, W. A., Wang, Q., Rodican, C. F., Barriera, P. J. et al. (2008). When programs benefit some people more than others: Tests of differential service effectiveness. *Administration and Policy in Mental Health & Mental Health Services Research, 35*, 283–294. Retrieved September 30, 2008, from www.ps.psychiatryonline.org.

Markoff, J. (2006). Taking spying to higher level, Agencies look for more ways to mine data. *New York Times*, pp. 1–4. *February 25th. Technology*

Mason, J., Edlow, M., Lear, M., Scopetta, S., Walther, V., Epstein, I. et al. (2001). Screening for psycho-social risk in an urban prenatal clinic population: A retrospective, practice-based research study. *Social Work in Health Care, 33*(3–4), 33–52.

McCracken, S., & Marsh, J. C. (2008). Practitioner expertise in evidence-based practice decision-making. *Research on Social Work Practice,18*(4), 301–310.

McNeece, A., & Thyer, B. (2004). Evidence-based practice and social work. *Journal of Evidence-Based Practice, 1*, 7–25.

McNeill, T. (2006). Evidence-based practice in an age of relativism: Toward a model for practice. *Social Work, 51*(2),147–156.

Mendenhall, A. (2007). Switching hats: Transitioning from the role of clinician to the role of researcher in social work doctoral education. *Journal of Teaching in Social Work, 27,* 273–290.

Mirabito, D. (2000). *Keeping the door open or keeping the door shut?: How and why adolescents terminate from mental health treatment.* Unpublished doctoral dissertation. Graduate faculty in Social Welfare. The City University of New York.

Mirabito, D. (2001). Mining treatment termination data in an adolescent mental health service: A quantitative study. *Social Work in Health Care, 33*(3–4), 71–90.

Moses, L. E. (1995). Measuring effects without randomized trials? Options, problems, challenges. *Medical Care, 33*(4), AS8–AS14.

Morgan, D. L. (2007). Paradigms lost and pragmatism regained: Methodological implications of combining qualitative and quantitative methods. *Journal of Mixed Methods Research, 1*(1), 48–76.

Muhr, T. (1997). ATLAS/ti. *The knowledge workbench.* Thousand Oaks, CA: Scolari Sage Publications Software.

Mullen, E. J., & Bacon, W. (2004). A survey of practitioner adoption and implementation of practice guidelines and evidenced-based treatments. In A. R. Roberts & K. Yeager (Eds.), *Evidence-based practice manual: Research and outcome measures in health and human services* (pp. 193–199). New York: Oxford University Press.

Mullen, E. J., Shlonsky, A., Bledsoe, S. E., & Bellamy, J. L. (2005). From concept to implementation: Challenges facing evidence-based social work. *Evidence and Policy, 1,* 61–84.

Myers, L., & Thyer, B. (1997). Should should social work clients have the right to effective treatment? *Social Work, 42*(3), 288–298.

New York Times (2008a). Practicing patients. *The New York Times Magazine, March 23,* 32–37.

New York Times (2008b). Police dept. appeals order to show street-stop data. *The Metro Section, July 1,* B–6.

Nilsson, D. (2001). Psycho-social problems faced by "frequent flyers" in a pediatric diabetes unit. *Social Work in Health Care, 33*(3–4), 53–70.

O'Callaghan, C. (2001). *Music therapy's relevance in a cancer hospital researched through a constructionist's lens.* Unpublished doctoral dissertation, University of Melbourne, Melbourne.

O'Callaghan, C. (2005). Qualitative data-mining through reflexive journal analysis: Implications for music therapy practice development. *Journal of Social Work Research and Evaluation, 6*(2), 217–229.

O'Callaghan, C. (2008). Lullament: Lullaby and lament-therapeutic qualities actualized through music therapy. *American Journal of Hospice and Palliative Medicine, 25*(2), 93–99.

Olson, D., & Shi, Y. (2007). *Introduction to business data mining*. New York: McGraw-Hill Irwin.

Osmond, J., & O'Connor, I. (2004). Formalizing the unformalized: Practitioners' communication of knowledge in practice. *British Journal of Social Work, 34*(5), 677–692.

Otto, H., & Zeigler, H. (2008). The notion of causal impact in evidence-based practice: An introduction to the special issue on what works. *Research on Social Work Practice, 18*(4), 273–277.

Parkin, T., & Skinner, T. C. (2003). Discrepancies between patient and professional recall of an outpatient consultation. *Diabetic Medicine, 20*(11), 909–914.

Pawlak, E. J. (1977). Differential selection of juveniles for detention. *Journal of Research in Crime and Delinquency, 14*(2), 152–165.

Pawson, R. (2002). Evidence-based policy: The promise of 'realist synthesis'. *Evaluation, 8*(3), 340–358.

Peake, K., Epstein, I., & Medeiros, D. (Eds.). (2005) *Clinical and research uses of an adolescent intake questionnaire: What kids need to talk about*. Binghampton, NY: Haworth Press.

Peake, K., Mirabito, D., Epstein, I., & Giannone, V. (2005). Creating and sustaining a practice-based research group in an urban adolescent mental health program. *Social Work in Mental Health, 3*(1–2), 39–54.

Petr, C. G.(2008). *Multi-dimensional evidence-based practice: Synthesizing knowledge, research, and values*. New York: Routledge.

Petr, C. G., & Walther, U. (2008). Evidence-based practice: A critical reflection. *European Journal of Social Work*.

Posenelli, S., Joubert, L., Power, R., Vale, S., Lewis, A., & Elliot, R. (2005). Managerial collaboration through allied health data-mining: The St. Vincent's Health experience. *Journal of Social Work Research and Evaluation, 6*(2), 167–176.

Pottick, K., Bilder, S., Vander Stoep, A., Warner, L., & Alvarez, M. (2007). US Patterns of mental health service utilization for transition-age youth and young adults. *Journal of Behavioral Health Services & Research*, Regular Article, 35, 1–16.

Proctor, E., & Rosen, A. (2008). From knowledge production to implementation: Research challenges and imperatives. *Research on Social Work Practice, 18*(4), 285–291.

Polansky, N. (Ed.) (1960). *Social work research*. Chicago: University of Chicago Press.

Reamer, F. G. (1998). *Social work research and evaluation skills: A case-based, user-friendly approach*. New York: Columbia University Press.

Reeser, L., & Epstein, I. (1990). *Professionalization and activism in social work: The 60's, the 80's and the future*. New York: Columbia University Press.

Rehr, H. (1992). "Practice uses of accountability systems in healthcare settings: Social work and administrative perspectives. In A. S. Grasso & I. Epstein (Eds.), *Research utilization in the social services:Innovation for practice and administration* (pp. 241–260). New York: The Haworth Press.

Rehr, H., Rosenberg, G., Showers, N., & Blumenfield, S. (1998). Social workers in health care: Do practitioners' writings suggest an applied science? *Social Work in Health Care, 28*(2), 63–79.

Reid, W. J. (1979). The model development dissertation. *Social Service Research, 3*(2), 215–225.

Reid, W. J. (1994). The empirical practice movement. *Social Service Review, 68*(2), 165–184.

Rexer, K., Gearan, P., & Allen, H. N. (2007). Surveying the field: Current data mining applications, analytic tools, and practical challenges. *Data Mining Survey Summary Report. Rexer Analytics,* 1–7.

Robb, M. (2005). A deepening doctoral crisis? *Social Work Today, 5*(4), 13.

Ross, J., Walther, V., & Epstein, I. (2004). Screening risks for intimate partner violence in primary care settings: Implications for future abuse. *Social Work in Health Care, 38* (4), 1–24.

Rossi, P. (1992). Assessing family preservation programs. *Children and Youth Services Review, 14*(1–2), 77–97.

Rodriguez, L. (2009). Exploring pathways to independence: A data-mining study to research predictors of long-term stay among homeless men in the New York City family shelter system. Unpublished doctoral dissertation. Graduate faculty in Social Welfare. The City University of New York.

Rothman, J. (1980). *Social R & D: Research and development in the human services.* Englewood Cliffs, NJ: Prentice-Hall.

Rubin, A. (2006). Forward in. Alexander, L., & Solomon, P. (Eds.) *The research process in the human services: Behind the scenes* (pp. xii–xiv). Belmont, CA: Thomson-Brooks/Cole.

Rubin, A., & Parrish, D. (2007). Problematic phrases in the conclusions of published outcome studies: Implications for evidence-based practice. *Social Work Research and Practice, 17,* 334–347.

Sainz, A., & Wu, C. (2008). *Uncovering my original nature. How to embrace and appreciate my life as the journey home.* Taipei: CITE Publishers.

Sainz, A., & Epstein, I. (2001). Creating experimental analogs with available clinical information: Credible alternatives to 'gold standard' experiments? *Social Work in Health Care, 33*(3–4), 163–184.

Sales, E., Lichtenwalter, S., & Fevola, A. (2006). Secondary analysis in social work research education: Past, present and future promise. *Journal of Social Work Education, 42*(3), 543–558.

Saracostti, M. (2008). *Social networking as a strategy to overcome poverty in Chile: A data-mining evaluation of the Chile Solidario System.* Unpublished doctoral dissertation. Graduate faculty in Social Welfare. The City University of New York.

Schön, D. (1983) *The reflective practitioner: How professionals think in action.* Basic Books

Schwartz, D., Kaufman, A. B., & Schwartz, I. M. (2004). Computational intelligence techniques for risk assessment and decision support. *Children and Youth Services Review, 26*(11), 1081–1095.

Schwartz, E. (2007a). *Effective privatization of a community mental health agency: Assessing and developing an agency's readiness to change.* Unpublished doctoral dissertation. Graduate faculty in Social Welfare. The City University of New York.

Schwartz, E. (2007b). *Effective privatization of a community mental health agency: Assessing and developing an agency's readiness to change.* Berlin, Germany: VDM Verlag Dr. Muller Aktiengesellschaft & Co.

Schwartz, I. M. (2007). Interview quoted in *CSWE News Briefs*, November.

Schwartz, I. M., Jones, P. R., Schwartz, D., & Obradovic, Z. (2008). Improving social work through the use of technology and advanced research methods. In D. Lindsey & A. Shlonsky (Eds.), *Child welfare research: Advances for practice and policy* (pp. 214–230). Oxford University Press.

Scriven, M. (1995). The logic of evaluation and evaluation practice. In: Fournier (Ed.). *Reasoning in evaluation: Inferential links and leaps* (New Directions for Program Evaluation, No. 68, pp. 49–70). San Francisco: Jossey-Bass.

Shaw, I. (2005). Practitioner research: Evidence or critique? *British Journal of Social Work, 35*(8), 1231–1248.

Shaw, I., & Faulkner, A. (2006). Practitioner evaluation at work. *American Journal of Evaluation, 27*(1), 44–63.

Shmueli, G., Patel, N. R., & Bruce, P. C. (2006). *Data mining for business intelligence: Concepts, techniques and applications in Microsoft Office Excel with XLMiner.* Hoboken, NJ: John Wiley.

Shyne, A. B. (1960). Use of available material. In N. A. Polansky (Ed.), *Social work research* (pp. 106–124). Chicago: University of Chicago Press.

Skinner, T. C., Bernard, K., Cradock, S., & Parkin, T. (2007). Patient and professional accuracy of recalled treatment decisions in out-patient consultations. *Diabetic Medicine, 24*(5), 557–560.

Smith, C. A., Cohen-Callow, A., Harnek-Hall, D. M., & Hayward, R. A. (2007). Impact of a foundation-level MSW research course on students' critical appraisal skills. *Journal of Social Work Education, 43*(3), 481–496

Soydan, H. (2008). Applying randomized controlled trials and systematic reviews in social work research. *Research on Social Work Practice, 18*(4), 311–318.

Statham, H. (2002). Prenatal diagnosis of fetal abnormality: The decision to terminate the pregnancy and the psychological consequences. *Fetal and Maternal Medicine Review, 13,* 213–247.

Statham, H., Solomou, W., & Green, J. M. (2001). *When a baby has an abnormality: A study of parents' experiences.* Vol. 1 of the report of a study funded by a grant from the NHS (R&D) Mother and Child Health Initiative (MCH 4–12) *Detection of fetal abnormality at different gestations: Impact on parents and service implications.* Cambridge, UK: Centre for Family Research, University of Cambridge.

Statham, H., Solomou, W., & Green, J. M. (2002). *When a baby has an abnormality: A study of health professionals' experiences.* Vol. 2 of the report of a study funded by a grant from the NHS (R&D) Mother and Child Health Initiative (MCH 4–12) *Detection of fetal abnormality at different gestations: Impact on parents and service implications.* Cambridge, UK: Centre for Family Research, University of Cambridge.

Statham, H., Solomou, W., & Green, J. M. (2003). Continuing a pregnancy after the diagnosis of an anomaly: Parents' experiences. In L. Abramsky & J. Chapple (Eds.), *Prenatal diagnosis: The human side* (2nd ed., pp. 164–176). Cheltenham, UK: Nelson Thornes.

Staudt, M. M. (2007). Two years later: Former students' perceptions of a clinical evaluation course and current evaluation practices. *Journal of Teaching in Social Work, 27*(1–2), 125–139.

Strauss, A., & Corbin, J. (1990). *Basics of qualitative research.* Newbury Park, CA: Sage Publications.

Thomas, E. J. (1984). *Designing interventions for the helping professions.* Beverly Hills, CA: Sage

Thyer, B. A. (2008). The quest for evidence-based practice?: We are all positivists! *Research on Social Work Practice, 18*(4), 339–345.

Thyer, B., & Thyer, K. (1992). Single system research designs in social work practice: A bibliography from 1965–1990. *Research On Social Work Practice, 2*(1), 99–116.

Tripodi, T., & Epstein, I. (1978). Incorporating knowledge of research methodology into social work practice. *Journal of Social Service Research, 2,* 65–78.

Tripodi, T., & Epstein, I. (1980). *Research techniques for clinical social workers.* New York: Columbia University.

Tripodi, T., Epstein, I., & MacMurray, C. (1970). Dilemmas of evaluation. *American Journal of Orthopsychiatry, 40,* 850–857.

Tripodi, T. Fellin, P., & Epstein, I. (1971). *Social Program Evaluation: Guidelines for Health, Education and Welfare Administrators.* Itasca, Il: Peacock.

Tripodi, T., Fellin, P., & Epstein, I. (1978). *Differential social program evaluation.* Itasca, IL: F.E. Peacock.

Tripodi, T., & Lalayants, M. (2008). Research overview. In T. Mizrahi & L. E. Davis (Eds.), *Encyclopedia of Social Work* (20th ed. pp. 512–520). New York: Oxford University Press.

Unrau, Y. A., Gabor, P. A., & Grinnell, R. M. (2006). *Evaluation in social work: The art and science of practice.* New York: Oxford University Press.

Veblen, T. (1914) *The instinct of workmanship and the state of the industrial arts.* New York: Macmillian.

Vonk, E., Tripodi, T., & Epstein, I. (2006). *Research techniques for clinical social workers.* (2nd ed.). New York: Columbia University Press.

Vourlekis, E., Bembry, J., Hall, G., & Rosenblum, P. (1991). Evaluating the interrater reliability of process recordings *Research on Social Work Practice* *2* (2), 198–206.

Wai, F. (2007). Data-mining as a methodology for explaining written narratives: An application on understanding the breast cancer experience among Hong Kong Chinese women. Unpublished doctoral dissertation. University of Hong Kong.

Whitehurst, T. (2007). Can software assist in child welfare decisions? *City Limits Weekly, October 15,* 1–3.

Williams-Gray, B. (2008). Accreditation as an intervention and a means for expanding organizational capacity: An organizational data-mining study. Unpublished doctoral dissertation. Graduate faculty in Social Welfare. The City University of New York.

Webster's Seventh New Collegiate Dictionary (1970). Chicago: Rand McNally.

Zeira, A., & Rosen, A. (1999). Intermediate outcomes pursued by practitioners: A qualitative analysis. *Social Work Research, 23*(2), 79–87.

Zeira, A., & Rosen, A. (2000). Unraveling 'tacit knowledge': What social workers do and why they do it. *Social Service Review, 74*(1), 103–123.

Zilberfein, F., Hutson, C., Snyder, S., & Epstein, I. (2001). Social work practice with pre- and post-liver transplant patients: A retrospective self-study. *Social Work in Health Care, 33*(3–4), 91–104.

Zorich, Z. (2009). American genes. *Archaeology, 62*(1), 22.

Index

Lightning Source UK Ltd.
Milton Keynes UK
UKOW07f0211270115

245180UK00014B/391/P

9 780195 335521